This Book Comes With Lots of
FREE Online Resources

Nolo's award-winning website has a page dedicated just to this book. Here you can:

KEEP UP TO DATE. When there are important changes to the information in this book, we'll post updates.

GET DISCOUNTS ON NOLO PRODUCTS. Get discounts on hundreds of books, forms, and software.

READ BLOGS. Get the latest info from Nolo authors' blogs.

LISTEN TO PODCASTS. Listen to authors discuss timely issues on topics that interest you.

WATCH VIDEOS. Get a quick introduction to a legal topic with our short videos.

And that's not all.
Nolo.com contains thousands of articles on everyday legal and business issues, plus a plain-English law dictionary, all written by Nolo experts and available for free. You'll also find more useful **books, software, online apps, downloadable forms,** plus a **lawyer directory.**

With
**Downloadable
FORMS**

 **NOLO**
LAW for ALL

Get forms and more at
www.nolo.com/back-of-book/SPOT.html

10th Edition

101 Law Forms for Personal Use

by the Editors of Nolo

TENTH EDITION	SEPTEMBER 2016
Editor	DAVID GOGUEN
Cover Design	SUSAN PUTNEY
Book Design	TERRI HEARSH
Proofreading	IRENE BARNARD
Index	THÉRÈSE SHERE
Printing	BANG PRINTING

ISSN: 2167-5775 (print)

ISSN: 2330-0434 (online)

ISBN: 978-1-4133-2306-1 (pbk)

ISBN: 978-1-4133-2307-8 (epub ebook)

This book covers only United States law, unless it specifically states otherwise.

Please note

We believe accurate, plain-English legal information should help you solve many of your own legal problems. But this text is not a substitute for personalized advice from a knowledgeable lawyer. If you want the help of a trained professional—and we'll always point out situations in which we think that's a good idea—consult an attorney licensed to practice in your state.

Table of Contents

How to Use This Book

This book provides more than 100 ready-to-use forms and contracts for a variety of everyday legal and practical transactions that most people can safely handle themselves, without formal legal help. Among the forms are those necessary to write a simple will, settle minor legal disputes, prepare a power of attorney, lend or borrow money, rent a place to live, request your credit report, and sell a used car. Forms are also included to hire someone to do home repairs, to care for your children, and for a variety of other purposes.

Many of the forms in this book are primarily designed for your personal, individual use, such as the Landlord-Tenant Checklist or Loan Comparison Worksheet. But other forms, such as the Elder Care Agreement, are contracts, designed to allow two or more parties to create a legally enforceable agreement.

Unlike commercial contracts used to buy a house or sign up with a health maintenance organization, which almost always consist of pages full of legalese, the contracts in this book are written in everyday (but legal) language. They are designed to describe and define a transaction, such as designating a temporary guardian for your child, with a reasonable level of specificity—without sacrificing clarity and simplicity.

Don't worry that because our contracts are jargon-free they might be less valid than others. In general, as long as two parties—business entities or people—exchange promises to each do something of benefit for the other, a valid contract is formed. A contract will usually be enforced as long as all of the following requirements are met:

- **The terms are specific enough.** The contract must be clear and detailed enough so that an arbitrator or judge can sensibly decide who is right if there's a dispute later. For example, a house painting agreement that says "John the Painter shall paint Sally the Homeowner's house" provides so little guidance that it probably would not be enforced. At the very least, to be enforceable, the contract should state how much John is to be paid for his work. Of course, you'll want to create a contract that not only defines who and what is involved but also anticipates problems that are likely to arise. To be of real value, the contract should include key details such as the type and color of paint to be used, the work schedule, how and when payment is to be made, and what happens if John and Sally disagree about something.

- **The contract is for a legal purpose.** A contract formed to accomplish something illegal is not enforceable in court. For instance, if two people sign a contract to transfer an illegal gambling operation, and they later have a falling out, the agreement will not be enforced by a judge.

- **Enforcement would not be grossly unfair.** The contracts you make using the forms in this book are unlikely to be challenged on the grounds of fairness. But in extreme situations, if a contract is both unfair and the result of one party's superior bargaining position (such as a one-sided premarital agreement between a millionaire and an unsophisticated recent immigrant), a court might not enforce it. If you keep in mind that the best contracts substantially benefit both parties, you should have no problems.

The Importance of Getting Contracts in Writing

The most important rule when making any business agreement or transaction is this: Get it in writing. In a few situations—such as a contract to buy or sell real estate—you must have a written agreement for it to be legally enforceable. Similarly, a contract that can't be performed within one year of when it's made must be written.

But even when an oral contract is legal, there are many practical reasons why a written contract is preferable. Two years from now, you and the other people involved in any transaction might have significantly different recollections about what you agreed to. So putting your agreement into black and white is an important memory aid.

A well-drafted contract has several other important benefits. For one, it serves as a framework for settling disputes. And if settlement proves impossible and a court contest ensues, it will be far easier to prove the terms of a written contract than an oral one.

Another important benefit of drafting a written agreement is that the act of putting a contract together can help you and the other parties focus on key legal and practical issues, some of which might otherwise be overlooked. By starting this process with a well-designed form—like those in this book—you increase your chances of creating a thorough and useful document.

Filling in the Contracts and Forms

The forms in this book are designed to be used as needed; we don't expect you to read the book from start to finish. But we do ask one thing: Read this introduction, all of the introductory material at the beginning of any chapter containing a form that you will use, and the instructions for completing the form itself.

Readers who have a print version of this book can use the forms provided in the book in at least three ways:

1. **Use the companion page on Nolo.com.** All of the forms and contracts in this book are available for you to download on this book's online companion page (see Appendix A for the link). For a list of all forms as well as step-by-step instructions on accessing, using, and saving them, see Appendix A. When there are important changes to the information in this book, we'll post updates on this same dedicated page.

2. **Fill out the forms in this book.** You can also get the job done the old-fashioned way—by photocopying a form out of the book and filling it in with a typewriter or pen. *Don't*, however, use the original form from the book, or you'll be left without a clean copy. Although you'll be fine filling in some forms in this book by hand, such as the Property Worksheet, we suggest that you type the agreements whenever possible. While typing is not legally required, a typed document usually carries more weight than a hand-written one and is more legible. But if convenience or cost dictates that you fill in a contract or form by hand, do it neatly and you should be fine.

 CAUTION
Do not just fill in a will form by hand. Unlike the rest of the forms in this book, a will form cannot be completed by hand. Legally, a valid will cannot contain a mix of handwritten and machine-printed material. To make a legally valid will, use one of the downloadable forms on this book's companion page. Use your word processing program

to enter the personal information called for and to delete any clauses you don't need. If you don't have a computer, you can use a typewriter to type the entire will document.

3. **Use the forms in this book to evaluate similar forms and contracts.** If someone drafts a contract and presents it to you to sign, you can use a corresponding form in this book as a checklist to make sure that the proposed contract has all the recommended ingredients. If it doesn't, use the form in this book as a model to suggest modifications or additions.

Editing the Forms

Many of the forms in this book may meet your needs perfectly. All you will need to do is fill in a few blanks and sign the form. But for some forms, you'll want to make some changes— such as adding or deleting language or clauses. Here's how.

Selecting From Several Choices

Many of our forms require that you choose among several options, such as the method of payment for the work being performed under a Home Repairs Agreement or Child Care Agreement (see sample below). When you see a clause like this, simply check the correct box on the tear-out form and provide any requested additional information.

On several of our forms, you may encounter language that is too cut and dried for your purposes, or wording that ends up sounding awkward, such as ☐ Yes ☐ No or "his/hers." In these situations, you can easily clean the form up by deleting words that don't apply or substituting more appropriate language (assuming you're using the downloadable forms). If you're filling in a tear-out form, leaving the unneeded words in will not affect the validity of the contract. If you prefer, however, you can ink out the portion that does not apply.

Example of Clause With Several Options (Clause 2 of Home Repairs Agreement)

2. **Payment**

In exchange for the work specified in Clause 1, Homeowner agrees to pay Contractor as follows [*choose one and check appropriate boxes*]:

☐ $ _____ , payable upon completion of the specified work by ☐ cash ☐ check.

☐ $ _____ , payable by ☐ cash ☐ check as follows:

_____% payable when the following occurs: _____

_____% payable when the following occurs: _____

_____% payable when the following occurs: _____ .

☐ $_____ per hour for each hour of work performed, up to a maximum of $ _____ ,

payable at the following times and in the following manner: _____

_____

_____ .

☐ Other: _____

_____ .

Deleting Clauses or Phrases

Some individual clauses or phrases in our forms and agreements may not apply to your situation. If you are using the downloadable forms, making changes is easy—simply delete those clauses and renumber the remaining clauses as appropriate.

If you are using the tear-out forms, draw lines through the clause you want to delete and have all parties put their initials next to it. If you are deleting a complete clause, you'll need to renumber the clauses to avoid confusion. For example, if you do not want your lease assignment consent contract to include a clause on "Tenant's Future Liability" (Clause 4 of the Consent to Assignment of Lease), make the modifications as shown below.

Adding Clauses or Language

Adding extra terms to a contract is easy if you're completing the forms on your computer: Simply add the new language or clauses and renumber the remaining clauses as appropriate.

If you are using the tear-out forms and want to add words to a clause, use the space provided. If we didn't leave enough room, or if you want to add a new clause, you should prepare a separate addendum sheet or attachment. See "How to Prepare an Attachment Page," below, for details.

CAUTION

Be sure your changes are clear, easy to understand, and legal. If you add a list of property or work specifications to a contract, your contract should still be fine. But if you delete one of our clauses and substitute your own, make sure your language is easy to understand, free of ambiguity, and consistent with the rest of the contract. Also, if you have any doubt about the legal validity of language you want to add or delete—especially if significant amounts of money or property, or the personal rights of the other person are involved—have the changes checked by a lawyer.

Describing People, Property, and Events

Some forms ask you to name people or describe events or property. Here's the best way to do this.

People. Where you are asked to insert someone's name, address, and other identifying information, use that person's legal name—the name on a driver's license—and home street address. If a person commonly uses two names (not including a nickname), include both, for example, "Alison Johnson, aka Alison Walker-Johnson."

Property. To identify property, such as a defective laptop you're returning with a Request for Refund or Repair of Goods Under Warranty, be as specific as you can.

Example of How to Delete a Clause (Clause 4 of Consent to Assignment of Lease)

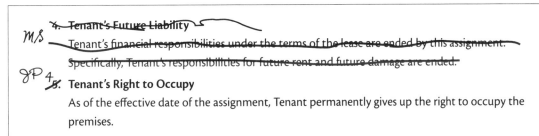

There are no magic words. Your goal is simply to identify the property clearly so that no misunderstanding will arise later. Normally, this means listing the make, model, type, color, identifying number if the item has one, and any other identifying characteristics that come to mind. For instance, if you are requesting repair of a computer under warranty, you might say "Dell Inspiron 15 laptop, ID # 445556."

Events. Take a similar approach when describing events, such as payment for a house-cleaner. As long as you identify the date, time (if appropriate), and location, and include a clear description of what happened or what is supposed to happen, your description should be adequate.

Signing the Forms

Each form has specific signing instructions, including who must sign, how many copies to make, whether notarization is required or recommended, requirements for a spouse's signature, or the need for witnesses.

CAUTION
Always keep your signed copy in a safe place, along with any related documents or correspondence. You may need this at some point—for example, if you end up in court over a dispute concerning an agreement or contract.

How to Prepare an Attachment Page

If you need to add anything to a tear-out copy of one of the forms or agreements in this book, take the following steps.

1. If you want to add words to a clause and there is not enough space to insert the new language into the specific clause of the agreement, you can refer to it as an attachment by adding the words: "Clause [*number*] continued on Attachment A [*or B or C and so on*] of [*name of agreement or form*]."

   EXAMPLE: Clause 1 of the General Bill of Sale provides space for you to list the items you're selling. If there is not enough room to list all these items on the tear-out, write the words "Clause 1 continued on Attachment A of the General Bill of Sale."

   Similarly, if you want to add a new clause, insert the words "Agreement continued on Attachment A of [*name of agreement or form*]" after the last clause of the agreement and before the place where the agreement gets signed.

   Use a separate attachment each time you need more room.

2. Make your own attachment form, using a sheet of blank white 8½" by 11" paper. At the top of the form, write "Attachment A [*or B or C and so on*] to [*name of agreement or form*] between [*insert names of all parties*]" for the first attachment, and so on. Then add the words "a continuation of [*number clause*]" if you're continuing a clause, or "an addition to [*number clause*]" if you're adding a new clause.

   EXAMPLE: "Attachment A to General Bill of Sale between Beth Spencer and Rich Portman. A continuation of Clause 1."

3. Type or print the additional information on the attachment.
4. Have both parties sign or initial the attachment at the bottom of each page.
5. Staple all attachments to the end of the main agreement or form.

Notarization

When this book tells you that a form can (or should) be "notarized," it means that you can (or should) take your form to a notary public (or have one come to you) so that the notary can certify in writing that:

- you're the person you claim to be, and
- you've acknowledged under oath signing the document.

When you are having a form notarized, who needs to be present depends on the circumstances. If you're preparing a form that must be both witnessed and notarized (like the Power of Attorney forms in Chapter 1), you and your witnesses must appear together before the notary public so the witnesses can watch you sign the form. In other cases where more than one person signs the document, you can each visit the notary on your own, if you prefer.

In that case, each signer will get a separate notarization certificate and you'll attach all of them to the document.

Very few legal documents need to be notarized or witnessed. Notarization and witnessing are usually limited to documents like a power of attorney involving real estate, which are going to be recorded at a public office charged with keeping such records—for example, a county land records office or registrar of deeds. Occasionally—but very rarely—state laws require witnesses or notaries to sign other types of documents.

The notary will want proof of your identity, such as a driver's license that bears your photo and signature. The notary will watch each of you sign (or, in some circumstances, you can simply acknowledge that you signed the document already) and then will complete an

Sample Notarization Language

Certificate of Acknowledgment of Notary Public

State of _____ } ss

County of _____

On _____ , _____ , before me, _____

_____ , personally appeared _____

_____ ,

who proved to me on the basis of satisfactory evidence to be the person(s), whose name(s) is/are subscribed to the within instrument and acknowledged to me that he/she/they executed the same in his/her/their authorized capacity(ies) and that by his/her/their signature(s) on the instrument, the person(s), or the entity upon behalf of which the person(s) acted, executed the instrument.

I certify under PENALTY OF PERJURY under the laws of the State of _____ that the foregoing paragraph is true and correct.

WITNESS my hand and official seal.

[NOTARY SEAL]

_____

Notary Public for the State of _____

My commission expires _____

acknowledgment, including a notarial seal or stamp. In some states, the notary may take your thumbprint for documents that affect real estate.

Your state may also have special requirements for the form or language of the notary certificate. For example, California notary certificates must have a box with specific text at the top of the page. A competent notary will know your state's requirement and provide the correct form. A sample notary acknowledgement is shown above.

To find a notary, try searching online. Some businesses have a notary public on staff, including many mail/shipping services, banks, and real estate offices. Most charge less than $20, and often the price is set by state law. You can usually pay a "mobile" notary more to come to you.

 TIP
Notarization is always an option. If there is no mention of notarization in the signing instructions for a form, that means it is not required or recommended. However, even if we don't suggest you have a form notarized, you may choose to—simply because it adds a measure of legal credibility.

Spouse's Signature

If you'll be asked to sign a contract that makes you liable for a debt, such as a promissory note, the other person may ask that your spouse sign as well. This is most likely to happen, for example, if you're borrowing money to buy property that both spouses will use, or to help finance a new business venture. For more details, see the discussion of promissory notes, in Chapter 5.

Resolving Disputes

No matter how airtight your document might be, real life can always creep in, and at some point you may have a legal dispute involving one of the forms or contracts in this book. For example, maybe your partner reneges on an agreement to share property when you split up, or you're upset because your dog sitter acted contrary to the terms of your pet care agreement. One way to resolve a dispute is through a court fight, but lawsuits and trials can be expensive, prolonged, and emotionally draining. It usually makes far more sense to attempt to resolve disputes through other means, including the following:

Informal negotiation. The parties to the dispute try to voluntarily work out their differences through open discussions, which often result in each compromising a little to put the matter to rest. It may make sense to have a trusted mutual friend informally negotiate an agreement.

Mediation. The parties try to achieve a voluntary settlement with the help of a neutral third party, a mediator. With mediation, the two of you get together to talk face to face about your disagreements, with the mediator working to help you communicate so that you can craft your own solution. No one has the power to impose a solution with mediation—rather, you must work out your own agreement voluntarily. Mediation is inexpensive, quick, confidential, and effective the majority of the time. Depending on your situation, you may want to contact a community mediation agency, which offers mediation, usually by trained community volunteers.

Arbitration. If mediation fails to resolve a dispute, arbitration is the next best choice. With arbitration, the parties allow a neutral third party, an arbitrator, to arrive at a binding decision in order to resolve the dispute. Normally, the decision is solely up to the arbitrator, and the parties agree beforehand to abide by the arbitrator's decision. In some situations, however, the parties establish certain rules in advance of the arbitration— for example, a limit on the amount of money that can be awarded. Where limits are set by the parties, the arbitrator is bound by them. Arbitration is almost always speedier and usually much less expensive than litigation.

Ideally, you'd like to be able to settle disputes informally. Unfortunately, however, even when everyone tries in good faith, they don't always reach a compromise. Therefore, a dispute resolution clause (see the one shown below) lets you agree in advance on a framework mandating mediation and arbitration for resolving disputes. This dispute resolution clause is already in several of the forms in this book. If it's not on a particular form and you want to add it, you can find it on this book's online companion page in the file Disputes.rtf.

(See Appendix A for details.) To add the dispute clause, simply follow the directions in "Editing the Forms," above, about adding a clause.

This dispute resolution clause allows the parties to make one of three choices:

- **Litigation.** You go to court and let a judge or jury resolve the dispute.
- **Mediation and possible litigation.** You agree to let a mediator help you try to reach a voluntary settlement of the dispute. If mediation doesn't accomplish this goal, either of you can take the dispute to court. You can name the mediator when you prepare the form or agree on one when the need arises.
- **Mediation and possible arbitration.** You start by submitting the dispute to mediation. If mediation doesn't lead to

---

16. Disputes

[*choose one*]:

☐ **Litigation.** If a dispute arises, any party may take the matter to court.

☐ **Mediation and possible litigation.** If a dispute arises, the parties will try in good faith to settle it through mediation conducted by [*choose one*]:

  ☐ _____ [*name of mediator*].

  ☐ a mediator to be mutually selected.

  The parties will share the costs of the mediator equally. If the dispute is not resolved within 30 days after it is referred to the mediator, any party may take the matter to court.

☐ **Mediation and possible arbitration.** If a dispute arises, the parties will try in good faith to settle it through mediation conducted by [*choose one*]:

  ☐ _____ [*name of mediator*].

  ☐ a mediator to be mutually selected.

  The parties will share the costs of the mediator equally. If the dispute is not resolved within 30 days after it is referred to the mediator, it will be arbitrated by [*choose one*]:

  ☐ _____ [*name of arbitrator*].

  ☐ an arbitrator to be mutually selected.

  The arbitrator's decision will be binding and judgment on the arbitration award may be entered in any court that has jurisdiction over the matter. Costs of arbitration, including lawyers' fees, will be allocated by the arbitrator.

a settlement, you submit the dispute to arbitration. The arbitrator makes a final decision that will be enforced by a court, if necessary. You can name the arbitrator when you prepare the form or agree on one when the need arises.

RESOURCE

You'll find lots of information to help you understand common legal issues online at www.nolo.com, including in-depth articles, FAQ, and state laws across dozens of legal topics. In particular, for resources on mediation and other methods of resolving disputes, visit the "Small Claims Court & Lawsuits" center. An excellent source for more thorough information is *Mediate, Don't Litigate: Strategies for Successful Mediation*, by Peter Lovenheim and Lisa Guerin, available as an eBook from www.nolo.com. If you do end up fighting a case in court, read *Represent Yourself in Court*, by Paul Bergman and Sara Berman. If the amount of money at stake in your case is below a certain dollar threshold (in most states the cap is somewhere between $5,000 and $10,000), you may be able to bring it in small claims court. In that case, see *Everybody's Guide to Small Claims Court*, by Ralph Warner, or, if you live in California, *Everybody's Guide to Small Claims Court in California*, also by Ralph Warner. All titles are published by Nolo.

Do You Need a Lawyer?

Most of the contracts in this book cover relatively straightforward transactions. Just as you routinely negotiate deals to lend money to a friend or hire someone to paint your kitchen without formal legal help, you can just as safely complete the basic legal paperwork needed to record what you and the other party have agreed upon.

But like most generalizations, this one isn't always true. Creating a solid written agreement —especially where a lot of money or property is at stake—will occasionally mean obtaining the advice of a lawyer. Fortunately, even when you seek a lawyer's help, the forms and information included here will let you keep a tight rein on legal fees. You'll have gotten a running start by learning about the legal issues and perhaps drawing up a rough draft of the needed document, allowing you and your lawyer to focus on the few points that may not be routine.

Ideally, you should find a lawyer who comes highly recommended from personal referrals. Look for someone who's willing to answer a few questions, or possibly to review a completed contract draft, but who respects your ability to prepare the routine paperwork. Adopting this approach should keep the lawyer's fee to a minimum. For more advice on finding and working with a lawyer, visit Nolo's Lawyer Directory at www.nolo.com/lawyers.

Get Forms, Updates, and More Online

Remember, all of the forms and contracts found in this book are available for you to download at any time on the book's companion page at www.nolo.com (see Appendix A for instructions on accessing this page). And when there are important changes to any of the information in this book, we'll post updates there, too.

Delegating Authority to Care for Children, Pets, and Property

Human beings can be distinguished from the rest of the animal kingdom in one fundamental way: the ability to reason or make decisions. Many of the key decisions we make as adults affect the care of our children, finances, and property. And sometimes, when we know we won't be available to make these decisions, we appoint a person we trust to do so. This chapter includes a temporary guardianship authorization, a power of attorney for finances, and several forms you can use to delegate decision making to others in a few common situations. It also includes forms to provide instructions for the care of your home and pets.

TIP

When it comes to care of your children, be sure you choose the right person. While it's important to prepare a sound agreement authorizing someone to care for your children when you can't, your children's interests aren't served if you don't choose a good caretaker. So be sure you pick someone you trust completely to follow your wishes for your child's care.

Form 1: Temporary Guardianship Authorization for Care of Minor

You may find it necessary to leave your child in the care of another adult for a few days, weeks, or months. If so, you should give the caretaker permission to authorize medical care and make other important decisions for your child. This includes school-related decisions—for example, if your child needs approval to go on a field trip, or becomes ill and needs to be picked up from school.

When you complete a temporary guardianship authorization, you are establishing what the law calls an "informal guardianship." By contrast, a formal guardianship requires court approval and is used most often when a child will be in a guardian's care for a long period of time—for example, when a young child moves in with his or her grandparents because the parents have died. A formal guardianship permits the guardian to make more extensive decisions for a child, such as taking the child out of one school and registering him or her at another.

An informal or temporary guardianship is most often used in these two situations:

- You will be traveling or otherwise unavailable for a relatively short period of time—for example, due to a hospital stay—and will leave your child in another adult's care.
- Your child lives with you and a stepparent who has not legally adopted your child. Because you travel frequently, the stepparent commonly functions as the primary caregiver.

If you have more than one child, you should prepare a separate temporary guardianship authorization for each child.

RELATED TOPIC

Authorizing medical care. When you make a temporary guardianship authorization, you should also consider making an Authorization for Minor's Medical Treatment, discussed below. Although the temporary guardianship form gives the temporary guardian explicit permission to authorize medical examinations, X-rays, hospital care, and other necessary treatments, the medical treatment authorization form allows you to spell out your child's medical history and needs in more detail. The two forms work well together. Whichever form you complete, you should speak with the pediatrician's office so that they know that the person you name as temporary guardian has your permission to make health care decisions for your child.

Signing Instructions

The parent(s) and the temporary guardian must sign the Temporary Guardianship Authorization for Care of Minor before it will be valid. Print out two copies of the form (or enough copies to give each person who will be signing the form). The parent(s) and the temporary guardian should sign and date all copies of the authorization form. Give one of the signed documents to the temporary guardian. Keep the other signed document for your own records and store it in a safe place.

FORM
Notarization is optional. You can choose to have a form notarized, but it's not required. (See the Introduction for general advice on having a form notarized.) Notarization will add a measure of legal credibility, but it isn't usually necessary. For example, you probably don't need to have your temporary guardianship authorization form notarized if you will be leaving your child with a grandparent for a few days. But if you will be away from your child for a long time—especially if your child stays with a nonrelative—it may be a good idea to visit a notary.

Form 2: Authorization for Minor's Medical Treatment

You can use a medical care authorization to permit an adult that you name to authorize necessary medical or dental care for your child. This can help you rest easier when your child is participating in sports or other organized activity outside of your supervision. You should provide this authorization to any adult who will be caring for your child when you are away, including babysitters and temporary guardians. This form provides details on your child's doctor, dentist, insurance, allergies, and ongoing medical conditions such as diabetes or

asthma, as well as information on how to reach you while your child is in another's care.

If your child is participating in a specified activity, such as a basketball league or dance lessons, the sponsoring organization may give you its own medical authorization to fill out. But if the organization doesn't give you a form, you should take the time to complete this one.

Signing Instructions

You (the parent[s]) must sign the Authorization for Minor's Medical Treatment document for it to be valid. Make two copies of the form and sign and date both. Give one of the signed documents to the person who has permission to authorize medical treatment for your child. Keep the other signed document for your own records and store it in a safe place.

FORM
Notarization is optional. You can choose to have a form notarized, but it's not required. (See the Introduction for general advice on having a form notarized.) Notarization will add a measure of legal credibility, but it isn't usually necessary.

Form 3: Authorization for Foreign Travel With Minor

Your child is unlikely to be permitted to travel outside the United States with someone other than a parent or legal guardian unless the travel companion has documentation showing the person's legal relationship to your child and his or her authority to travel with your child. If you are planning a trip for your child, you should prepare an authorization for foreign travel. This form provides necessary proof that you have given consent for your child to leave the country with another adult. It also provides information about the child's travel plans and contact information for you (the parents).

If you have more than one child who will be traveling outside the country with another adult, prepare a separate authorization form for each child.

In planning your child's trip, you should check travel rules carefully. Start by calling the embassy or consulate for the foreign country to which your child will be traveling. Ask whether the country has any rules or regulations governing adults traveling with an unrelated minor. Chances are good that the country does not, but it's always good to ask. If there are special requirements, you and the child's adult traveling companion can prepare for them in advance.

RELATED TOPIC

Authorizing medical care. This form does not permit the person traveling with your child to authorize medical care for the minor. To ensure that your child can receive any necessary medical treatment while traveling, you should also complete the Authorization for Minor's Medical Treatment, discussed just above.

Signing Instructions

You (the parent[s]) must sign the Authorization for Foreign Travel With Minor for it to be valid. Make two copies of the form. You and your child's other parent (if any) should sign and date both copies of the document. If you and your child's other parent are divorced or separated, you must still obtain the signature of the second parent before authorizing your child to leave the country with another adult. This will eliminate the possibility that foreign authorities will detain the travelers, suspecting a violation of child custody laws.

Give one of the signed documents to the person who has permission to travel with your child. Keep the other signed document for your own records and store it in a safe place.

FORM

Your foreign travel authorization should be notarized. To have a form notarized, you must go to the notary before signing it. (See the Introduction for general advice on having a form notarized.) The acknowledgment of a notary public will give the form a greater degree of legitimacy, especially in the eyes of a foreign government. This could help if problems arise during the trip.

Form 4: House-Sitting Instructions

Many people arrange to have a relative, a friend, or even a friend of a friend house-sit while they are away on vacation or for an extended period of time. Even if your house-sitter is quite familiar with your home, it's always a good idea to provide written information about the care and maintenance of your house. Use this form to specify details such as what to do about mail, newspapers, garbage, and recycling; gardening and yard maintenance; operation of appliances, locks, and security systems; and where you keep supplies. Write down everything you think the house sitter should know, including the location of emergency gas and water shut-off valves, and any special house rules, such as no smoking. Your house-sitting instructions should also provide details on how to reach you while you're away as well as the names and phone numbers of local contacts who can help with any problems or questions, such as a neighbor who has an extra key, your plumber, and your insurance agent. Preparing detailed house-sitting instructions will greatly reduce the chances of problems and give you peace of mind while you're many miles from home.

RELATED TOPIC

Pets, cars, and kids. If your house-sitter will be taking care of your pet or driving your car, be sure to complete the Pet Care Agreement and the Authorization to Drive a Motor Vehicle. And if your child will be staying at home in this house sitter's care, complete the Temporary Guardianship Authorization for Care of Minor.

Signing Instructions

There are no signing instructions for the House-Sitting Instructions. Simply fill out the form and leave it with your house sitter. It's probably a good idea to give an extra copy to a friend or neighbor.

Form 5: Children's Carpool Agreement

It's a rare family these days that doesn't rely to some extent on carpooling. Whether it's a trip to school, lessons, clubs, or after-school jobs, carpools make it possible for parents to share transportation hassles and—no small matter—have some time for their own jobs, commitments, and even themselves.

But as any carpool-savvy parent can tell you, there are good arrangements and there are those that don't work. While we can't guarantee that using our form will result in smooth sailing, we can help all carpool members get off on the right foot by recording their agreements on issues that should be discussed and settled at the outset. In addition, our form gives you a place to record important information that may come in handy. Think about the following issues and talk them out; then record your conclusions on the form:

- Who will be the drivers, and are you all satisfied that the drivers are qualified to drive and that they'll do so safely? Is each vehicle that will be used adequately insured?
- How long will the carpool wait for children who aren't ready when the carpool arrives? What should the driver do in the event that there is no one home at the drop off site?
- Identify two people who can care for your child in an emergency, as you do when asked by your school for your child's records.
- Identify any special considerations, such as a child's dietary restrictions (watch those carpool snacks), items that must be brought along (don't forget to check that the trumpet comes home from the music lesson), and personal quirks (with small children, seating arrangements can assume monumental importance).

Signing Instructions

After you and the other parents have made your decisions about the issues raised in the Carpool Agreement, record your conclusions in the spaces provided. Then have each parent sign and date the document. Give a copy of the signed agreement to each parent and keep a copy for yourself.

CAUTION

Unlike many of the forms in this book, your Carpool Agreement is not a legally binding document. If a member doesn't live up to it, your only recourse is to talk it over and come to a consensus about what to do.

Form 6: Pet Care Agreement

If you're going on a trip or will be otherwise unable to care for your pet for a period of time, you might leave your animal in the care of a neighbor or friend. If you do, it's a good idea to make a written agreement describing the arrangement and setting out clear instructions for your pet's care.

With this form, you can specify your pet's needs (including food, medication, exercise, and grooming), veterinarian contact information, special instructions such as vaccination due dates, how you can be reached, how you will reimburse the caregiver for any expenses involved in caring for your pet, and more. Having an agreement will greatly reduce the chances of a misunderstanding that might hurt your pet—or your relationship with the caregiver.

If you do find yourselves involved in a dispute, this agreement states that you and the pet caregiver will select a mutually agreeable third party to help you mediate the dispute and that you will share equally any costs of mediation. Mediation and other dispute resolution procedures are discussed in the Introduction.

 TIP

Payment for pet food and vet bills.
When a friend cares for your pet, you may think it unnecessary to pay for a few dollars' worth of pet food. Think again—you are already asking for a big favor, one that is likely to be extended again only if you are scrupulous about the details. Even if your friend has several animals already and ten bags of pet food in the garage, bring along more than enough chow to feed your pet while you will be away, plus some cash for unexpected expenses. Also, if your pet is prone to illness or is recovering from an illness or injury, arrange for payment of your vet bills in advance or ask to be billed. Otherwise, leave your credit card number with your vet in case your pet needs care while you are away. Finally, make sure you notify your vet, in writing, that your friend has the authority to make any necessary care decisions while you are away. Your vet may have an authorization form for you to fill out, or may ask you to write a simple letter authorizing the caregiver to make decisions.

Signing Instructions

You and the caregiver must sign the Pet Care Agreement for it to be valid. Make two copies of the agreement. You should each sign and date both copies. Give the caregiver one of the signed documents and keep the other one for your own records.

Form 7: Authorization to Drive a Motor Vehicle

Lending your vehicle to a friend or even a relative isn't always as simple as just handing over the keys. If the person who borrows your car is pulled over by the police or is involved in an accident, it will be important to be able to prove quickly that you agreed to lend out your car. If the borrower can't show that you gave permission, there may be a delay while police investigate whether the vehicle is stolen. Completing this authorization form provides the important legal proof that you've given someone else permission to drive your vehicle.

This form provides a place to list important information, such as your insurance policy number, that will help ensure that your guest driver (and car) are taken care of in the event of an accident or other mishap. If you want to set any restrictions on when or where the car may be used—for example, limiting driving to a specific geographic area or for a specific number of miles—you can do so.

This motor vehicle authorization form is designed for a car, but it will work fine for a motorcycle, truck, or other motor vehicle, such as a motorboat.

Signing Instructions

You (the vehicle owner) must sign your Authorization to Drive a Motor Vehicle form to make it valid. Make two copies of the authorization document. Sign and date both copies. Give one of the signed originals to the person who will be driving your car or other vehicle. Keep the other for your own records.

Form 8: Power of Attorney for Finances (Limited Power)

A power of attorney is a legal document in which you give another person legal authority to act on your behalf. In legal jargon, you're called "the principal," and the person to whom you give this authority is called your "attorney-in-fact" or "agent." In this context, "attorney" refers to anyone authorized to act on another's behalf; it's most definitely not restricted to lawyers.

Your attorney-in-fact (including any alternates you choose to name) should be someone you trust completely to act in your best interests—such as a spouse, relative, or close friend—who has enough common sense and experience to carry out the tasks you assign.

A limited power of attorney for finances lets you appoint an attorney-in-fact to help you with one or more specific, clearly defined tasks involving your finances. For example, you may want to name a relative or close friend to monitor certain investments—and sell them, if necessary—while you are on vacation or in the hospital for a short period of time. Or you may need someone to sign business or legal papers for you while you are unavailable.

 CAUTION
Don't use this power of attorney to give someone control over real estate transactions. If you need an attorney-in-fact to sell, buy, or manage real property for you, use the Power of Attorney for Real Estate.

 CAUTION
New York and Pennsylvania have special forms. If you live in New York or Pennsylvania, don't use Form 8 because your state has unique requirements for powers of attorney. Instead, use Form 8NY or Form 8PA. You can find both of these forms in Appendix B, and they are also available on this book's companion page.

To create your limited power of attorney, you'll enter some basic information about you (the "principal") and your attorney-in-fact, followed by the exact powers you want to grant—such as selling your car, signing loan papers while you're out of town, or monitoring your investments. Be as specific as possible— for example, if you want someone to sell your car for a minimum of $15,000 cash only, spell this out. Include relevant bank account numbers and complete descriptions of any property the attorney-in-fact may deal with.

The power of attorney form gives your attorney-in-fact the authority to act for you in all matters that you list. The attorney-in-fact, however, has a legal obligation to take only those actions that are in your best interests, and to represent you honestly and carefully.

This power of attorney form includes language designed to reassure third parties that they can accept the document without risk of legal liability. This "indemnification" clause clearly states that a third party may rely on the document without worry—in other words, the third party may conduct business with your attorney-in-fact as you have instructed—unless the person knows that you have revoked the document.

When the Power of Attorney Begins and Ends

Your power of attorney takes effect on a date you specify in your document. It ends under the circumstances described below.

The termination date. When you prepare your document, you can specify the date on which it will expire. You can enter a specific day, such as the day you expect to return from a trip. Or, you can make an open-ended document. If you don't specify an ending date, your attorney-in-fact is legally permitted to act for you until you revoke the power of attorney in writing.

You revoke the power of attorney. You can revoke your power of attorney at any time, as long as you are of sound mind. (And if you aren't of sound mind, the document terminates automatically, so you don't have to worry about revoking it.) To revoke your document, all you need to do is fill out a simple form, sign it in front of a notary public, and give copies to the attorney-in-fact and to people or institutions the attorney-in-fact has been dealing with. Form 10 is a revocation form you can use.

After a divorce. In a number of states, if your spouse is your attorney-in-fact and you divorce, your ex-spouse's authority is immediately terminated. Regardless of state law, however, if you've named your spouse as attorney-in-fact and you get divorced, you should revoke your power of attorney and make a new one.

No attorney-in-fact is available. Your power of attorney will automatically end if your attorney-in-fact dies, resigns, or becomes unable to represent you for any other reason.

You become incapacitated or die. Your power of attorney states that it will automatically end if you become incapacitated or die. In most states, however, if the attorney-in-fact doesn't know of your incapacity or death and continues to act on your behalf, these actions are still valid.

TIP

Financial institutions may have their own power of attorney forms. If you're giving your attorney-in-fact authority to deal with a bank, brokerage firm, or other financial institution, find out whether it has its own power of attorney form. If it does, you'll probably want to use that form instead of this one. Doing so will reduce hassles for your attorney-in-fact, because a financial institution will know what powers its own form grants and will have no need to quibble with your document.

Signing Instructions

A Power of Attorney for Finances is a serious document. To make it legally valid and effective, you must observe certain formalities when you sign it. Specifically, you must have your power of attorney form notarized, and, in some states, you may need to sign your document in front of witnesses. (See "States That Require Witnesses for a Power of Attorney," below.)

In a few states, your attorney-in-fact must sign the power of attorney before taking action under the document. In other states, the attorney-in-fact's signature is not required, but it's a fine idea to include it anyway. The attorney-in-fact's signature acts as assurance that the attorney-in-fact has read and fully understands the document, and is willing to assume the responsibility of acting prudently and honestly on your behalf. For this reason this power of attorney form includes a blank for the attorney-in-fact to sign. However, your attorney-in-fact doesn't need to sign until he or she needs to use the document, and that signature doesn't need to be notarized (except in New York).

States That Require Witnesses for a Power of Attorney

Most states don't require a power of attorney to be signed in front of witnesses. The few states that do and the number of witnesses required are listed below. Witness requirements normally consist of the following:

- Witnesses must be present when you sign the document in front of the notary.
- Witnesses must be mentally competent adults.
- The person who will serve as your attorney-in-fact can't be a witness.

Choose witnesses who will be easily available if they are ever needed. It's obviously a good idea to choose witnesses who live nearby and will be easy to contact.

State	Number of Witnesses	Other Requirements
Arizona	1	Witness may not be your attorney-in-fact, the spouse or child of your attorney-in-fact, or the notary public who acknowledges your document.
Connecticut	2	Neither witness may be your attorney-in-fact.
Delaware	1	Witness may not be your attorney-in-fact or be related to you by blood, marriage, or adoption; or be entitled to inherit a portion of your estate under your will or trust.
District of Columbia	2	Witnesses are necessary only if your power of attorney is to be recorded. Neither witness may be your attorney-in-fact.
Florida	2	Neither witness may be your attorney-in-fact.
Georgia	2	Neither witness may be your attorney-in-fact. In addition, one of your witnesses may not be your spouse or blood relative.
Illinois	1	Witness may not be your attorney-in-fact, or someone related to you or your attorney-in-fact by blood, marriage, or adoption; a person
Illinois (continued)		who provides health services to you; or an owner or operator of a health care facility where you are a resident.
Maryland	2	Witnesses may not be your attorney-in-fact.
Michigan	2	Witnesses are necessary only if your power of attorney is to be recorded. Neither witness may be your attorney-in-fact.
Oklahoma	2	Witnesses may not be your attorney-in-fact or anyone who is related by blood or marriage to you or your attorney-in-fact.
Pennsylvania	2	Witnesses may not be your agent or the person who signs your document for you. (Use forms 8PA and 9PA.)
South Carolina	2	Neither witness may be your attorney-in-fact.
Vermont	1	Witness may not be your attorney-in-fact or the notary public who acknowledges your document.

Limited Versus Durable Power of Attorney

This form is typically referred to as a "limited" or "conventional" power of attorney. As you may know, there is another type of power of attorney, called a durable power of attorney, that remains in effect even if you become incapacitated and can no longer make decisions for yourself. Durable powers of attorney are commonly signed in advance of need by older or ill people who realize that at some point they may require help managing their affairs. In contrast, limited powers of attorney (like this one) are used when you want someone to handle specific transactions for you at a set time. Because state laws vary in this area, if you want a durable power of attorney, you will need more extensive information. One excellent resource is *Quicken WillMaker Plus* software, which lets you create a valid will, durable power of attorney for finances, health care directive, and final arrangements document using your computer. If you live in California, you can use the book *Living Wills & Powers of Attorney for California*, by Shae Irving (Nolo). It contains all the forms and instructions California residents need to prepare a durable power of attorney for finances and advance health care directive.

FORM

A notary public must acknowledge your power of attorney demand. In some states, notarization is required by law to make the power of attorney valid. But even where law doesn't require it, custom does. A power of attorney that isn't notarized may not be accepted by people your attorney-in-fact needs to deal with.

If you will have your form witnessed (see "States That Require Witnesses for a Power of Attorney," above), everyone who has to sign the form must appear together in front of the notary. After watching each of you sign, the notary will complete an acknowledgment, and will attach a certificate to your document.

For more information on finding and using a notary, see this book's introduction.

Give the original signed and notarized document to the person you authorized. Your attorney-in-fact will need it as proof of authority to act on your behalf. Make a copy for yourself and store it in a safe place. If you wish, you can give copies of your power of attorney to the people your attorney-in-fact will need to deal with—for example, banks or government offices. If your financial power of attorney is already in their records, it may eliminate hassles for your attorney-in-fact later. Be sure to keep a list of everyone to whom you give a copy.

CAUTION

Revoking a power of attorney. If you later revoke your power of attorney, you must notify each institution of the revocation. We discuss the Notice of Revocation of Power of Attorney below.

Form 9: Power of Attorney for Real Estate

A power of attorney for real estate allows you to give someone the authority to buy or sell a piece of real estate for you, or to conduct any other business concerning real estate that you own. A power of attorney for real estate is a "limited" power of attorney, meaning that it automatically expires if you become incapacitated or die. (If you want a document that will stay in effect even if you become incapacitated, you need a "durable" power of attorney—see "Limited Versus Durable Power of Attorney," above.)

A power of attorney for real estate may be useful in a number of situations. Here are a few common ones:

- You will be out of town or otherwise unavailable when important real estate documents need to be signed.
- You will not be available to look after your real estate for a limited period of time.
- You live far away from property that you own and you want to authorize someone to manage it in your absence.

EXAMPLE 1: Alan is purchasing a condominium. Escrow has been opened at a title company, but the closing is delayed for several weeks. Because of the delay, the closing is now scheduled for the middle of Alan's long-planned trip to Greece. To solve this problem, Alan prepares a power of attorney for real estate, authorizing his sister Jennifer to sign any documents necessary to complete the closing and to withdraw any amounts of money (from an identified bank account) necessary to pay expenses and costs incurred because of the closing. Alan specifies that Jennifer's authority expires on the date he is to return from Greece.

Alan discusses his plans with his bank and the title company before he leaves, to be sure they'll accept the power of attorney and the authority of his attorney-in-fact. Both organizations assure him they'll accept a valid power of attorney for real estate. He has copies of his power of attorney placed in the bank's records and in his file at the title company. He leaves the original document with Jennifer, his attorney-in-fact.

EXAMPLE 2: Ann owns a summer cottage. Her friend June lives in the next cottage as her permanent home. Ann and June agree that because June is on the spot she'll take care of renting Ann's cottage, collecting rent, and paying all house bills and costs. Ann prepares a power of attorney for real estate giving June

authority to represent Ann for all transactions concerning her property at 20 Heron Lake Road. Ann specifies that the power of attorney will continue indefinitely. She also provides that June has no authority to sell the cottage nor to represent her in any transaction that doesn't concern the cottage.

TIP

Make sure your power of attorney will be accepted. The most important thing you can do to ensure that financial institutions, such as your mortgage lender or title company, will accept your power of attorney is talk with them in advance. Be sure that they're willing to accept the document and the authority of your attorney-in-fact. Your financial institution may ask you to include certain language in your form or even to use its own power of attorney form. If so, you should comply with its wishes. (If you're working with more than one financial institution, you may end up using more than one form.) Even though you can make a perfectly valid, legal document with this form, your financial institution may balk at accepting any form other than its own. Following your financial institution's recommendations will save time and trouble for you and your attorney-in-fact.

CAUTION

New York and Pennsylvania have special forms. If you live in New York or Pennsylvania, don't use Form 9 because your state has unique requirements for powers of attorney. Instead, use Form 9NY or Form 9PA. You can find both of these forms in Appendix B, and they are also available on this book's companion page.

Instructions for Preparing Your Power of Attorney for Real Estate

Here are instructions for filling in the Power of Attorney for Real Estate form.

Step 1. Principal and Attorney-in-Fact

In the first four blanks on the form, fill in your name and the city, county, and state where you live. Enter your name as it appears on official documents such as your driver's license, bank accounts, and real estate deeds. This may or may not be the name on your birth certificate.

> **EXAMPLE:** Your birth certificate lists your name as Rose Mary Green. But you've always gone by Mary, and always sign documents as Mary McNee, your married name. You would use Mary McNee on your power of attorney.

Be sure to enter all names in which you hold bank accounts or other property your attorney-in-fact will be dealing with. This will make his or his or her job far easier. If you're including more than one name, enter your full legal name first, followed by "aka" (also known as). Then enter your other names.

If during the course of a year you live in more than one state, use the address in the state where you vote, register vehicles, own valuable property, have bank accounts, or run a business. If you've made your will, health care directives, or a living trust, be consistent: Use the address in the state you declared as your residence in those documents.

Next, type in the name of the person who has agreed to serve as your attorney-in-fact. Then enter the city, county, and state where your attorney-in-fact lives.

Step 2. Description of Your Real Property

There is a large blank space following the first paragraph of the form. In it, you should type a description of the real estate your power of attorney will govern. Enter the exact street address, if your property has one. Then, attach a copy of the deed to your power of attorney form to avoid the trouble of retyping the lengthy and often confusing legal description contained in the deed.

SAMPLE INSERT:

> 9 Lotus Lane, Danville, CA 94558, Contra Costa County, California, as further described in the attached deed.

If you're up for it, you can type in the legal description instead. But be sure to type the entire description, exactly as it appears on the deed.

SAMPLE INSERT:

> LOT 195, as shown upon that certain map entitled, "Map of Greenbrae Sub. No. One, Marin Co. Calif.," filed May 2, 1946, in Book 6 of Maps, at Page 7, Marin County Records.

Step 3. Limiting the Powers Granted to the Attorney-in-Fact

Read through the powers described in the second paragraph of the document. If you don't want to grant one or more of the numbered powers, you can strike out or delete those that you don't need. If you just want to limit the numbered powers in some way, include your instructions in the blank space following the list of powers. For example, you might want to forbid your attorney-in-fact from selling your property; you can type that limitation in the blank space.

If you don't want to limit the powers in any way, strike out or delete the phrase "However, my attorney-in-fact shall not have the power to:"

Step 4. Additional Powers

In the fourth paragraph of the form, you can authorize your attorney-in-fact to carry out any additional powers related to the real estate powers you've granted. For example, you may want to authorize your attorney-in-fact to withdraw funds from a named bank account to cover any costs that arise in relation to his or her duties.

SAMPLE CLAUSE:

> I further grant to my attorney-in-fact full authority to act in any manner both proper and necessary to the exercise of the foregoing powers, including withdrawing funds from my checking account, #4482 478 880, Anderson Valley Savings and Loan, Boonville, CA, and I ratify every act that my attorney-in-fact may lawfully perform in exercising those powers.

If you don't want to add any powers to the document, strike out or delete the word "including."

Step 5. Termination Date

In the last paragraph of the form, type in a specific date on which you want the power of attorney to expire. (See "When the Power of Attorney Begins and Ends," in the instructions for Form 8, above.)

If you want the power of attorney to continue indefinitely, strike out or delete "or until _____ , whichever comes first." If you do so, and you later want to terminate the power of attorney, you must revoke it in writing.

Step 6. Preparation Statement

Insert the name, signature, and address of the person creating the power of attorney document—usually this is the principal. Some states or counties require a preparation statement on documents that will be recorded, but even where the law doesn't require it, tradition often does.

Signing Instructions

A power of attorney is a serious document, and to make it effective you must observe certain formalities when you sign it. Fortunately, these requirements aren't difficult to meet.

Notarization

A notary public must acknowledge your signature on your power of attorney document. Go to the notary public with your witnesses (if any), and sign your document in the notary's presence. See the Introduction of this book for more information about notarization.

Witnesses

Most states don't require the power of attorney to be signed in front of witnesses. (See "States That Require Witnesses for a Power of Attorney," in the instructions for Form 8, above.) Nevertheless, it doesn't hurt to have a witness or two watch you sign, and sign the document themselves. Witnesses' signatures may make the power of attorney more acceptable to lawyers, banks, insurance companies, and other entities the attorney-in-fact may have to deal with.

If you're giving your attorney-in-fact authority to handle real estate in a state other than the state where you live, be sure the document has at least the number of witnesses required by the state where the real property is located. Otherwise, you may not be able to record the power of attorney in that state.

SKIP AHEAD

If you will be using the downloadable forms on this book's online companion page to create your Power of Attorney for Real Estate, you don't need to read the cautionary instructions that follow. You can skip to the section on the attorney-in-fact's signature just below. The form on the companion page contains instructions to help you print the right number of signature lines. (See Appendix A for details on accessing the companion page.)

CAUTION

The Power of Attorney for Real Estate tear-out form in the back of the book has multiple last pages that may, at first glance, appear to be duplicates. Each of these pages is slightly different, however. Choose only the last page that has room for the number of witnesses your state requires—none, one, or two. (You can find the number of witnesses required by your state in "States That Require Witnesses for a Power of Attorney," in the instructions, above.) Then, check the page numbers of your document to make sure everything's in proper order and you aren't missing pages or including any extras.

The Attorney-in-Fact's Signature

In a few states, your attorney-in-fact must sign the power of attorney before taking action under the document. In other states, the attorney-in-fact's signature is not required, but it's a fine idea to include it anyway. The attorney-in-fact's signature acts as assurance that the attorney-in-fact has read and fully understands the document, and is willing to assume the responsibility of acting prudently and honestly on your behalf. For this reason, the form includes a blank for the attorney-in-fact to sign. However, your attorney-in-fact doesn't need to sign until he or she needs to use the document, and that signature doesn't need to be notarized (except in New York).

Putting Your Power of Attorney on Public Record

You must put a copy of your power of attorney on file in the county land records office, called the county recorder's or land registry office in most states. This is called "recording" or "registration" in some states. If you don't record the power of attorney, your attorney-in-fact may not be permitted to handle real estate transactions for you.

Recording makes it clear to all interested parties that the attorney-in-fact has power over the property at issue. County land records are checked whenever real estate changes hands or is mortgaged. If, for example, your attorney-in-fact is supposed to sell or mortgage a piece of property for you, there must be something in the public records that proves he or she has authority to do so.

If you put your power of attorney on public record and then later revoke it in writing, you must also record the notice of revocation. You can make a notice of revocation using the Notice of Revocation of Power of Attorney.

Where to Record Your Power of Attorney

In most states, each county has its own county recorder's (or registry of deeds) office. Take the power of attorney to the office in the county where the real estate is located. If you are granting your attorney-in-fact authority over more than one parcel of real estate, record the power of attorney in each county where you own property.

How to Record a Document

Recording a document is easy. You may even be able to do it by mail, but it's safer to go in person. The clerk will make a copy for the public records. It will be assigned a reference number, often called an "instrument number." It shouldn't cost more than $20 to record your document.

What to Do With the Signed Document

Give the original signed, and notarized document to the attorney-in-fact, who will need it as proof of authority to act on your behalf.

Making and Distributing Copies

You should give copies of your power of attorney to the people your attorney-in-fact will need to deal with—banks or title companies, for example. If your power of attorney is in their records, it may eliminate hassles for your attorney-in-fact later.

Be sure to keep a list of everyone to whom you give a copy. If you later revoke your power of attorney, notify each institution of the revocation.

Keeping Your Document Up to Date

If you've made a power of attorney without a specific termination date, you should redo it every year or so. Banks and other financial institutions may be reluctant to accept a power of attorney that's more than a couple of years old, even though the document is still technically valid. You should destroy any copies of the old power of attorney document and notify the people and institutions with copies of the former document that you have revoked your old power of attorney and made a new one.

Form 10: Notice of Revocation of Power of Attorney

You can use a Notice of Revocation of Power of Attorney form in two situations:

- You want to revoke your power of attorney before the termination date set out in the document.
- Your power of attorney has ended as specified in the document, but you want to be absolutely sure that all institutions (such as banks, stockbrokers, and insurance companies) and people (such as your attorney or accountant) who have received it know that it is no longer in force.

Signing Instructions

Sign and date the Notice of Revocation in front of a notary public for your state, as explained in the discussion of the Power of Attorney for Finances (Limited Power).

 CAUTION
If you recorded your power of attorney, record the Notice of Revocation. If you put your power of attorney on file in the public records office and it hasn't expired on its own, you should also record your Notice of Revocation. Otherwise, people who don't actually know of your revocation are entitled to continue to deal with your attorney-in-fact on your behalf.

Basic Estate Planning

Making arrangements for what will happen to your property after you die is called estate planning. Generally, if you die without a will or other legal means for transferring property, your property will be distributed to certain close relatives—your spouse or domestic partner, children, parents, or siblings—under state "intestacy" laws.

Making a will is an important part of estate planning. For many people, a will, coupled with naming beneficiaries for retirement plans, insurance policies, and other investments, is the only estate plan they need. Whether that is true for you or not depends on your circumstances. Generally speaking, the more wealth you possess, the more you'll want to consider legal issues beyond the scope of a will, such as avoiding probate—the court-supervised process of gathering and distributing a deceased person's assets. And, depending on your situation, you may want to provide for a child with a disability, establish a fund for grandchildren, or make charitable gifts.

This chapter introduces the concept of estate planning and provides some useful worksheets and some basic will forms. Resources listed here explain where to go for more detailed information.

Form 11: Property Worksheet

Before you write a will or other estate planning document, you may find it helpful to make an inventory of your property, including real estate, cash, securities, cars, household goods, digital assets, and business personal property, such as a company you own or the right to receive royalties. Filling out the Property Worksheet can jog your memory to make sure you don't overlook important items.

Describe each asset on the Property Worksheet under the appropriate section of the "Property" column. If an asset such as a house or car is jointly owned, specify the percentage you own.

Even if you haven't made a will, you may have already named someone to get some of your property at your death. For example, if you have an IRA, 401(k) retirement plan, or insurance policy, you have probably named a beneficiary and alternate beneficiary on a form provided by the account custodian company. If you own real estate, you may hold it in joint tenancy with right of survivorship, meaning that the other joint owner will automatically inherit your share at your death. If you've already named someone to inherit an asset after your death, write down the beneficiary's name on the Property Worksheet under "Name of Any Existing Beneficiary."

The Property Worksheet also prompts you to list your "digital assets," such as your social media accounts, email addresses, apps, or online memberships. Most of these assets won't pass through your estate when you die, but your executor may need to access them in order to wrap up your estate. After using the Property Worksheet to brainstorm about what digital assets you have, consider creating a separate document that includes 1) a list of your digital assets, 2) details on how to access them, and 3) instructions on what to do with those assets after your death. Keep this document in a secure place, and make sure your executor knows how to find it.

Signing Instructions

You don't need to sign the Property Worksheet. Simply fill it out and use it when preparing your will or other estate planning document.

RESOURCE

Organize your personal information.
Get It Together: Organize Your Records So Your Family Won't Have To, by Melanie Cullen and Shae Irving (Nolo), helps you leave survivors a clear record of your important documents and information, including secured places and passwords, retirement accounts, insurance policies, real estate records, and much more. It also provides a road map to the arrangements you have made for after your death.

Form 12: Beneficiary Worksheet

Like the Property Worksheet, the Beneficiary Worksheet is a tool that can help you get ready to draft estate planning documents. On the Beneficiary Worksheet, list each item of property and then list the people or organizations to whom you want to leave the property. If you name more than one beneficiary to share a specific gift, state the percentage share each is to receive.

It is also highly advisable to name an alternate beneficiary or beneficiaries for each gift, in case your first choice dies before you do.

You can also list people who owe you money, if you want to forgive these debts at your death. For example, if you loaned your best friend $10,000 and he pays you back with interest $100 a month, it will take him many years to pay off the debt. If he still owes you money when you die, you can forgive or waive the balance due. This means that your heirs cannot go after your friend for the rest.

Finally, list a "residuary" beneficiary or beneficiaries. This is one or more people or organizations who will get everything that's left after your specific gifts are distributed. Do this even if you are sure you have identified all your property and named a beneficiary to receive it; there is always a chance that you'll acquire additional property between the date you make your will and your death.

TIP

Do you need to use the Beneficiary Worksheet? If you plan to leave all your property to one or a very few people (for example, "all property to my spouse, or if she predeceases me, to my children in equal shares"), there is no need to complete the Beneficiary Worksheet. You already know who will get your property at your death, and you can turn to the will forms that follow.

Signing Instructions

You don't need to sign the Beneficiary Worksheet. Simply fill it out and use it when preparing your will or other estate planning documents.

Common Property That May Already Have Beneficiaries

You may have already planned the eventual disposition of much of your property before you prepare a will. Here are some examples of property for which you may have already named a beneficiary:

- bank accounts, naming a payable-on-death beneficiary (on a form provided by the bank)
- real estate, holding it with someone else in joint tenancy, in tenancy by the entirety, or (in community property states) as community property with right of survivorship with your spouse
- securities, registering them in transfer-on-death form if your state law allows it
- real estate or vehicles for which you have named transfer-on-death beneficiaries (not available in all states)
- retirement accounts, naming a beneficiary (on a form provided by the account custodian) to take whatever is still in the account at your death, and
- life insurance policies, naming a beneficiary (on a form provided by the company) to receive the proceeds at your death.

Nolo Resources on Estate Planning

Nolo publishes several books and software products containing more sophisticated—but still easy-to-use—information on wills and living trusts. A living trust is the document used most often to avoid probate, the process of distributing a person's property under court supervision.

- *Plan Your Estate*, by Denis Clifford, is a comprehensive estate planning book, covering everything from basic estate planning (wills and living trusts) to sophisticated tax-saving strategies (AB trusts and much more). If you haven't yet decided how to approach your estate planning tasks, this is Nolo's best resource.
- *Quicken WillMaker Plus* interactive software lets you make a more sophisticated will than those offered here. For example, you can choose among three ways to provide property management for children should you die before they are competent to handle property themselves. In addition, with *Quicken WillMaker Plus* you can create a separate document to express your wishes for your funeral and burial. It also contains a

health care directive (living will), a durable power of attorney for finances, and many other useful forms.

- *Nolo's Online Will* and *Living Trust* allow you to make a will or living trust without books or software—in less than an hour. These are time-tested documents created by Nolo's expert attorneys, and they come with plenty of legal and practical information along the way. Go to www.nolo.com to get started.
- *8 Ways to Avoid Probate*, by Mary Randolph, explains important and often overlooked ways to avoid probate. It is now possible to avoid probate for many kinds of property without creating a living trust. If you vaguely know you should be paying attention to probate avoidance, but dread thinking about it, start with this small but thorough book.
- *Special Needs Trusts: Protect Your Child's Financial Future*, by Kevin Urbatsch and Michele Fuller, explains how you can leave money to a loved one who has a disability, without interfering with eligibility for SSI or Medicaid benefits.

Forms 13 and 14: Basic Wills

A basic will is easy to make. It's also easy to change or revoke; you won't be stuck with it if you change your mind later. With the will forms in this book, you can:

- leave your property to anyone you wish
- name a guardian to raise young children if you can't, and
- appoint an executor to carry out your will's terms.

This section gives an overview of making a basic will. Next come two bare-bones forms, which can be used by residents of all states except Louisiana.

These wills are a good choice if you want a will quickly on the eve of a long trip or don't want to spend much time on estate planning right now. You'll probably want to draft a more extensive will for the long term. Precisely because these forms are short, simple, and easy to use, they do not include a lot of options. For example, they do not let you create a trust to hold property that may be left to children or young adults.

If you have children, use the Will for Adult With Child(ren). Otherwise, use the Will for Adult With No Children.

Anyone who is of legal age (18 years old in most states) and of sound mind can make a valid will. You have to be very far gone before your will can be invalidated on the grounds that you were mentally incompetent. If you're reading and understanding this book, your mind is sound enough to make a will.

 CAUTION
Do not just fill in a will form by hand. A will should not contain a mix of handwritten and machine-printed material. When you prepare a will using the forms in this book, you can use the tear-out forms to sketch out a draft of your document. But then you'll need to use your computer to download, edit, and print a fully-typed final version of your will. (If you don't have a computer, you can use a typewriter to type the entire will document.)

Leaving specific items. If you want to list specific items of property you're leaving through your will, you'll use the "Specific Gifts" section. When you list items, describe them so that your executor—and anyone else—will know exactly what you meant. There is no need to use formal legal descriptions unless they are really necessary to identify the property. Here are some examples of good property descriptions:

- "my house at 435 76th Avenue, Chicago, Illinois"
- "all household furnishings and possessions in my house at 435 76th Avenue, Chicago, Illinois," and
- "$10,000 from my savings account, No. 44444, at First National Bank, Chicago, Illinois."

Then you'll need to say what you want to happen to the rest of your property, which is called your "residuary." For example, say you make a few small specific gifts and want everything else to go to your three children. You would use the "Specific Gifts" section to make your specific gifts and the "Residuary Estate" clause to leave everything else to your children.

CAUTION
Don't use "all my children" or other categories of people. You may be tempted to refer to beneficiaries with phrases like "all my children," "my surviving children," "my lawful heirs," or "my issue." Don't do it. Name each beneficiary individually to avoid any confusion later.

Leaving Everything. If you want to leave everything to just one beneficiary, or a group of them—your spouse or your three children, for example—don't use the "Specific Gifts" part of the will. Instead, use the "Residuary Estate" clause. Because "residuary" simply refers to the rest of your estate and you have made no specific gifts, everything will go to the person or persons you name as your residuary beneficiary(ies).

Property with debt. When you leave property, any encumbrances on it—for example, a mortgage—pass with the property. In other words, the beneficiary takes the debt as well as the property.

Naming your executor. In your will, you must name someone to be in charge of winding up your affairs after your death. This person is called your executor (the term "personal representative" is used in some states). The executor must shepherd your property through probate—the court process of distributing the property of a deceased person—if it's necessary, and must see that your property is distributed according to the wishes expressed in your will.

Many people name their spouse or a grown child as executor. The executor usually doesn't need special financial or legal expertise. The important thing is that the person you choose is completely trustworthy and will deal fairly with other beneficiaries.

Preparing your will. Use the tear-out forms in this book to make a rough draft of your will. For this initial draft, you can fill in the blanks by hand, cross out clauses you don't need, and renumber the remaining clauses. Then, either retype the entire will, or download, edit, and print a will form from this book's companion page. (See Appendix A.)

When you're done, read your will carefully to make sure you understand and agree with every word. If you do not agree with something in the will, do not reword the will language yourself, or you'll risk your will's validity. Instead, you may need to use a more complex will that can be more carefully tailored to your situation. (See "Nolo Resources on Estate Planning," above.)

Signing Instructions

Your signature on your will must be witnessed. When you are ready to sign it, gather together two adults who aren't beneficiaries of your will. Your witnesses do not need to read your will. You simply tell them, "This is my will." Then you sign and date your will while the witnesses watch. Finally, each witness signs while the other witness watches. You do not need to have your will notarized. Be sure to store your will in a safe place.

> **CAUTION**
>
> **If you're married or in a registered domestic partnership, your spouse may be able to claim a share of your estate.** In most states (all except Arizona, California, Idaho, Louisiana, Nevada, New Mexico, Texas, Washington, and Wisconsin, which follow the community property system), a surviving spouse has the right to reject what the will says and instead claim a share of the deceased spouse's entire estate. In many states, that share is about one-third of the estate. The details get tricky fast. As long as you plan to leave your spouse or partner at least half of your property, you don't need to worry about it. But if you plan to leave less than half of your property to your spouse or partner, see a lawyer and don't try to use the forms in this book.

Form 13: Will for Adult With No Children

This is the will to use if you don't have children. Remember, these forms can be used by residents of all states except Louisiana.

Read the introduction to basic wills (above) for brief but important instructions on filling out the form correctly, so that you will create a legally valid will that accomplishes what you want.

Form 14: Will for Adult With Child(ren)

First, read the material on basic wills, above, for brief but important instructions on filling out the form correctly, so that you will create a legally valid will that accomplishes what you want. Because you have children, you have some special issues to consider before you make your will.

Heading off claims. You should mention each of your children in your will, even if you don't use your will to leave them any property. That's because, although children are not usually entitled to claim any property from a parent's estate, they do have certain rights if it appears that they were unintentionally overlooked. By listing all of your children, including those you have legally adopted, you head off any argument that you forgot any of them.

Custody of minor children. If you have children under age 18, use Clause 8 to name the person you want to raise the children if you die and the other parent is unavailable to raise them. This person is called their "personal guardian." It is also wise to nominate an alternate personal guardian, in case the first choice can't serve.

If a guardian is ever needed, a judge will review your choice. If no one objects, the person you name will most likely be appointed. But in an unusual situation, a judge who is convinced that naming a different personal guardian is in the best interests of the child has the authority to do so.

CAUTION

With this will form, you cannot name different guardians for different kids. This will form requires that you name the same personal guardian for all of your minor children. If for some reason you want to name different people as guardians for different children, use *Nolo's Online Will* or *Quicken WillMaker Plus*.

Property left to children. Minors cannot legally own property outright, free of supervision, beyond a minimal amount—$2,500 to $5,000, depending on the state. By law, an adult must be legally responsible for managing any significant amount of property owned by a minor child. So if your children or other minors might inherit property through your will—even if they're only alternate beneficiaries—you should arrange for an adult to supervise it. You can do this easily in your will.

Form 14 gives you two ways to provide for adult supervision for gifts to minors:

- **Name a custodian for each young person who might receive property through your will.** The custodian will manage any property slated for the child until the child turns 21 (in most states). A custodian is authorized under your state's Uniform Transfers to Minors Act (UTMA). (See below and see Clause 10 of the will.)
- **Name a property guardian for each of your own minor children.** You should always name a property guardian and successor property guardian in your will, even if you appoint a custodian under the Uniform Transfers to Minors Act.

The property guardian will be formally appointed by a court and will manage any property not left through your will (and so not covered by the UTMA custodianship)—for example, property the minor gets from someone else.

Other Property Management Options

The Will for Adult With Child(ren) does not offer two other fairly common—but legally more complicated—ways to arrange for a minor's property to be managed by an adult:

- A family pot trust that will hold property left to all your minor children, allowing the trustee you name to spend it as needed. For example, if one child had an expensive medical problem, the trustee could spend more for that child and less for others.
- A trust for each child. This option is primarily of value for people with larger estates who do not want adult children to take control of money outright until they are in their middle or late twenties. It gets around the fact that in most states a custodianship under the terms of the Uniform Transfers to Minors Act ends at age 21.

These options are available in *Quicken WillMaker Plus* and *Nolo's Online Will*.

Uniform Transfers to Minors Act. All states except South Carolina have adopted the Uniform Transfers to Minors Act (UTMA). This law authorizes you to appoint an adult custodian and successor custodian in your will to supervise property you leave to a minor. The custodianship ends, and any remaining property must be turned over to the child outright, at the age the UTMA specifies. In most states, this is 21, but a few (for example,

California and Alaska) allow you to choose up to age 25. Our form sets the ending age at the oldest age allowed in your state, which in the majority of states is 21.

Because the custodian has almost complete discretion over management of the property, it is essential that you name someone who is totally honest and has good financial management skills. The custodian also has a legal duty to act prudently in the best interests of the child. Normally, no court supervision is required.

Complete a separate UTMA clause for each young beneficiary.

Form 15: Will Codicil

A codicil is sort of a legal "P.S." to a will. In a codicil, you can revoke a clause in your will and then substitute a new clause. Or you can simply add a new provision, such as a new gift of an item of property.

A codicil must be signed and witnessed just like a will. The form must be retyped or computer printed (start with "First Codicil to the Will of _____ ," leaving off our title), then dated and signed by you in front of two witnesses. You don't have to use the same witnesses who signed your will, but in many states the witnesses cannot be people named as beneficiaries in your will or codicil.

Today, codicils are less commonly used than they were in the days when wills were laboriously copied by hand or typed on a typewriter. With almost universal access to computers, it's usually easier—and less likely to confuse—to prepare a whole new will, revoking the previous one. Nevertheless, codicils can still be sensibly used to make limited changes to a will—for example, when you want to change who receives one item.

Things to Do After a Death: Documents for Executors

After a death, someone must step in and wind up the deceased person's affairs. An executor—sometimes called personal representative or administrator—is the person named in the will, or appointed by the probate court, who has legal responsibility for safeguarding and handling the deceased person's property, seeing that debts and taxes are paid, and distributing what is left to beneficiaries as directed by the will. Here are a number of simple forms and letters you can use if you are named as someone's executor, as well as a checklist to help you be sure you are taking care of all that needs to be done.

 RESOURCE
Nolo has books that can help you. *How to Probate an Estate in California: A Step-by-Step Guide*, by Julia Nissley, gives California residents step-by-step instructions for handling an estate. *The Executor's Guide: Settling a Loved One's Estate or Trust*, by Mary Randolph, covers the legal and financial matters that crop up after a death, helping the surviving family through what is often a difficult and confusing time.

 CAUTION
These forms are not applicable in all situations. The forms in this chapter cannot be used to claim benefits under an insurance policy or retirement plan. You will need to contact the appropriate companies and complete their forms.

Form 16: Request for Death Certificate

As an executor or personal representative, you will need to handle many tasks, such as terminating leases and credit cards, notifying banks and the post office, and so forth. If you will be contacting agencies, businesses, or organizations about the death, you will need

certified copies—probably about ten—of the death certificate. Typically, the mortuary you deal with will get copies of a death certificate—and add the cost to the bill.

If the mortuary was not able to get copies for you, or if you need additional copies, you can order them yourself.

Concern about identity theft has led some states to restrict access to death records to relatives of the deceased person, or to people who have a legal role in the deceased person's affairs, such as the executor. If you are requesting the death certificate for any reason other than taking care of a deceased person's estate—for example, genealogical research—do not use this form. There may be other requirements as well. For example, several states now require you to send in a photocopy of your driver's license or other photo identification with the request.

Most county websites offer request forms that you can print out and send; others allow you to submit your request online and pay by credit card. You may also be able to order death certificates through your state's department of health or through a private online service such as www.vitalchek.com.

That said, in some counties, you may still be able to use the form in this book to request copies of a death certificate by mail. If you want to use this form, check with your county's recorder's office first, and then follow the rest of the instructions in this section.

Where to send the request for death certificate form. Before you send in a request, call the vital statistics office or county health department in the county where the decedent died and ask where to send your request. Also find out the cost of a certified copy of a death certificate.

Information to include in your request. You will need the name of the deceased and place of death. The deceased person's place of birth and Social Security number are optional, but they can be very helpful for identification purposes. Be sure to state your relationship to the deceased person—for example, surviving spouse—whose death certificate you are requesting.

Reason for the request. Most states now require you to include the reason you are requesting the death certificate. This form tells the vital records office that you need the death certificate in order to wind up the affairs of the deceased's estate. Be sure to indicate the number of copies you want. Most executors need at least ten copies.

Signing Instructions

Sign and date your Request for Death Certificate. Mail it to the appropriate agency, along with a check for the proper amount and a stamped self-addressed business-sized envelope. Keep a copy of the form for your records.

Form 17: Notice to Creditor of Death

After someone dies, the executor needs to notify creditors of the death and close the deceased person's credit accounts. That's the purpose of this form. You can send it to credit card issuers, department stores, banks, mortgage companies, and other businesses that extended credit to the deceased person.

You will need to put the date of death and the appropriate account number on this notice. You may also need to attach a document showing your appointment as executor or administrator.

> **CAUTION**
>
> **If a formal probate court proceeding is conducted, you'll also have to follow special rules for notifying creditors**, for example, mailing a notice to creditors you know about and publishing a notice in a local newspaper to alert those you're not aware of. Check with the lawyer who is handling the

probate proceedings, or, if you are handling probate on your own, ask the probate clerk at the county courthouse for the rules.

Signing Instructions

Sign the notice and mail two copies to each of the deceased's creditors. The creditor who receives this notice should sign and date it—and mail a copy to you in the stamped, self-addressed envelope you enclose. Keep the completed copy you receive for your records. You may later need it as proof that you notified the creditor of the death.

> **TIP**
>
> **Reconcile the deceased person's records.** This notice asks the creditor to forward information to you about any remaining balance owed by the deceased. Once you hear back from the creditor, check the information sent by the creditor against the deceased person's records.

Form 18: Executor's Checklist

The executor of an estate has many small and large jobs. The Executor's Checklist lists the tasks that an executor must typically complete when winding up the affairs of someone who has died. Keep in mind, however, that an executor's specific duties depend on the needs of the estate and the requirements of state law. These vary based on the size of the estate, the kind of assets in the estate, and personal factors, such as the needs and expectations of the family. Use the Executor's Checklist as a guide, tailoring it to your situation.

Signing Instructions

There's no need to sign or fill in any part of the Executor's Checklist. Simply use it as a guide to ensure that you are taking care of the tasks required of you as the executor of an estate.

Form 19: General Notice of Death

You may want to notify businesses and organizations that aren't creditors—that is, they aren't owed any money—of the death. For example, you might want to send a simple notice communicating the fact that someone has died to charities to which the deceased person has donated regularly, magazine publishers, and mail-order businesses that frequently send catalogs.

 RELATED TOPIC
If you want to get the deceased's name deleted from junk mail lists, use the Notice to Remove Name From List.

It's easier to send a form than to write individual letters to each organization or business. You can also send this form to individuals who need to be notified of the death—unless they are friends or relatives who merit a personal call or note.

 CAUTION
Do not use this general notice of death form for creditors and government agencies. Many need specific information about the deceased, such as the accounts owing or type of benefits received. To notify creditors, use the Notice to Creditor of Death, above. For other government agencies, it's a good idea to call and find out what type of notice they require.

 TIP
How to stop Social Security payments after a death. If a deceased person was receiving Social Security benefits, the executor or personal representative must notify the Social Security Administration (SSA) of the death. To stop payments, call the SSA at 800-772-1213 or 800-325-0778 (TTY).

Signing Instructions

Sign and date your General Notice of Death and mail it to the business or organization you wish to notify. Keep a copy of the notice for your records or, if you are sending many copies, keep a record of everyone on your mailing list, rather than copies of every notice sent.

Form 20: Obituary Information Fact Sheet

When a family member or friend dies, it's always a challenge to focus on the many details that need your attention. This form will help you with one of those tasks: organizing information for your loved one's obituary.

Most of the time, local newspapers obtain obituary information from the funeral home. On some occasions, the newspaper may obtain this information directly from the family—for example, when the death occurred away from home or when a funeral home is not handling arrangements.

Regardless of who speaks to the obituary writer, there's less chance of error if you complete a fact sheet providing relevant information. Be sure to spell all names accurately, and include any business or personal information of interest. For example, "He founded the Carverville Barbershop Quartet" or "She was widely traveled and a frequent visitor to Nairobi and the Serengeti." When listing survivors, include surviving spouses and children of previous marriages.

The amount of detail that's included in an obituary and the placement of the obituary in the newspaper (some obituaries are published in the news section, not the obituary section) depend on the prominence of the deceased in the community. It's possible that space limitations will preclude the newspaper from including some or all of the information that you submit.

In addition to a print obituary, you might also consider whether you want an online death notice. Online obituaries are less limited by space and can include photos, videos, and music. Importantly, they are also accessible worldwide and provide a place for family and friends near and far to leave a note or memory. Some mortuaries or funeral homes provide online obituaries as part of their service, and many newspapers also print their death notices online. However, families can create their own online memorials through websites like www. forevermissed.com.

Signing Instructions

You don't need to sign the Obituary Information Fact Sheet form. Simply fill it out and mail it to local newspapers you think will be likely to publish the obituary. The mortuary will have a list of contacts for local obituary columns.

Form 21: Notice to Deceased's Homeowners' Insurance Company

Use this form if the deceased person owned a home and insured it. The form notifies the insurance company of the death and asks that you, the executor, be added as a "named insured" to the homeowners' insurance policy.

 CAUTION
If you are a co-owner of the home, do not use this form. Instead, call the insurance company to report the death.

As the executor, you will want to be added as a named insured to that policy as soon as possible. This status will give you all the protections and rights that the deceased person had under the policy. This means that you will be covered if you or anyone is injured on the premises due to your carelessness. And you will be able to make claims for property damage, if necessary. As a named insured, you also have the right to increase coverage or change policy limitations. For example, if you discover that the home and its contents are underinsured, you can make changes in the coverage. Finally, if the insurance company makes a payment after a claim has been made under the policy—for example, paying for the results of a wind-damaged roof—you will be a copayee on the check. This is important because these payments are part of the estate, and you will need to receive and account for them.

After you are added as a named insured, you'll want to discuss with the insurance agent or broker how best to continue insurance coverage for the deceased's home. You may want to add coverage or increase coverage limits, particularly if you discover that the home was underinsured. You may also want to add riders for jewelry or other special items.

To complete this form, you will need the following information:
- the deceased person's full name (if the deceased's name is different on the insurance policy, be sure to note that)
- the date of death
- the name of the insurance company that issued the policy and the complete address of its home office
- the homeowners' policy number, and
- a certified copy of the death certificate (see Request for Death Certificate, above).

Signing Instructions

Sign and date the Notice to Deceased's Homeowners' Insurance Company. Make two copies of the signed notice. Mail the original and one copy to the insurance company office, along with a stamped, self-addressed envelope and a certified copy of the death certificate. Keep the second copy of the notice for your records.

Form 22: Notice to Deceased's Vehicle Insurance Company

Use this form if the deceased person owned and insured any automobiles, trucks, motorcycles, motor homes, or trailers. The notice informs the insurance company of the death of the insured person and asks them to add you, the executor, to the insurance policy.

You will want to be added as a "named insured" to that policy so you will have all the protections and rights that the deceased person had under the policy. Most important, you will be permitted to add or delete coverage or adjust policy limits, if appropriate. Also, you will be named as a copayee (along with others insured under the policy) in any payment from the company. Because these payments are part of the estate, you must receive and account for them.

Many people own more than one vehicle, and they may be insured under separate policies. Even if the deceased person used the same company for multiple policies, you should send a separate notice for each policy.

After you are added as a named insured, talk to the insurance agent or broker about how best to continue insurance coverage for the deceased's vehicles. You may want to add coverage or increase coverage limits; and if the deceased was rated a poor risk, you may even want to ask for a reduction in premiums.

Even if you do not expect that the vehicle will be used, you must insure it in case of a fire or other calamity. A parked car in a home garage, for example, will not be covered by the homeowners' policy if there is a fire—you need an auto policy or other insurance coverage. When the vehicle is distributed or sold and is no longer part of the estate, you can easily cancel the insurance you have purchased.

To complete this form, you will need the following information:

- the deceased person's full name (if the deceased's name is different on the insurance policy, be sure to note that)
- the date of death (if you don't know it, look on the death certificate)
- vehicle year, make, and model
- the name of the insurance company that issued the policy and the complete address of its home office
- the vehicle insurance policy number
- the latest billing statement from the insurance company
- a certified death certificate for the person who has died (see Form 16 to request a death certificate), and
- in some cases, a certified copy of your driving record (available from your state's department of motor vehicles).

 TIP

Document your role as executor. The insurance company may require proof of your status as the executor. Be prepared to send a copy of the court order (often called "letters testamentary" or "letters of administration") that names you as the executor. If you do not have a court order by the time the insurance company calls you, ask what other proof it will accept.

Signing Instructions

Sign and date the Notice to Deceased's Vehicle Insurance Company. Make two copies of the signed notice. Mail the original and one copy to the insurance company office, along with a stamped, self-addressed envelope. Remember to enclose a certified copy of the death certificate. Keep the second copy of the notice for your records.

Renting a Place to Live

Whether you rent or own property, you probably understand just how bad a failed landlord-tenant relationship can be. But there is an excellent way to get any landlord-tenant relationship off to a good start and minimize the possibility of future misunderstandings and legal problems: Put all agreements in writing. This chapter includes a rental application, a move-in letter, repair request, and other forms that will help you do this and will be useful during the tenancy and at move-out time.

RESOURCE

To learn more details of landlord-tenant law, see the following Nolo books and forms:
From the landlord's point of view:

- *Every Landlord's Legal Guide*, by Marcia Stewart, Ralph Warner, and Janet Portman. This 50-state book provides extensive legal and practical information on leases, tenant screening, rent, security deposits, privacy, repairs, property managers, discrimination, roommates, liability, and tenancy termination, and includes 50-state law charts on important rules affecting landlords. It includes more than 30 legal forms and agreements, all available for download on the Nolo website.
- *Every Landlord's Guide to Finding Great Tenants*, by Janet Portman. This book provides an in-depth process for finding tenants, from advertising to dealing with current residents, to evaluating applications, credit reports, and more. More than 40 forms, complete with essential 50-state legal tables with the law landlords need to know.

Nolo also publishes two books for California landlords, both by David Brown: *The California Landlord's Law Book: Rights & Responsibilities* (with Ralph Warner and Janet Portman), and *The California Landlord's Law Book: Evictions*, as well as other national books for landlords, such as *First-Time Landlord: Your Guide to Renting Out a Single-Family*

Home, *Every Landlord's Tax Deduction Guide*, and *Every Landlord's Guide to Managing Property*.

In addition to books, Nolo offers dozens of state-specific leases and other forms for landlords at www.nolo.com. And for hundreds of free articles and FAQs of interest to landlords, see the Landlords & Rental Property section on the Nolo website.

From the tenant's point of view:

- *Every Tenant's Legal Guide*, by Janet Portman and Marcia Stewart. This book gives tenants in all 50 states the legal and practical information they need to deal with their landlords and protect their rights when things go wrong. It covers all important issues of renting, including signing a lease, getting a landlord to make needed repairs, fighting illegal discrimination, protecting privacy rights, dealing with roommates, getting the security deposit returned fairly, moving out, and much more.

Nolo also publishes a book specifically for California renters: *California Tenants' Rights*, by Janet Portman and David Brown. And for dozens of free articles and FAQs of interest to tenants, see the Renters' & Tenants' Rights section of www.nolo.com.

State Landlord-Tenant Laws Vary on Key Issues

All states have laws regulating residential landlord-tenant relationships. Typically, these laws establish the maximum dollar amount allowed for a security deposit and the deadline for returning it; the amount of notice required to change or end a month-to-month tenancy; tenants' privacy rights; late rent charges (and rent limits in communities with rent control); a tenant's right to install locks; disclosures regarding the condition of property; tenant options, such as rent withholding, if a landlord fails to make repairs; eviction rules and procedures; antidiscrimination laws; and much more. (For details, see the Nolo resources listed above.)

Form 23: Rental Application

Landlords routinely use rental applications to screen potential tenants and select those who are likely to pay the rent on time, keep the unit in good condition, and not cause problems. This Rental Application calls for a wide variety of information, including the applicant's rental, employment, and credit history, and personal references. Conscientious landlords will insist on verifying this information before signing a lease or rental agreement.

If you own or manage rental property, you can use the Rental Application to help screen potential tenants. Be sure to ask all serious applicants to fill out an application, not just those who you think need special scrutiny. Ask all applicants to sign the Rental Application authorizing you to verify the information, call references, and run a credit check. Also, use the "Notes" section at the end of the application to write down legal reasons for refusing an individual—for example, negative credit history, insufficient income, or your inability to verify information. Landlords will want this kind of record in order to survive a fair housing challenge if a disappointed applicant files a discrimination complaint.

 CAUTION
Make sure you understand how discrimination laws work. Many types of discrimination are illegal, including discrimination based on race, religion, national origin, sex, familial status, disability, and, in some states, sexual orientation, gender identity, marital status, or source of income. For more information on legal and illegal reasons to reject a tenant, see the resources listed at the beginning of this chapter. There are several useful articles in the Landlords & Rental Property section of www.nolo.com.

Savvy tenants will also find this Rental Application useful when looking for a new place to live. If you're a tenant, we suggest you complete this application in advance of apartment-hunting—providing information about your employment, income, credit background, and rental housing history. Take a copy of the completed application with you when you see a potential rental unit. This is almost guaranteed to impress a landlord or rental agent.

Signing Instructions

Before giving prospective tenants this Rental Application, a landlord should complete the box at the top of the form, filling in the property address, rental term, first month's rent, and any deposit or credit check fee tenants must pay before moving in. Any credit check fee should be reasonably related to the cost of the credit check. Check your state law for any limits on this fee.

If you're a landlord, give a copy to each tenant applying for your rental property. Be sure the tenant fills the application in completely and signs it before you call references or order a credit check.

If you're a tenant, complete the application in advance of apartment-hunting. You can either give your application to prospective landlords or use the information you've pulled together on the Rental Application to complete the landlord's application.

Form 24: Tenant References

If a prospective tenant's Rental Application looks good, careful landlords will follow up and contact the applicant's current and previous landlords or managers for references, checking to see if the tenant paid rent on time or caused any problems, such as damage to the rental unit or an overly aggressive dog that bothered neighbors. Other key parts of the screening process include verifying the tenant's income and length of employment and obtaining a credit report to see how responsible the person is managing money. Landlords will want to do this homework before accepting someone as a new tenant.

Tenants should first authorize the landlord to contact landlords, employers, and other references and run a credit report. The Rental Application, discussed above, includes a section at the end providing this authorization.

When you talk with previous landlords, employers, and other references, ask the questions listed on the Tenant References form, and take notes of all of your conversations about the tenant's rental history and behavior. Also, ask about problems with any pets (and try to meet the dog or cat, to make sure it's well-groomed and well-behaved).

You should also verify the applicant's employment and see if the employer will comment on the person's suitability as a tenant (most employers will simply verify dates of employment). Many landlords don't check with personal references, except in the case of college students or others who have never rented before, but it's a good idea to do so if you need additional references. All landlords should check credit and financial information and make a general comment on this form, such as "Credit report fine—see attached."

If you will be rejecting an applicant, note on the Tenant References form your reasons for doing so—for example, negative credit information, bad references from a previous landlord, or your inability to verify information on the Rental Application. You want a record of this information so that you can survive a fair housing challenge if a disappointed applicant files a discrimination complaint against you.

See the Rental Applications & Tenant Screening articles in the Landlords & Rental Property section of www.nolo.com for more on the subject.

Signing Instructions

Fill in the name of the applicant and the address of the rental unit that the tenant wants to rent at the top of the Tenant References form. Then, fill in the tenant's reference information, such as names and phone numbers of previous landlords. (If you're a tenant, you have probably provided your references as part of the landlord's Rental Application, as is the case with the rental application included in this book. If not, it's a good idea to have your references available for the landlord early on.)

Landlords should then write down all the information collected from calling references and checking credit reports of prospective tenants on the Tenant References form, including reasons for rejecting a particular tenant.

Form 25: Landlord-Tenant Checklist

Legal disputes between tenants and landlords have justly gained a reputation for having the potential to be almost as nasty as a bad divorce. And like a failed marriage, disputes often continue after the legal relationship is over. This is most likely to occur when a landlord keeps all or part of a tenant's security deposit, claiming the place was left excessively dirty or damaged.

Fortunately, using the Landlord-Tenant Checklist, a landlord and tenant can work together to minimize deposit-related disputes by inspecting the rental unit together at both the start and end of the tenancy. This type of inspection is a legal requirement in some states, and a good practice in all.

The idea is to identify damage, dirt, mildew, and obvious wear and tear before the tenant moves in (use column 1, Condition on Arrival), in both the General Condition of Rental Unit and Premises section of the form and the Furnished Property section. Your comments should be as specific as possible. Mark "OK" next to items that are in satisfactory condition—basically, clean, safe, sanitary, and in good working order.

You will then inspect the unit again just before the tenant moves out—ideally landlord and tenant will do this together; at this point, using column 2 (Condition on Departure). The landlord will fill in the last column (Estimated Cost of Cleaning/Repair/Replacement) when the tenant has moved out. This is a way to document the landlord's need to make deductions from the security deposit for repairs or cleaning, or to replace missing items.

Tenants should read and check the box regarding smoke detectors and fire extinguishers on the bottom of the last page of the General Condition of Rental Unit and Premises section of form.

In the "additional explanation" section at the end of the Landlord-Tenant Checklist form, note any areas of disagreement between the landlord and the tenant. (Incidentally, to avoid a court battle over security deposit deductions, many wise landlords and tenants try to compromise any disputed damage claims when doing the final inspection.)

Signing Instructions

After completing the Landlord-Tenant Checklist at move-in time, make two copies. The landlord and tenant should sign and date both originals and each keep one original.

Review the Checklist again at move-out time, fill in the appropriate columns as noted above, and sign and date both originals.

 TIP

Take photos or videos at move-in and move-out to avoid disputes. Having photos lets you compare "before" and "after" pictures, rather than deal with competing versions of the condition of the property. If you end up in court fighting over the security deposit, photos will be invaluable visual proof. Tenants should consider taking along a friend or colleague as a potential witness to the condition of the rental unit at move-in and move-out time—someone who will be available to testify in court on the tenant's behalf if necessary.

Form 26: Move-In Letter

A clearly written lease or rental agreement is the key to starting a tenancy. But smart landlords often go further and prepare a move-in letter for new tenants that dovetails with the lease or rental agreement by summarizing key clauses, such as rules on rent, roommates, and deposits, and clearly spelling out tenant legal rights and responsibilities. This Move-In Letter provides a template for this purpose.

The Move-In Letter is also a useful place for landlords to provide basic information tenants need to know, such as the manager's phone number and email address; rules that are too detailed to include in the lease or rental agreement, such as the location and use of laundry rooms, pickup day for garbage and recycling, and maintenance dos and don'ts; and anything else that is important or unique to the specific rental.

Signing Instructions

After preparing a personalized Move-In Letter, the landlord should date and sign it and deliver to the tenant. You should also make a copy of your signed letter for the tenant to sign, indicating that he or she has read the letter. Be sure to update the Move-In Letter from time to time as necessary.

Form 27: Notice of Needed Repairs

Landlords are legally required to provide tenants livable premises when they offer a unit for rent, and to maintain the rental property in decent condition throughout the rental term. In most states, the legal jargon used to describe this obligation is the "landlord's legal duty to fulfill the implied warranty of habitability."

Tenants have the right to a decent place to live even if they move into a place that's clearly substandard (below reasonable habitability standards), or even if the lease comes right out and says that the landlord doesn't have to provide a habitable unit. Or put another way, all courts have rejected the sleazy argument that tenants waive the right to a livable place when they accept a substandard rental unit.

Tenants who have a problem with the physical condition of your rental unit will want to notify their landlord or manager as soon as possible so that it can be promptly fixed. The best approach is to put every repair and maintenance request in writing, using the Notice of Needed Repairs, keeping a copy for yourself. You should then email, hand deliver, or mail your repair request. You may find it easier to call your landlord first, particularly in urgent cases, but be sure to follow up with a written repair request.

Be as specific as possible regarding the problem—whether it's plumbing, heating, security, weatherproofing, or other defects. Note the effects of the problem on you, what you want done, and when. For example, if the thermostat on your heater is always finicky and sometimes doesn't function at all, explain how long you've been without heat and how low the temperature has dipped—don't simply say "the heater needs to be fixed." If the problem poses a health or safety threat, such as a broken front door lock, say so and ask for it to be fixed immediately.

Be sure to note the best time to make repairs, the date of the request, and how many requests, if any, have preceded this one. Keep records of all repair requests and details on how and when the landlord responded. Your records will serve as potential evidence in case you ever need to prove that the serious problems with your unit were the subject of repeated repair requests.

If you are a landlord, it's a good idea to give tenants copies of the Notice of Needed Repairs and encourage them to immediately report plumbing, heating, weatherproofing, or other defects or safety problems. Landlords should be sure to note details as to how and when the problem was fixed, including reasons for any delay, on the bottom of the tenant's repair request form. Keep copies of all completed forms in the tenant files.

Signing Instructions

Landlords should give tenants copies of the Notice of Needed Repairs form. If they don't, tenants should go ahead and use the form on their own to report problems. Tenants should simply sign the document and keep a copy for their records. If your landlord has an on-site office or a resident manager, deliver the repair request personally. If you mail it, consider sending it certified mail (return receipt requested) or use a delivery service that will give you a proof of delivery. Besides keeping a copy of every written repair request (including emails), keep notes of oral communications, too.

TIP

If your landlord ignores your requests and your rental is unlivable, you'll have to undertake stronger measures. These might include calling state or local building or health inspectors, moving out, withholding the rent, or repairing the problem yourself. These remedies, available only in certain situations according to your state's laws, are thoroughly discussed in the Nolo books listed at the beginning of this chapter. Tenants will also find useful information in the Repairs and Maintenance section under Renters' & Tenants' Rights on www.nolo.com.

Form 28: Semiannual Safety and Maintenance Update

The best way to avoid disputes about repair and maintenance problems is for landlords to establish and communicate clear procedures for tenants to ask for repairs, document all complaints, and respond quickly when complaints are made. This starts with clearly setting out tenant responsibilities for repair and maintenance in the lease and rental agreement and again in a Move-In Letter. Landlords should also use a Landlord-Tenant Checklist before the tenant moves in, and encourage tenants to immediately report plumbing, heating, security, and other problems, using the Notice of Needed Repairs.

In addition, landlords should give tenants a checklist on which to report any potential safety hazards or maintenance problems that might have been overlooked, such as low water pressure in the shower, a sticky front door lock, or security problems in the neighborhood. That's the purpose of the Semiannual Safety and Maintenance Update.

Signing Instructions

There are no specific signing instructions for the Semiannual Safety and Maintenance Update. Landlords should give tenants a copy of this form twice a year. If they don't, tenants should go ahead and use the form on their own to report problems in as much detail as possible. Tenants should simply sign and date the document and keep a copy for their records.

Landlords should note how they handled the problems on the bottom of this form and keep a copy for their records.

Form 29: Landlord-Tenant Agreement to Terminate Lease

If you're a tenant with a long-term lease, ideally you'll have a lease for just the amount of time you need the rental. But despite your best efforts to plan ahead, you may want to move before your lease is up.

One option is simply to move out early. Leaving before a fixed-term lease expires, without paying the remainder of the rent due under the lease, is called breaking the lease. With a little luck, it may not cost you much— in most states, the landlord is required to take reasonable steps to rerent the property. If the landlord does so (and doesn't attempt to hide the fact that there's now a new rent-paying tenant), your financial liability will be limited to paying the rent for the brief time the unit was vacant.

Nevertheless, if you plan to leave early, you don't just have to move out and hope your landlord plays fair and gets a new tenant quickly. For a variety of reasons, the landlord may procrastinate, claim an inability to find a new tenant, or rent the unit to a tenant who pays less rent than you did—meaning you're liable for the difference. Fortunately, there are steps you can take to minimize your financial responsibility—as well as help avoid a bad reference from the landlord next time you're apartment hunting.

First, consider simply asking the landlord to cancel the lease, using this Agreement to Terminate Lease. If you and the landlord both sign and date this form, your obligations for rent beyond the termination date end. (You are still responsible for unpaid back rent and any damage you've caused beyond normal wear and tear.) Why would a landlord voluntarily agree to let you off the hook? If you have been a steady and considerate tenant, it's possible that you'll be treated in kind, especially if the market is tight or the landlord has a new tenant standing by who will pay a higher rent. If the landlord initially balks at canceling the lease, you might prevail by offering to pay an extra month's rent in exchange for the lease cancellation.

In some states, landlords must allow early termination of a lease under certain conditions. For example, in Delaware you need give only 30 days' notice to end a long-term lease if you must move because your present employer has relocated or because of health problems—yours or a family member's. In New Jersey, a tenant who has suffered a disabling illness or accident can break a lease and leave after 40 days' notice, upon presenting proper proof of disability. Some states allow tenants who are victims of domestic violence to terminate a lease early. In all states, federal law allows military and other personnel to terminate a lease early when called to active duty or when active duty personnel are transferred. If you have a good reason for a sudden move, check your state's law. See the Nolo resources listed at the beginning of this chapter for details.

Also, a tenant may be able to move out without providing proper notice if the landlord has violated an important lease provision—for example, by failing to maintain the rental unit in accordance with health and safety codes.

If you can't get the landlord to cancel the lease outright, your best approach is usually to find a new tenant who will be ready to move in as soon as you leave and who will sign a new lease at the same or higher rent. If you follow this approach, you should owe nothing additional since the landlord won't be able to argue that a suitable replacement tenant couldn't be found.

TIP
When the landlord won't accept the tenant you find. Keep careful records of all prospective tenants you find, especially their credit histories—you can use the Rental Application. If the landlord sues you for back rent, present these records to the judge as proof the landlord failed to limit (mitigate) damages by refusing to accept a suitable replacement tenant.

If the landlord accepts the new tenant, you and the landlord should cancel your lease by completing the Agreement to Terminate Lease. The landlord and the new tenant can sign their own lease, and you will no longer be in the picture.

Signing Instructions

Print out two copies of the Landlord-Tenant Agreement to Terminate Lease form—one for the landlord and one for the tenant(s). The landlord and every tenant should sign and date both originals. The landlord should keep one signed original and the tenant(s) the other. (Co-tenants, if any, may make their own copies of the tenants' signed document.)

Form 30: Consent to Assignment of Lease

If you are a tenant who wants to move out permanently, but the landlord won't cancel your lease or sign a new lease with a tenant you find, your next best option may be to "assign" your lease to a new tenant (called an "assignee") who is acceptable to the landlord. With an assignment, you turn over the remainder of your lease to someone else. You can do this with the Consent to Assignment of Lease. Unless the landlord agrees otherwise, you remain in the picture as a guarantor of rent payments in case the new occupant (the assignee) fails to pay. Having a second source for the rent is one reason a savvy landlord might agree to an assignment but not a cancellation.

Landlords can voluntarily waive their rights to look to you as the guarantor of the assignee's rent, something that is not uncommon when the new tenant has excellent credit. Clause 4 of this form releases you from this worrisome obligation, essentially putting you in the position of someone who has terminated the lease. If the landlord balks at the release, and you are reasonably sure of your replacement's ability to pay the rent, you may not be risking much if you cross out Clause 4 and remain theoretically responsible for the rent.

Signing Instructions

Print out three copies of the Consent to Assignment of Lease form—one for the landlord, one for the tenant, and one for the assignee. Each person should sign and date all originals in the spaces indicated. The landlord should keep one signed original and the tenant and assignee the others.

Form 31: Tenant's Notice of Intent to Move Out

If you have a month-to-month tenancy, in most states and for most rentals you must provide 30 days' notice to your landlord if you want to move out. In some states, if you pay rent weekly or twice a month, you can give written notice to terminate that matches your rent payment interval. For example, if you pay rent every two weeks, you may need to give only 14 days' notice.

In most states, you can give notice at any time during the month. For example, if you pay rent on the first of the month but give notice on the tenth, you will be obliged to pay for only ten days' rent for the next month, even if

you move out earlier. To calculate the amount, prorate the monthly rent using 30 days.

Check the Nolo resources listed at the beginning of the chapter for specific requirements as to how and when to give notice. The Leases & Rental Agreements section under Renters' & Tenants' Rights on www.nolo.com includes useful information on the subject.

Signing Instructions

Tenants should sign and date the Tenant's Notice of Intent to Move Out form and give or mail it to the landlord. Be sure to check your state rules to make sure you are meeting any specific notice requirements.

TIP
If you give oral notice, follow up in writing with this form. If you know your landlord or manager well, you may wish to convey your moving plans in a face-to-face or phone conversation. Fine, but immediately follow up with written confirmation. The law almost always requires written notice. You can use Form 31 for this purpose.

Form 32: Demand for Return of Security Deposit

Getting cleaning and security deposits returned can be a problem for tenants. To avoid trouble, or to successfully deal with a landlord who unfairly retains your deposit, use the Landlord-Tenant Checklist, to make a written and photographic record of what the place looks like when you move in and when you move out. Be sure you leave the rental in good condition, give proper notice, and are paid up in rent when you leave. And don't forget to give the landlord your new address.

Depending on the law of your state, you should receive your deposit back within 14 to 30 days of moving out. If you don't, send a written request using the Demand for Return of Security Deposit form. If this doesn't work, you may need to sue the landlord in small claims court. (Some state security deposit statutes require tenants to make a written request; and in some states, small claims court rules require you to send a demand letter before you can sue.) You can find your state security deposit rules in the Security Deposit section under Renters' & Tenants' Rights on www.nolo.com.

Your demand letter should state the date you moved out of the rental and lay out the reasons your landlord owes you deposit money. Refer to any statutory deadlines and tangible evidence supporting your demand, such as photos or a before-and-after Landlord-Tenant Checklist. In the Demand for Return of Security Deposit, you make it clear that if the landlord does not promptly return your deposit by a specified date (we suggest seven to ten days), you plan to go to small claims court.

In many states, if a landlord withholds a deposit without giving the tenant a good written reason for doing so (for example, to cover specific damage or unpaid rent) within the required time, the tenant has some powerful options. Tenants may be able to sue for the amount of the wrongly withheld deposit, plus an extra amount for punitive damages if the landlord intentionally failed to return the deposit on time. Check your state law for specifics and refer to it in any correspondence with your landlord. For example, California landlords have 21 days to return the security deposit with an itemized statement of deductions and copies of receipts or invoices for needed cleaning or repairs.

Signing Instructions

Sign your Demand for Return of Security Deposit letter and send it certified mail (return receipt requested) to the landlord, or use a delivery service that will give you a proof of delivery. Keep a copy of your letter and all related correspondence. You'll need this if you end up in a court dispute over your security deposit.

Going to Small Claims Court

Hopefully, your Demand for Return of Security Deposit letter will spur action on the landlord's part and you'll get your deposit back. If it doesn't, you may need to file in small claims court. These courts will handle disputes worth up to a certain amount—typical limits are between $5,000 and $10,000 (each state sets its own limit, and a few fall outside this range). Most security deposit disputes will fit within the court's limit. You can sue your landlord for your security deposit and for interest (if it's required in your state or city). In many states you can also sue for extra, punitive damages if the landlord intentionally failed to return the deposit on time.

It is inexpensive (usually less than $50) to file a case in small claims court, you don't need a lawyer, and disputes usually go before a judge (there are no juries) within 30 to 60 days. Small claims courts are informal places, intended to be used by regular folks presenting their own cases.

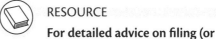

RESOURCE

For detailed advice on filing (or defending) a case in small claims court, see *Everybody's Guide to Small Claims Court*, or, if you live in California, *Everybody's Guide to Small Claims Court in California*, both by Ralph Warner (Nolo). Also, check out the Small Claims Court & Lawsuits section on www.nolo.com for useful articles including state laws and dollar limits.

Borrowing and Lending Money

This chapter contains several promissory notes you can use when you borrow money from or lend money to a friend, relative, or someone else who isn't a commercial customer. (Banks and other institutional lenders follow many legal rules and must use forms with far more fine print.) This chapter also includes a loan comparison worksheet to keep track of information you collect on different loans (whether from a personal or commercial lender), a form to authorize a lender to check the borrower's credit, and "demand" letters to use when trying to collect an overdue payment or bad check.

Form 33: Loan Comparison Worksheet

A good consumer shops around before making a significant purchase. There is no reason to do otherwise when you are looking to borrow money. A loan from one bank may come with very different terms than a loan from a credit union or finance company—or even from a different bank across town. And a loan from your former college roommate or your Aunt Charlotte may be very different still.

The cost of a loan doesn't depend only on how much interest you pay. Long-term loans carry a higher rate of interest than short-term loans (the lender runs the risk that inflation will erode the real value of the interest it receives for a longer period, so it passes some of this risk on to you in the form of a higher interest rate). But short-term loans are not necessarily cheaper. You need to consider application fees and other up-front fees, which can vary considerably from one lender to the next, when computing the cost of a loan. Fortunately, this isn't true of all short-term loans, so be sure to shop around. When you apply for a commercial loan, the lender must tell you the annual cost of the loan.

This is stated as the annual percentage rate, or APR. You can use that figure to compare the annual cost of different loans.

APR isn't the entire story, especially for adjustable rate loans or loans with a balloon payment or other features. For a full comparison of loans, use this worksheet to record the terms of any loans you are considering, whether to buy a car or computer system or pay down your credit cards. (See "Basic Loan Terms Explained," below, before you start collecting information on different loans.)

Because mortgage loans involve far more considerations than the loans discussed in this chapter, use the Mortgage Rates and Terms Worksheet in Chapter 6 when shopping around for a mortgage.

Signing Instructions

There are no signing instructions for the Loan Comparison Worksheet. Simply fill one out each time you start collecting information on different loans.

Form 34: Authorization to Check Credit and Employment References

Commercial lenders—banks, credit unions, and finance companies—will always check a loan applicant's credit before agreeing to lend money. If you're thinking of lending someone money, it makes good sense to check the borrower's credit and employment references. You'll need the borrower's signed authorization to do this. Most employers, financial institutions, and credit sources require this kind of signed authorization before providing information on the borrower. That's the purpose of this Authorization to Check Credit and Employment References. The borrower should complete all sections, including details on employment and credit history.

Basic Loan Terms Explained

To understand your loan agreement, you'll need to know the meaning of a few terms.

Adjustable rate. An interest rate that changes over time. It is set initially by the lender, usually fairly low, and then fluctuates (usually meaning it increases) every several months.

Balloon payment. A lump sum payment made at the end of a loan to cover the remaining balance. For example, you borrow $10,000 for five years at 6% interest. The monthly payments are $193.33. You can afford to pay only about half that amount, so the lender lets you pay $100 a month. At the end of five years, however, you owe a balloon payment of $6,511.53. Balloon payments are usually bad deals. Borrowers often get into trouble by focusing on the low monthly payments rather than the large and often unaffordable sum due at the end of the loan term.

Cap. On an adjustable rate loan, the cap refers both to the maximum amount the interest rate can increase each year and the ultimate maximum an interest rate can reach. For example, an adjustable rate loan that begins at 4% may have an annual cap of 0.5% and a lifetime cap of 7%. This means that at the beginning of the second year, the rate will be 4.5%. If the loan continues to increase 0.5% each year, it will reach its lifetime cap of 7% in six years.

Collateral. Property a borrower pledges as security for repayment of a loan. Sometimes it's the item being purchased, such as a car. Other times the collateral is property the borrower already owns. If the borrower defaults, a lender can take the collateral without first suing the borrower and obtaining a judgment.

Cosigner. A creditworthy person who agrees to be fully liable for repayment of a loan if the borrower defaults.

Credit check. A lender getting a copy of the borrower's credit report from a credit reporting agency in order to verify the borrower's creditworthiness.

Credit insurance. Insurance coverage offered by some lenders to ensure payment of a loan in the event the borrower becomes disabled or dies. Most consumer advocates say credit card insurance is a waste of money.

Fixed rate. An interest rate that is established by the lender at the outset and will never change.

Grace period. The number of days a borrower has after a loan payment is due to make the payment without being charged a late fee. For example, if your loan payments are due on the 1st of the month, you may have a grace period until the 10th, meaning that the lender will accept your payment until that date without penalizing you.

Late fee. The fee a lender charges when a borrower pays late. (See "Grace period.")

Loan application fee. Fees charged by lenders for the work involved in lending money. These include credit checks, appraisals on collateral, and loan processing fees.

Loan discounts. Incentives offered by a lender that reduce a loan's interest rate. For example, you might be offered a 0.5% discount if you set up direct payment from your checking account or if you maintain a checking account with the lender with a minimum balance requirement.

Points. Real estate loans usually come with points, an amount of money equal to a percentage of your loan. This money is paid to the lender simply for the privilege of borrowing money.

Prepayment penalty. A penalty imposed on a borrower for paying off a loan early. It's usually expressed as a flat fee or a percentage of the interest the lender lost as a result of your prepaying.

Doing a credit and reference check will give you an idea whether the borrower is likely to repay you in full and on time, and put you in a good position to say "no" to someone with poor credit. Checking a person's credit references and saying "no" is likely to put a strain on a personal relationship, but making a loan to someone who can't handle the payments is more likely to cause long-term problems.

Signing Instructions

The person borrowing money should sign and date the Authorization to Check Credit and Employment References. The lender should keep the original and give the borrower a copy. The lender should also send copies of the signed authorization form to the credit and employment references that will be checked. It may be helpful to enclose a stamped, self-addressed envelope.

Form 35: Monthly Payment Record

If a loan will be repaid over many months or years, it's easy to forget whether and when every payment has been made. This is especially likely if the debtor misses several payments because of an emergency and then makes them up a little at a time. In this case, the amounts will be different each month. Use the Monthly Payment Record to keep track of payments made under installment notes, such as the promissory notes included in this chapter.

Signing Instructions

There are no signing instructions for the Monthly Payment Record. The lender simply records payments due and made every month.

Forms 36–40: Promissory Notes

A promissory note is a written agreement to pay money to someone. As with all legal documents, promissory notes often contain loads of unnecessary legalese. Because the notes in this chapter are designed to be used primarily between family and friends, we prefer to keep the language simple.

The primary function of a promissory note is to document the amount of a debt and the terms under which it will be repaid, including the interest rate (if any). A promissory note is typically signed when a person borrows money or buys something on credit. Here are several important reasons why all promissory notes should be put in writing:

- You are assured that the borrower and lender have agreed to the same terms, including the repayment schedule and interest rate.
- You specify exactly what those terms are.
- Both parties have a written document to refresh their memories.

This chapter contains five promissory notes, each designed to deal with a somewhat different repayment scenario:

- Form 36: Promissory Note—Installment Payments With Interest
- Form 37: Promissory Note—Installment Payments With Interest and Balloon Payment
- Form 38: Promissory Note—Installment Payments Without Interest
- Form 39: Promissory Note—Lump Sum Payment With Interest
- Form 40: Promissory Note—Lump Sum Payment Without Interest.

All of these notes are for unsecured loans—meaning that the borrower does not pledge any property, such as a car, as collateral to guarantee repayment. This means if the borrower doesn't repay the loan, the lender must sue in court to get a judgment, which then makes the lender eligible to use wage garnishment or property attachments to collect on the note. You can add a security provision to your note using Form 42, which gives the lender the right to force the sale of personal property pledged as collateral if the borrower doesn't repay. Form 43 is the actual security agreement you will use when property is pledged.

Signing Instructions for Promissory Notes

The borrower(s) must sign the Promissory Note for it to be valid. (There may be two borrowers—for example, if a husband and wife are jointly borrowing money. See "Does a Borrower's Spouse Need to Sign a Promissory Note?" below.) Print out one copy of the form. The borrower(s) should sign and date only one copy of the document in the space provided. This signed original should be given to the lender. The borrower(s) should keep a copy of the signed document for their own records.

 FORM

Using a notary public. You may want to have the borrower sign the promissory note in front of a notary public. This may be required in some states; even if it is not, notarization adds a measure of legal credibility to your promissory note. (See "Signing the Forms," in the Introduction, for general advice on having a form notarized.) If you do get the promissory note notarized, attach the notary certificate where indicated on the form.

 TIP

If the borrower's credit is questionable, consider requiring a cosigner. You can add a cosigner clause to your promissory note by using the Cosigner Provision explained below.

Does a Borrower's Spouse Need to Sign a Promissory Note?

A promissory note is a contract that makes a borrower liable for a debt. The lender may ask that the borrower's spouse sign as well. This is likely to happen, for example, if someone is borrowing money to buy property that both spouses will use or to help finance a new business venture. Keep in mind that a lender may not require a borrower's spouse to sign if the borrower is the only one applying for the loan and no jointly held or community property is involved.

By having the borrower's spouse sign, a second person becomes legally liable for repaying the debt. Normally, if only the borrower signed the contract and didn't repay it, the other party to the agreement could get a judgment against the borrower but not the borrower's spouse. This means that the creditor would be able to seize property that the borrower owns as sole owner, but not property that the borrower and a spouse own in both of their names or that the spouse owns solely, unless the borrower lives in a community property state such as California. (See "Who Pays the Debts in Community Property States?" below for more details.) But if the borrower and spouse both sign a contract and then default, the other party can sue and get a judgment against both. That judgment can be enforced by seizing the couple's joint bank account, putting a lien on jointly owned real estate, seizing property in the borrower's name alone, and seizing property in the spouse's name alone.

Form 36: Promissory Note— Installment Payments With Interest

This form allows the borrower to repay the note in installments rather than all at once,

Who Pays the Debts in Community Property States?

Arizona, California, Idaho, Louisiana, Nevada, New Mexico, Texas, Washington, and Wisconsin follow the community property system. (In Alaska, a couple can choose to have their property treated as community property by preparing a written agreement.) In these states, property acquired during a marriage is generally considered community (joint) regardless of whose name it's in or who paid for it. In addition, all debts incurred during the marriage—even if only one spouse signed the loan papers—are considered community (joint) debts unless a creditor was explicitly told that only one spouse would be liable for the debt.

In most situations, the rights of creditors to seize property after getting a judgment for nonpayment of a debt depend on whether the property is considered community or separate.

- **Community property.** Usually, property earned or acquired by either spouse during the marriage—except property acquired by gift or inheritance or defined as separate

under a premarital agreement—is considered community property. A creditor can go after all community property to pay for either a community debt or a separate debt of one spouse incurred during the marriage.

- **Separate property.** This is property a spouse owned before getting married, acquired during the marriage by gift or inheritance, or agreed in writing to be kept separate. It's also property acquired using separate assets. For example, if a woman owned a house when she got married, then sold it and used the proceeds to buy stock held in her name, the stock is clearly her separate property. For community debts, a creditor can seek reimbursement from either spouse's separate property. For example, for debt the wife accumulates while married, a creditor can go after her separate property, all community property (including her husband's share) and her husband's separate property.

and charges interest. Charging a friend or family member interest strikes some people as being ungenerous. In our opinion, this view is based on a misconception about the function of interest, which is to compensate the lender for the use of the money. Think of it this way. Suppose Joan lends Harry $5,000 for a year, interest free. If Joan had put the money in a certificate of deposit, she would have earned the going rate of interest. By giving Harry the money interest free, Joan ends up paying for the privilege of lending the money to Harry.

Interest charged on money lent to friends and relatives tends to run between 5% and 10%. If you wish to charge a higher rate of interest, check your state law to see if the rate is legal; it may constitute the crime of usury. How

much interest is appropriate? In an effort to be generous to a relative or friend, many lenders charge interest at somewhat less than the market rate, sometimes as little as—or just slightly more than—they would receive if they purchased a bank certificate of deposit for the same time period. This is a great deal for the borrower; after all, even if Harry qualified to borrow from a bank or other commercial lender, he would have to pay a much higher rate of interest than Joan would receive if she put the money in a CD.

Charging interest does add a level of complication when it comes to figuring out the amount of the monthly payments. For this, you will need an amortization calculator or software program. You can find one at www.nolo.com. You plug in the loan amount, interest rate, and number of months the borrower will take to repay the loan. The calculator gives you the monthly payment amount.

If the borrower decides to pay off part of the principal sooner than the promissory note calls for under the installment plan, you will have to recalculate the payments based on the new outstanding balance. This is easy to do with an amortization calculator.

 TIP

What is a "buyer in due course"? Forms 36–40 all contain a phrase that says that "the term Lender refers to any person who legally holds this note, including a buyer in due course." This phrase refers to any person who buys goods from another person. In the context of these forms, it refers to anyone who might purchase the promissory note from the original lender, and says that such a purchaser would hold the same rights as the original lender to collect the money from the borrower.

Form 37: Promissory Note— Installment Payments With Interest and Balloon Payment

Form 37 is similar to Form 36 in that the loan must be repaid in installments with interest. But there's an additional twist: Individual payments are lower than they otherwise would be, with the shortfall made up by one large balloon payment at the end of the loan term. To see how this works, let's take a look at an example. You lend a friend $10,000 at 7% interest and want the money paid back in three years. Using an amortization calculator, you discover that your friend would have to pay you $308.78 each month to pay it back over that time.

Legal Terminology of Promissory Notes

Here we translate some legal terms into plain English.

Acceleration. Our promissory notes accelerate the borrower's responsibility to make all necessary loan payments, meaning that if the borrower misses one or more regularly scheduled payments, the entire loan amount is immediately due. You specify the number of days—typically 30 or 60—the borrower has to pay before you exercise this option. Without this provision you can't sue for loan installments not yet due, even though the borrower has missed several payments and obviously has no plans to repay.

Attorneys' fees. Our promissory notes include a clause providing that the borrower has to pay the lender's attorneys' fees and court costs in a legal dispute if the lender wins. Under the laws of some states, this type of clause will be read by a court to go both ways. This means that if the borrower wins, she or he will be entitled to attorneys' fees and court costs, even if the loan papers don't specifically say so.

Buyer in due course. This is a person who buys or otherwise legally receives a promissory note from a lender. The borrower's obligation to repay the note doesn't change just because the lender sells the note to someone else.

Joint and several liability. This means that if there is more than one borrower, all borrowers are liable for repaying 100% of the loan. If Chuck and Laura borrow $5,000 from Miguel and then default, Miguel can go after either Chuck or Laura for the full $5,000. They can't claim that each person is liable for only $2,500.

Your friend can't afford to pay that amount each month now, but expects to receive some money in about three years when a trust matures. So you propose the following: Your friend can borrow $10,000 from you at 7% and repay it over three years. But to make the payments affordable now, you agree to amortize the loan as though it were to be paid off in ten years, meaning your friend's monthly payments are only $116.11, far less than $308.78. You agree to take these low payments for 36 months and at the end, your friend will make you one large payment, called a balloon payment, of the remaining principal. That amount is $7,693.

Form 38: Promissory Note—Installment Payments Without Interest

Use this form if the borrower will repay you in installments, but you won't charge interest. When the parties involved in the transaction are family members or close friends, the amount borrowed is relatively small, and the probability of repayment is high, lenders sometimes prefer to use an interest-free installment note.

Be aware that if the IRS learns of an interest-free loan, it can impute interest. This means that the lender will be assumed to have earned interest and will be required to report that interest as income on that year's tax return. For most personal loans, this won't be a problem because uncharged interest can be treated as a tax-free gift, as long as the total amount given and imputed to the borrower in a calendar year is $13,000.

Form 39: Promissory Note—Lump Sum Payment With Interest

This note is normally used when the borrower won't be able to repay the loan for a period of months or years. For example, you might borrow money from a friend to help you open a small business. You aren't likely to have the cash flow for at least six months or a year to repay the loan. In such a situation, your friend might agree to be repaid in a lump sum in two years.

The easiest way to determine the amount of annual interest that will be due on the loan is to use simple, not compound, interest. Multiply the amount of the loan by the annual interest rate. For instance, if the loan is for $4,000 and your annual interest rate is 10%, the annual amount of interest on the loan is $400. To determine the total amount of interest due, multiply the annual interest amount by the time period of the loan. In our example, if the loan is for two years, the interest due would be $800.

If you need to compute the interest for a period of months rather than years, compute the interest for one year, divide by 12, and then multiply the result by the number of months. For example, assume the $4,000 loan is for an 18-month period. Take the annual interest amount ($400), divide by 12 ($33.33), and multiply by 18 ($600).

If the loan is paid back before it is due, Clause 2 gives the lender two choices:

- Charge the full interest. This is not unreasonable, given that you committed yourself to being without the amount of the entire loan for the time indicated.
- Prorate the interest to correspond to the actual period of time the loan was outstanding. Returning to the $4,000 loan example, if you originally figured interest at 10% for two years ($800), but the loan was paid back in 18 months, simply charge the 18-month figure ($600) instead.

Form 40: Promissory Note—Lump Sum Payment Without Interest

This promissory note, which calls for a lump sum loan repayment and no interest, is about as basic as you can get. This sort of note is normally used by people with a close personal relationship when the person lending the money is primarily interested in helping out the borrower and expects nothing in return except, eventually, the return of the amount borrowed.

If the IRS learns of the loan, it can impute interest. This means that the lender will be assumed to have earned interest and will be required to report that interest as income on that year's tax return. For most personal loans, this won't be a problem because uncharged interest can be treated as a tax-free gift, as long as the total given to the borrower by the lender and imputed by the IRS is $13,000 or less in a calendar year.

Form 41: Cosigner Provision

A cosigner is someone who promises to repay a loan if the primary debtor defaults. If you'll be lending money to someone with a questionable (or no) credit history or a background of sporadic employment, you might require one or more cosigners, such as a parent or friend. (Each cosigner is 100% liable to repay the note if the borrower fails to.)

Federal law requires that commercial lenders give cosigners a notice of their potential liability when they agree to cosign a debt. Although this is not required for personal loans between friends and relatives, we believe full disclosure of the risks of cosigning is a good idea and so we incorporate much of that notice language in this form.

Signing Instructions

After filling in the top of the Cosigner Provision, staple it to your promissory note and then have the cosigner complete, sign, and date it. The lender should keep the original and give each cosigner a copy, along with a copy of the promissory note.

Forms 42–45: Security Agreements

If you lend money to someone who does not repay it, your only recourse usually is to sue the person, get a court judgment, and then take money or property that can legally be seized to satisfy a debt.

There is an easier way: You can attach a security agreement to the promissory note. In a security agreement, you specify certain property belonging to the borrower, such as a car or computer, as collateral for repayment of the loan. It's best to use the purchased property as collateral, called a purchase money security, because a nonpurchase money security agreement using certain household goods likely won't be upheld. If the borrower doesn't repay the loan, you can take the property, sell it, and use the proceeds to satisfy what you are owed. You don't have to go to court. However, you do have to follow proper procedures when you take back (repossess) the property.

Sometimes, a dishonest borrower will try to use the same piece of collateral to secure more than one debt. If that happens and the unscrupulous borrower later defaults on these secured loans, the lenders will find themselves competing to sell the collateral and use the proceeds to satisfy all their debts. How can secured creditors protect themselves? It's very simple: They must be the first to file evidence of their claim with the correct recording agency.

This chapter includes four different forms relating to security interests:

- Form 42: Security Agreement Provision for Promissory Note
- Form 43: Security Agreement for Borrowing Money
- Form 44: Uniform Commercial Code (U.C.C.) Financing Statement, and
- Form 45: Release of U.C.C. Financing Statement

Using Your House as Collateral

Think twice before you pledge real estate, and especially your home, as collateral for a loan. If you are unable to make loan payments, you could lose a large investment, not to mention a roof over your head.

When you pledge your home or other real estate as security for a loan, a security agreement is not adequate to protect the lender. The borrower generally needs to sign a mortgage or a deed of trust, which can then be recorded (filed) at a county office to establish the lender's security interest in the real estate. Then, if the borrower defaults, the lender has the right to sell the property to recover the amount due under the promissory note. This sort of transaction is complicated—you should seek the advice of a real estate lawyer before signing a mortgage or deed of trust.

Creating a security interest is a multistep process. First, you must add Form 42 to your promissory note. Second, you must complete a Security Agreement (Form 43) and attach it to your promissory note. Third, if the collateral is personal property, such as manufacturing equipment or vats of wine, a U.C.C. Financing Statement (Form 44) will usually need to be filed with the appropriate state agency (the lender typically takes care of this filing). This step "perfects your lien," meaning it gives you priority over creditors filing after you. (See the box above to learn how to perfect a real estate lien.)

Note that the forms in this book are intended to be used only when the borrower is securing a loan with tangible personal property, such as a computer or car. If you are considering using real property, such as a house, as collateral for a loan, you should seek the assistance of a real estate lawyer. Title to real estate is a highly technical matter beyond the scope of this book.

Similarly, if you are considering using intangible personal property (bank accounts, stock in a corporation) or intellectual property (copyright, trademark, patent) as collateral for the loan, you should consult an attorney.

Form 42: Security Agreement Provision for Promissory Note

You can use this form to identify the security interest, such as a car or valuable personal property, as a part of your contract. Choose the sample language on the form that is most appropriate for your situation and delete the others.

Signing Instructions

There are two ways to use the Security Agreement Provision. You can either copy the security language that's appropriate into your promissory note itself, or you can complete the security agreement form and staple it to your promissory note. If you use the form separately, the borrower (owner of the collateral) should sign and date the form. The lender should keep the original and give the borrower a copy, along with a copy of the promissory note. Otherwise, if the security provision becomes part of the note, the signing instructions for the note apply.

Form 43: Security Agreement for Borrowing Money

Use the Security Agreement to state the terms of the lender's security interest in the property that will be used as collateral for the loan, and to describe the property.

 CAUTION

Do not use this agreement if the collateral is real property, such as a house. In that case, you will need to file a mortgage or deed of trust with the county land records office. See a real estate lawyer for assistance with this transaction.

When describing the property that will be used as collateral, be sure that you describe it in enough detail that the property can be easily identified. For example, you would describe a vehicle as a "2012 Toyota Tacoma, license plate number 9876543, Vehicle Identification Number ABC1234567" instead of simply "my red truck."

In Paragraph 1 of the agreement, you'll need to insert information from the promissory note (the date, amount, and annual percentage rate). In Paragraphs 5 and 9, insert the state where the property is located and the state whose laws will govern the agreement—usually the state where the parties live.

The agreement states that the lender will file a U.C.C. Financing Statement explained below and that the borrower will sign any additional documents needed to protect the lender's security interest. Signing additional documents may be necessary in some situations, such as when the secured property includes certain kinds of assets (particularly cars and boats) that may require the lender to be added to the asset's certificate of title instead of filing a Financing Statement.

Be sure that you read and understand the entire agreement—it contains many important clauses, including requiring the borrower to take care of the secured property, stating when the borrower will be considered in default, and describing what the lender can do if the borrower defaults.

Signing Instructions

After completing the Security Agreement, both parties should sign and date the last page. The lender will keep the original and will attach it to the original promissory note. Because the Security Agreement is an important part of the promissory note, be sure to also attach a copy of the signed agreement to the borrower's copy of the promissory note.

Form 44: U.C.C. Financing Statement

Use the U.C.C. Financing Statement to record your security interest in personal property.

Once you have completed the Security Agreement, contact the appropriate state agency to find out your state's rules for documenting the lender's security interest in the property. If the collateral is a car, boat, or similar vehicle, you will most likely need to contact the motor vehicles department. Some kinds of assets (often those that are licensed by the state, such as cars and boats) require the lender to take a security interest in the property by listing its name on the certificate of title instead of filing a financing statement. For most other property, such as electronics equipment or a computer system, contact the secretary of state's office. Ask for a copy of your state's rules for filing a U.C.C. financing statement, and find out whether your state has any special form you must use. If it does, use the state form (not this one).

Signing Instructions

The borrower(s) should sign and date the U.C.C. Financing Statement. The lender should keep the original and give the borrower a copy. The lender should attach the promissory note and the security agreement to the U.C.C. Financing Statement and file these with the appropriate state office, such as the secretary of state. Leave the section at the bottom of the form blank; the filing officer will complete this.

Form 45: Release of U.C.C. Financing Statement

Once a loan is paid off, the borrower will want the public record to reflect that the property is no longer encumbered (being used as collateral) in favor of the lender. To do this, you will need to file this Release with the public agency, such as the secretary of state's office, where you filed the U.C.C. Financing Statement. That will let prospective lawyers, creditors, and credit rating agencies know that the lender no longer claims an interest in the borrower's collateral.

This form should correspond to your original U.C.C. Financing Statement. Therefore, make sure the description of property listed as collateral is identical and the other information makes clear which U.C.C. Financing Statement is being released.

Signing Instructions

The borrower(s) should sign and date the Release of U.C.C. Financing Statement. The lender should keep the original and give the borrower a copy. The lender should file this Release with the appropriate state office, such as the secretary of state. Leave the section at the bottom of the form blank; the filing officer will complete this.

Note: Make sure that before using this form your state does not have special U.C.C. form requirements.

Form 46: Agreement to Modify Promissory Note

If someone who borrows money from you falls behind on repayment, give a call to find out what's wrong. Offer whatever help you can to get the borrower back on track. Sometimes this will require no more than being willing to extend the repayment period for a few months. In other instances, you might take interest-only payments or rewrite the loan at a lower interest rate. Whatever you agree on, you must put it in writing. You can use this Agreement for that purpose.

Signing Instructions

The borrower(s) who signed the promissory note should sign and date the Agreement to Modify Promissory Note, and indicate the location (city or county) where this agreement is being signed. The lender should keep the original signed document and give a copy to the borrower(s).

Form 47: Overdue Payment Demand

If someone who owes you money under a promissory note falls behind on repayment despite your efforts to work out a new repayment plan, your next step is to send the borrower a formal demand letter. You can use this form in such a situation. It serves as a formal notice to the borrower that you are demanding repayment. It states that if you do not hear from the borrower within 15 days, you will enforce your rights under the promissory note, including possibly filing a lawsuit to collect the debt.

 CAUTION
Be careful not to make any threats that you don't intend to follow up. Although the federal and state fair debt law probably don't apply to you, it's still a good idea to be fair, yet firm, in trying to persuade the borrower to pay you back.

Signing Instructions

Sign the Overdue Payment Demand and send it to all borrowers and all cosigners by certified mail (return receipt requested). Keep a copy for your records. You may later need this if you end up suing the borrower to collect the money owed.

RELATED TOPIC

If you are writing to request the return of a security deposit on rental property, use the Demand for Return of Security Deposit in Chapter 4.

Form 48: Demand to Make Good on Bad Check

This form is similar to the Overdue Payment Demand in that it's used when someone who owes you money is not meeting the obligation to pay you and has ignored all your efforts to resolve the problem informally. The difference is that this form is used when the person who owes you money writes you a bad check, a slightly more complicated legal situation. Use this form to make a formal written demand for payment on a bad check.

Although writing a bad check is a crime in every state, prosecutions for writing bad checks are rare. Even in the unlikely event that a district attorney is willing to bring charges, there's a good chance the person would avoid a trial by agreeing to attend a diversion program for bad-check writers and making restitution—that is, paying up.

In most states, you'll want to deal with a bad check through civil, not criminal, remedies.

The person who receives a bad check can usually sue for extra damages (above and beyond the amount of the check) if not paid within 30 days of making a formal written demand for payment.

A clause is included in the Demand to Make Good on Bad Check stating that if you sue over the bad check, you may ask for the maximum monetary damages allowed under state law. This is often two or three times the amount of the check. To find out what the maximum damages are in your state, check your state's laws.

Signing Instructions

Sign the Demand to Make Good on Bad Check form and deliver it personally to the person who wrote you the bad check. Have the person acknowledge receipt by signing and dating an extra copy. Alternatively, send the form by certified mail (return receipt requested) or use a delivery service that will give you a receipt establishing delivery. Some states (California, for example) require that the demand be sent by certified mail (return receipt requested) in order for the lender to recover statutory damages. Keep copies of the demand and the return receipt. You may later need this if you end up filing a lawsuit to collect payment.

Buying a House

No doubt about it—a house is one of the most important investments you'll ever make. Careful planning and organization are key to getting the best house for your money. The forms in this chapter help you:

- identify house features most important to you and keep a record of relevant information about each house you see (Forms 49 to 51)
- determine how much you are able to spend on the down payment and monthly mortgage payments (Forms 52 and 53), and
- keep track of information you collect on different loans and compare features such as interest rates and loan costs (Form 54).

This chapter also includes a handy checklist (Form 55) to help plan your move.

Real Estate on Nolo.com

You can find a wide range of house-buying resources in the "Buying a House or Property" area of the "Real Estate" section of Nolo's website (www.nolo.com), which has information on:

- comparing interest rates and applying for a mortgage
- mortgage calculators
- screening houses that meet your needs
- gathering information on neighborhood schools, crime, and more
- checking sales prices of comparable properties to make a realistic offer
- arranging house inspections, and
- finding a real estate agent, home inspector, or other professional.

 RESOURCE
For an excellent resource on all aspects of home buying, check out *Nolo's Essential Guide to Buying Your First Home*, by Ilona Bray, Alayna

Schroeder, and Marcia Stewart. It covers the entire process, from deciding whether you're ready to buy to settling in to your new home.

Form 49: Ideal House Profile

When you're looking for a house, it's easy to become overwhelmed by the huge variety of choices, from size to style to floor plan. Then there's the issue of location—houses come in all sorts of neighborhoods, school districts, and potential hazard zones (fire, earthquake, and flood, to name a few). And, of course, price and purchase terms are crucial considerations. To cope with all these and at least a dozen other relevant variables, it's essential to establish your priorities in advance and stick to them.

The Ideal House Profile lists all major house features, such as upper price limit, number and type of rooms, and location. Use it to identify the essential characteristics you're looking for in a house.

Price is an obvious consideration for most people, so fill in the top section first. For example, under "Upper price limit," you might note $600,000, with a maximum down payment of $60,000. And if you have two kids, you might note that three bedrooms and excellent public schools are also "Must Haves."

In most cases, it will be obvious where to note your priorities. For example, if extreme quiet is important (you don't want to be near a freeway off-ramp) or you want walking access to a park, list these under "Desired neighborhood features." If you're not sure where to list a particular Must Have, such as a hot and dry climate, ocean view, or garage parking, put it in the "Other desired features" category on the Ideal House Profile.

Once you've compiled your list of "Must Haves," jot down features that you'd like but that aren't crucial to your decision of whether to buy. For example, under "Type of yard and grounds," you might note "patio and flat backyard" in the "Hope to Have" column. Or under "Number and type of rooms," you might list "a finished basement" or "master bedroom with bath."

Be sure to list your "Absolute no ways" (you will not buy a house that has any of these features) at the bottom of the form. Avoiding things you'll always hate, such as a house in a flood zone or in a poor school district, or one that's too far from where you work, can be even more important than finding a house that contains all your mandatory priorities.

If you're buying with another person, prepare your list of priorities together, so that each person's strong likes and dislikes are respected.

TIP

Can any of your priority items be added after you move in? A new kitchen, deck, patio, and sometimes even an extra room, can be added a few years down the road. Of course, replacing a small dark yard with a large sunny one can't be done.

TIP

Get more neighborhood information. If you're moving to a new area, you may not have a good sense of what particular cities and neighborhoods are like. Before finalizing a decision to buy, you'll want to get more information. For example, if under your "Must have" column you've written "excellent public schools," you need in-depth information about the school system in each community you are considering. It's fine to ask a real estate agent. There's also a wealth of community and neighborhood information available online. Or, take the time to talk to people in the area whose kids currently attend its schools. You can also ask for help from a reference librarian at an area public library.

Form 50: House Priorities Worksheet

Now it's time to use the information collected in your Ideal House Profile to create a House Priorities Worksheet, which will help you see how each house you visit stacks up.

First, copy your "Must haves," "Hope to haves," and "Absolute no ways" onto a master copy of this Worksheet. Then, make several copies, to allow for mistakes or the eventual scaling back of your priority list if it turns out you can't afford all the features you would like.

Make several copies of the completed worksheet. Take one with you each time you visit a house, and fill in the top of the worksheet. Enter the address, asking price, name and phone number of the contact person (listing agent, or seller if it's for sale by owner), and the date you saw the house.

As you walk around each house and talk to the owner or agent, enter a check mark if the house has a desirable or undesirable feature. Also make notes next to a particular feature if it can be changed to meet your needs (an okay kitchen could be modernized for around $25,000). Add comments at the bottom, such as "potential undeveloped lot next door" or "neighbors seem very friendly." If you look at a lot of houses, these notes will ensure you don't forget important information.

You should seriously consider only those houses with all or most of your "must haves" and none of your "no ways."

TIP

Set up a good filing system or database. As the list of houses you look at grows, keep track of the information you collect. Failing to adopt a good system may lead to revisiting houses you've already seen and rejected or making decisions based on half-remembered facts. For each house that seems promising, gather or enter information from the House Priorities Worksheet, the information sheets provided at the open house, the Multiple Listing Service information, ads, and your notes.

Form 51: House Comparison Worksheet

If, like many people, you look at a considerable number of houses over an extended period of time, you may soon have trouble distinguishing or comparing their features. That's where the House Comparison Worksheet comes in.

Across the top of the form, list the addresses of the three or four houses you like best. In the left column, fill in your list of priorities and "Absolute no ways" from your Ideal House Profile and House Priorities Worksheet. Then put a check mark on the line under each house that has that feature, to allow for a quick comparison.

Form 52: Family Financial Statement

When planning to buy a house, one of your most important tasks is to determine how much you can afford to pay. Begin by preparing a thorough family financial statement that includes:

- your monthly income
- your monthly expenses, and
- your net worth (your assets minus your debts or liabilities).

We use the word "family" as shorthand for the economic unit that will buy a house. For these purposes, an unmarried couple or a single person is just as much a family as is a married couple with three kids.

Preparing a family financial statement begins the process of learning how much house

you can afford—in terms of both the down payment and monthly mortgage payments.

And if you haven't been preapproved for a mortgage loan when you make a purchase offer, a financial statement can be extremely helpful to convince the seller that you're a serious bidder. This may be crucial, especially if there's more than one prospective buyer. The person who can best convince the seller of the financial ability to swing the deal with no glitches often prevails, even without making the highest offer.

CAUTION

This statement is for you, not your lender. No matter how much debt a lender ultimately says you can handle, the purpose of this statement is to help you develop your own realistic picture of what this debt will mean for your monthly cash flow. The information you collect will help you fill out your loan application, but you won't give this statement directly to the lender. That means that if you exaggerate your income or underestimate your expenses, you'll only be fooling yourself.

Directions for Completing the Family Financial Statement

Top. Indicate the name(s), address(es), email address(es), home phone number(s), employer's name(s) and address(es), and work phone number(s) for yourself and any coborrower. A coborrower includes anyone with whom you are purchasing the house.

Worksheet 1: Income and Expenses

This worksheet shows you how much disposable income you have each month, a key fact in determining how much you can afford to spend on a house. In the first two columns, you and any coborrower each list your monthly income and expenses. Total them in the third column.

IA. Monthly gross income. List your monthly gross income from all sources. Gross income means total income before amounts such as taxes, Social Security, or retirement contributions are withheld.

1. **Employment.** This is your base salary or wages plus any bonuses, tips, commissions, or overtime you regularly receive. If your income is irregular, take the average of the past 24 months. If you have more than one job, include your combined total.

2. **Public benefits.** Include income from Social Security, disability insurance, Temporary Assistance for Needy Families (TANF), Supplemental Security Income (SSI), and other public programs.

3. **Dividends.** Include all dividends from stocks, bonds, and similar investments.

4. **Royalties.** If you have continuing income from the sale (licensing) of books, music, software, inventions, or the like, list it here.

5. **Interest and other investment income.** Include interest received on savings or money market accounts, or as payments on rental property. If the source of the income has costs associated with it (such as the costs of owning rental property), include the net monthly profit received.

6. **Other.** Include payments from pensions, child or spousal support, or separate private maintenance income. Specify the source.

IB. **Total monthly gross income.** Total up items 1–6. (This is the figure that lenders use to qualify you for mortgages.)

IIA. **Monthly nonhousing expenses.** List what you spend each month on items such as child care and clothing. Here are some notes clarifying specific items. (Also, see Form 66, Daily Expenses, for advice on computing average monthly expenses.)

3. **Food.** Include eating at restaurants, as well as at home.

4. **Insurance.** List the monthly cost of your auto, life, and medical and dental insurance. If you pay any of these costs yearly, divide the annual amount by 12 and include here.

5. **Other medical.** List uninsured medical expenses.

6. **Personal.** Include costs for both personal care (haircuts, shoe repairs, and toiletries) and personal fun (attending movies and buying lottery tickets, subscribing to newspapers). Also, include any regular personal loan payments.

7. **Education.** Include monthly payments for education loans here, plus educational payments, such as your child's private school tuition.

9. **Transportation.** Include costs for both motor vehicles (include monthly car loan payments, but exclude insurance) and public transit. Include monthly upkeep for a vehicle and a reasonable amount for repairs.

10. **Other.** Specify such expenses as regular monthly credit card payments, charitable or religious donations, savings deposits, and child or spousal support payments.

IIB. **Current housing expenses.** If you currently own a home, list the monthly mortgage payments, taxes, insurance, and utilities (including gas, electricity, water, sewage, garbage, telephone, and cable service). If you rent, include your monthly rent and renter's insurance (if any).

IIC. **Total monthly expenses.** Here, total your nonhousing and housing expenses. Then subtract line C from line B to see how much disposable income you have available to put toward a monthly mortgage payment. Of course, you can also add in whatever amount you currently spend on your mortgage payment or rent.

Worksheet 2: Assets and Liabilities

I. **Assets.** In the first two columns, you and any coborrower write down the cash or market value of the assets listed. Total them up in the third column.

   A. **Cash and cash equivalents.** List your cash and items easily converted into cash. Deposits include checking accounts, savings accounts, money market accounts, and certificates of deposit (even if there is a withdrawal penalty).

   B. **Marketable securities.** Here you list items like stocks and bonds that are regularly traded and that you can turn into cash fairly readily. List the cash surrender value of any life insurance policy. Include items such as a short-term loan you made to a friend under the category "Other."

   C. **Total cash and marketable securities.** Add up items A and B.

   D. **Nonliquid assets.** These are items not easily converted into cash.

   1. **Real estate.** List the market value —the amount the property would sell for.

   2. **Retirement funds.** Include public or private pensions and self-directed accounts (IRAs, Keoghs, or 401(k) plans). List the amount vested in the plan.

   3. **Business.** If you own a business, list your equity in it (market value less the debts of the business). Many small businesses are difficult to sell, and therefore difficult to value, but do your best.

   4. **Motor vehicles.** List the current market value of any car, truck, RV, or motorcycle, even if you're still making payments. Check used car guides for the information; you can check the *Kelley Blue Book* at www.kbb.com.

   5. **Other.** Include nontangible assets such as copyrights, patents, and trademarks. Yes, it is hard to value these types of assets, but it can be done, especially if you've been receiving income and it promises to continue. Depending on your field, professional organizations that serve authors, inventors, musicians, or software writers may be able to help. In the "Other" category, also include the current value of long-term loans you've made to others, and any really valuable personal property such as expensive jewelry, cameras, or electronic gear.

   E. **Total nonliquid assets.** Total up items D1–5.

   F. **Total all assets.** Total up items IC and IE.

IIA. **Liabilities—Debts.** In the first two columns, you and any coborrower write the total balances remaining for your outstanding loans under their respective categories.

   Under "Other," don't include monthly insurance payments or medical (noninsurance) payments, as these go on Worksheet 1, Section IIA, Monthly Expenses— Nonhousing. Do include stock pledges, lawyer's and accountant's bills, and the like.

IIB. **Total liabilities.** Total the monthly payments and balances remaining for items 1–7.

III. **Net worth.** Total of all assets minus total liabilities.

   Now that you understand what assets you have available, you can estimate how much money you'll have to put toward a down payment.

Form 53: Monthly Carrying Costs Worksheet

Your next step is to understand how much money a lender will allow you to borrow. This will be based on your income, your debts, and the monthly expenses—called "carrying costs"—associated with buying your home. To make this calculation, complete the Monthly Carrying Costs Worksheet. You will need to provide the following information:

Line 1: Estimated purchase price. How much money you'll need to spend on a house likely to have at least most of the "must have" features listed on your Ideal House Profile.

Line 2: Down payment. Enter the down payment you plan to make (which will likely need to be 20% of the purchase price).

Line 3: Subtract your anticipated down payment (line 2) from your estimated purchase price (line 1). The result is the amount you'll need to borrow.

Line 4: Interest rate. Estimate the mortgage interest rate you'll pay based on the rates listed online at sites such as bankrate.com. (You'll know what rate you'll pay more precisely when you start shopping for a mortgage using the Mortgage Rates and Terms Worksheet.)

Line 5: Monthly mortgage payment. Calculate your monthly mortgage payments by using a calculator on a website such as bankrate.com.

Line 6: Homeowners' insurance. You can get exact quotes in advance from insurance agents. Expect to spend several hundred dollars, depending on your home's size, features, and location.

Line 7: Property taxes. These vary tremendously depending on where you live. You'll need to get an estimate from a local tax assessor's office.

Line 8: Now add up your mortgage payment (line 5), insurance (line 6), and taxes (line 7). This is your monthly carrying cost (also called PITI—principal, interest, taxes, and insurance).

Line 9: Other monthly debts. These are items such as monthly payments on a car or student loan. Exclude any debts that will be paid off within ten months.

Line 10: Private mortgage insurance (PMI). Your lender may require this if you're making a down payment of less than 20%. PMI is often about 0.5% of the loan.

Line 11: Homeowners' association fee. You may have to pay this monthly fee if you're looking at a condo, townhome, or a house in a planned unit development.

Line 12: Add lines 8–11 for the sum of your total monthly carrying costs and long-term debts.

Line 13: Lender qualifying ratio. Other things being equal (which they rarely are), lenders normally want you to pay monthly carrying costs (mortgage payment, property taxes, and homeowners' insurance) with no more than 28%–36% of your monthly gross income. Whether you qualify at the bottom or top of this range depends on the amount of your down payment, the interest rate on the type of mortgage you want, your credit score (a numerical measure that reflects how you've managed credit in the past), and the level of your other long-term debts.

Line 14: Divide line 12 by line 13 to determine the monthly income needed to qualify.

Line 15: Multiply line 14 by 12 (which represents months in a year) to calculate the yearly income to qualify.

Form 54: Mortgage Rates and Terms Worksheet

As with any other consumer product, you can save money by carefully shopping for a mortgage. But because of the variety of mortgages on the market and the fact that fine-print terms can significantly influence how much you'll really have to pay, it's essential that you carefully compare the total cost of different deals.

You can use the Mortgage Rates and Terms Worksheet to keep track of information you collect on different loans. It is helpful whether you'll be working with a loan broker (who specializes in matching house buyers and appropriate mortgage lenders) or shopping for a mortgage on your own.

This form is important for three primary reasons:

- Filling it out all but requires you to really understand the fine-print details of every loan you consider.
- Having this information will aid your memory days or weeks later when trying to recall what you've been offered.
- Assuming you get information about more than one loan, you can efficiently compare features.

Instructions for Completing the Mortgage Rates and Terms Worksheet

Heading

At the top of the table, enter the lender's name (such as Bank of Richmond), the name of the loan agent you met or spoke with, the agent's phone number, and the date of your meeting or conversation.

Section 1: General Information

Enter the type of loan: fixed or adjustable; the rate, if it's a fixed mortgage; whether it qualifies for government financing (if that's a need you have); the minimum down payment required; whether private mortgage insurance (PMI) is required and, if so, whether you'll need to set up an impound account; the term (number of years of the loan); whether it's assumable (currently possible only with FHA or VA loans); and, whether it lets you (and for how much)

lock in at a certain rate. (See the table below for a brief description of key mortgage terms. For more information, check the Real Estate & Rental Property section of Nolo's website at www.nolo.com.)

Section 2: Debt-to-Income Ratios Information

Here you need to indicate the percentage of your income each lender allows for the monthly carrying costs to obtain the mortgage, and for monthly carrying costs plus monthly payments on other long-term debts. Then, based on these debt-to-income ratios, enter the maximum loan each lender will make.

Section 3: Loan Costs

If possible, enter the costs associated with getting the loan—the number of points and their cost, PMI, additional loan fee, credit report, application fee, appraisal fee, and other miscellaneous costs. Then total them up. Your estimate will have to be rough, because most lenders won't estimate closing costs until they start processing your loan.

Section 4: Time Limits

You want to know how long it will take for the lender to process your loan application and, if it's approved, come up with the money (called "funding the loan"), enabling you to close the deal. Enter this information in the fourth section. Also, pay attention to the following items:

- the date each month your payment will be due (the first of the month is standard, although some portfolio lenders set the 15th of the month or allow you to choose a date)
- how many "grace" days you have (after which the payment is considered late—15 days is standard), and
- the fee for late mortgage payments.

Key Mortgage Terms

Fixed rate mortgage. The interest rate and the amount you pay each month remain the same over the entire mortgage term, which is traditionally 15 or 30 years.

Adjustable rate mortgage (ARM). The interest rates on these mortgages fluctuate according to interest rates in the economy. Initial interest rates are typically offered for a set period (sometimes as short as one month). This discounted interest rate is lower than the going rate for fixed rate mortgages. When the initial discount period ends, the interest rate adjusts according to current market rates. The amount of the adjustment is tied to a market-sensitive number called the "index." A "margin" is the factor or percentage a lender adds to the index to arrive at the interest rate you pay over the market rate. Though your interest rate can increase based on the index plus the margin, there usually is a maximum limit, called the "life-of-the-loan cap" (usually, five or six percentage points above the initial rate). A periodic cap limits the amount your interest rate can go up or down at each adjustment period, such as going up 2% annually, with your payments increasing accordingly.

PMI and impound account. Lenders may require private mortgage insurance (PMI) if you're making a down payment of less than 20%. PMI insures the lender if you don't pay the mortgage. Some lenders require that you set up an impound account at the time you close the house purchase, where you deposit up to a year's payments of PMI. In addition, you make monthly payments into the impound account for property taxes and homeowners' insurance, which in turn are paid by the lender or company that services the loan.

Assumable loan. A loan that a creditworthy buyer can take over (assume) from a seller. Most fixed-rate loans are not assumable unless they're FHA or VA loans.

Rate lock-in. A lender's guarantee to make a loan at a particular interest rate, even if the market changes before the closing. The lock-in is usually for a specific time period, such as three to six weeks.

Debt-to-income ratio. The ratio of your monthly mortgage payments (including insurance and property taxes) plus long-term debts to your income; also called lender qualification.

Monthly carrying costs. The sum of your monthly payments for your mortgage principal and interest, homeowners' insurance, and property taxes.

Points and loan costs. The fees associated with getting a mortgage, which usually add up to 2%–5% of the cost of the mortgage. Points make up the largest part of lender fees, with one point equaling 1% of the loan principal. Not all loans have points; they're a way to buy down the interest rate. If you will own a house for many years, paying relatively high points is usually a good idea—their cost is more than paid for by the reduction in interest payments over the life of the loan. But the reverse is also true—if you move in three to five years or less, try to pay as few points as possible, even if you pay a little more interest. It takes several years for the monthly interest savings to offset the initial high cost of points.

Section 5: Other Features

If the loan has any special features, such as discounted points if you have a savings account with the bank, indicate them.

Section 6: Fixed Rate Two-Step Loans

If you look at any fixed rate loans that step up to a higher rate after several years, indicate the initial annual percentage rate, and for how many years it stays in effect.

Section 7: Fixed Rate Balloon Payment Loans

If you are considering a fixed rate loan for a short period (often three, five, or seven years) that ends with one large balloon payment, indicate the interest rate and monthly payment, the term of the loan, and the amount of the balloon payment.

Section 8: Adjustable Rate Mortgages (ARMs)

First, enter the adjustable loan criteria—what index it's tied to and the amount of the margin.

Next, write down interest rate information—the initial rate, how long it lasts, the periodic interest rate cap, the adjustment period, and the life-of-the-loan cap (see the table below for definitions of all these terms).

Finally, enter the payment information—the initial payment, cap, and payment cap period. Also calculate your worst-case scenario: the highest interest rate and monthly payments possible with the adjustable rate loan offered for different time periods.

Section 9: Hybrid Loans

If you are interested in an ARM that has a fixed rate for the first few years and then becomes adjustable, enter the information here. Pay particular attention to how much the interest rate can jump at the first adjustment period.

Form 55: Moving Checklist

Congratulations! If you are looking at this form, chances are you found a good house, closed escrow, and are getting ready to move in. Use the Moving Checklist to help you plan your move.

Buying or Selling a Car, Dog, or Personal Property

This chapter contains forms for use when you sell used personal property, such as a car, boat, appliance, or furniture. It also includes a bill of sale for a dog. Use these simple agreements to record the terms of sale of all types of property (with the exception of real estate and securities, which are closely regulated by law).

A bill of sale is a written document that, at a minimum, includes:

- the names of the seller(s) and buyer(s) (there may be two sellers—for example, if the goods are co-owned as joint property by a husband and wife)
- a statement that a sale has taken place
- a description of the item(s) sold
- the amount paid, and
- the signature of the person selling the property and the date of the signing.

In addition, the bills of sale in this chapter often include:

- a promise that the seller owns or otherwise has the right to sell the item, and details of any liens or encumbrances giving someone else an ownership stake in the goods being sold
- a written warranty or guarantee that the item is in good condition and will be repaired or replaced if it fails within a certain period
- disclosures of any major defects known to the seller, and
- a statement that the item has been inspected by an expert and that the expert's report is attached, if appropriate.

TIP

A well-drafted bill of sale can head off future legal trouble. When used cars, boats, and other items of property are sold without a written bill of sale, the chances of future legal problems— maybe even a court battle—go way up. Far better to define in advance all key terms of the sale, including the condition of the goods being sold and whether the sale includes any seller's warranty (for example, 30 days on parts and labor) or is made "as is."

In some states, a bill of sale must have a notary clause. Although this isn't common, we've included a Certificate of Acknowledgment of Notary Public on each bill of sale form in this chapter. If your state doesn't require notarization, you don't need to use it—but it can never hurt. (See the Introduction to this book for more about notarization.)

Form 56: Motor Vehicle Bill of Sale

Use this bill of sale when you buy or sell a vehicle that must be registered with your state's motor vehicles department. This typically includes cars, trucks, motorcycles, recreational vehicles, and motor homes. It does not include stationary nonregistered mobile homes that are designed to be used semipermanently at a fixed location, such as a mobile home park. Such homes are commonly treated as real property— just as if they were houses—and are covered by special transfer, financing, and recording rules not discussed here. This category of motor vehicle also doesn't include off-road farm machinery—for that, use the General Bill of Sale—unless it can be registered in your state as a motor vehicle.

Describe the vehicle in detail on the bill of sale, including the vehicle identification number, or VIN (this is typically found on the driver's side of the dashboard, close to the windshield), and indicate the price paid. (Your state motor vehicles department needs the price to compute the sales tax.) List any personal property included in the sale, such as a bicycle rack.

 CAUTION

Double-check ownership interest in the vehicle. If you are buying a motor vehicle and you don't know the seller, check with the motor vehicles department where the vehicle is registered to be sure that the seller is the owner, and that no one else claims an ownership interest (lien) in the vehicle. (If the seller hadn't yet repaid a purchase loan, for example, the lender might have an ownership claim). You can get additional useful information about the vehicle's ownership history from services such as Carfax Vehicle Reports (www.carfax.com) or AutoCheck (www.autocheck.com) if you have the VIN. For example, you can learn whether the car was ever severely damaged and "salvaged" or whether the odometer has been rolled back.

Clauses 8 and 9 relate to inspections and condition of the vehicle. These provisions will help the seller avoid future legal problems. If the vehicle is inspected by a mechanic who prepares a written report that is given to the buyer, and the seller conscientiously discloses all known defects, it's highly unlikely that an unsatisfied buyer can later get a judge to agree that the seller misrepresented the car's condition.

Be sure to contact your state motor vehicles department for any special requirements when selling a motor vehicle. For example, the vehicle may have to qualify for a smog certificate. If there are other requirements, include them in Clause 10.

If the seller hasn't fully repaid a loan on the vehicle, the seller should ask the lender if its permission is required in order to sell the vehicle. If the vehicle is leased, the seller should ask the lessor what it requires before the vehicle can be transferred or sold.

Signing Instructions

The buyer(s) and seller(s) must sign the Motor Vehicle Bill of Sale for it to be valid. Print out two copies of the form (or enough for everyone who signs the form to have a separate copy). Each person should sign and date all copies of the form and keep a signed document with all original signatures.

Be sure to check with your state motor vehicles department regarding any official signing requirements that must be met. For example, the seller's signature on the vehicle's title may need to be notarized. And in some states, the bill of sale itself needs to be notarized. (If so, see the instructions about notarization, in the Introduction to this book.) In addition, the seller may need to file an official form to avoid liability if the buyer hits someone with the vehicle after the sale, and the buyer may have to file an official form to register the vehicle in his or her name.

Form 57: Boat Bill of Sale

This form is similar in content to the Motor Vehicle Bill of Sale, but it covers boats of all kinds. The form contains details about the boat, as well as any engines, electronics, and other equipment that are to be sold along with it.

Carefully read the discussion that accompanies the Motor Vehicle Bill of Sale, especially the advice about arranging for an inspection by a third party and having the seller list (disclose) all defects. These provisions make it difficult for a lawyer to claim later that the seller misrepresented the condition of the boat.

This bill of sale includes a number of entries unique to boat sales. Fill in the details key to your sale, such as a thorough list of all personal property items included in the sale or the maintenance history of the boat.

If the seller hasn't fully repaid a purchase loan on the boat, the seller should ask the lender whether its permission is required in order to sell the boat.

Signing Instructions

The buyer(s) and seller(s) must sign the Boat Bill of Sale for it to be valid. Print out two copies of the form (or enough for each person signing the form to have a separate copy). Each person should sign and date all copies of the form and keep a signed document with all original signatures.

Be sure to check with your state motor vehicles department (or the department in your state that registers boats) regarding any official signing requirements that must be met. For example, the seller's signature on the boat's title may need to be notarized. In addition, the seller may need to file an official form to avoid liability if the buyer hits someone with the boat after the sale, and the buyer may have to file an official form to register the boat in his or her name.

Form 58: General Bill of Sale

The General Bill of Sale should be used for the sale of personal property such as jewelry, artwork, sports equipment, rare books, furniture, collections, appliances, tools, photographic equipment, and electronic items. Do not use this form if you are selling a car or other motor vehicle, or a boat. (these categories are specifically covered above). Before using this form, read the brief discussion that precedes the Motor Vehicle Bill of Sale, which discusses key clauses in a bill of sale.

Signing Instructions

The buyer(s) and seller(s) must sign the General Bill of Sale for it to be valid. Print out two copies of the form (or enough for each person signing the form to have a separate copy). Each person should sign and date all copies of the form and keep a signed document with all original signatures.

Form 59: Bill of Sale for Dog

Use this bill of sale when you buy or sell a dog in a transaction with a private party or a breeder. It spells out exactly what terms the seller is promising, including price, how and when the dog will be turned over to the buyer, and who will pay shipping costs (if any). This form provides basic information on the dog, including birth date, medication information such as vaccination history, health, name of breeder, special training (if any), and registration with the American Kennel Club or other entity. Most of the form is self-explanatory. You can add any items of special concern—for example, if the seller wants the buyer to have the dog spayed or neutered.

Clause 6 gives the buyer two options if a veterinarian certifies, in writing, that the dog has a disease or a congenital defect that was present when the buyer bought the dog. Within 14 days, the buyer may either return the dog to the seller and be reimbursed for the purchase price and for reasonable veterinary bills already paid, or keep the dog and also receive reimbursement for reasonable veterinary bills, up to the amount of the purchase price.

If you're buying a dog from a pet store: You may have other legal rights in addition to those set out in this bill of sale. Because consumers have had so many problems with dogs bought in pet stores, many states impose special requirements on pet retailers that don't apply to breeders who raise and sell dogs themselves. You may be entitled to a disclosure sheet, stating where the animal came from (it may have been shipped across the country at a young age), and its health and vaccination history. You may also have a right to return or exchange an unhealthy dog, or get reimbursement for veterinary bills, that is different from the right this bill of sale gives you.

Signing Instructions

The buyer(s) and seller(s) must sign this Bill of Sale for Dog for it to be valid. Print out two copies of the form (or enough for each person signing the form to have a separate copy). Each person should sign and date all copies of the form and keep a signed document with all original signatures.

Renting Personal Property and Storing Goods

People frequently rent tools, equipment, and other personal property. While equipment is often rented from commercial companies that have their own forms, it is also not uncommon to rent items from a neighbor or friend.

Many rented items are used to perform a particular task, as would be the case if you rented a rototiller and weight drum to lay sod, or a power saw and sander to do a small remodeling job around your home. In other situations, you might rent property for a recreational purpose—for example, if you're assigned to bring a volleyball net and badminton set to the family reunion.

This chapter includes a form for renting personal property. You can tailor the form based on the type of property you're renting, its value, and how long you need to rent it for. The chapter also includes a notice to end this type of rental agreement.

In addition to borrowing or renting tools, equipment, and other items, people often turn to friends or neighbors to store their personal property, such as furniture, for an extended period of time. This chapter includes a storage contract for use in these situations.

Whether or not a rental or storage fee is paid, it makes sense to write down your understanding of key issues, such as the length of the rental or storage period and who will be responsible if the rented or stored property is damaged. Having a written agreement is especially important if valuable property is to be rented or stored for an extended period. If any problem comes up, having a simple written contract will help you arrive at a fair settlement and preserve relations between the parties.

Form 60: Personal Property Rental Agreement

You can use this form for a short-term rental (30 days or less) of personal (non–real estate) property. It is primarily geared toward renting relatively inexpensive personal property from a neighbor or friend. It is not intended to be used for rental of a motor vehicle, motorcycle, ATV, boat, personal watercraft, or the like. Because not much is at stake, this rental agreement doesn't deal with the many potentially complex issues that can arise when expensive property is rented for an extended period. But this personal property rental agreement covers all the basics, including the names of the parties (owner and renter), a description of the property and its condition, the amount of rent, length of the rental period, and delivery arrangements. It includes a dispute resolution clause that provides for negotiation, mediation, and/or arbitration as a means for the parties to resolve any disputes that may arise over the agreement. (See the Introduction for more on dispute resolution procedures.)

 TIP

Use this agreement even if no rent is being paid. Simply put a zero (∅) on the dollar amount lines in Clauses 3, 4, 5, and 6. Fill in all the other sections. And depending on the particular personal property, the renter should give the owner a small thank-you gift, such as movie tickets.

Signing Instructions

The owner and the renter must both sign this Personal Property Rental Agreement for it to be valid. Print out two copies of the form (or enough for each person who will be signing the form to have a separate copy). Each person should sign and date all copies of the form and keep a signed document with all original signatures.

Form 61: Notice of Termination of Personal Property Rental Agreement

This form can be used by either the owner or the renter to end any personal property rental agreement that is not made for a specific period. You do not need to give a reason (unless this is required by your rental agreement).

CAUTION

Do not use this termination notice if you have rented personal property for a specific rental period. In that case, you cannot terminate the agreement unless both parties agree.

Signing Instructions

Simply sign the Notice of Termination of Personal Property Rental Agreement and give it to the other party. Keep a copy for your records, and note on your copy the date and time you delivered the notice.

Form 62: Storage Contract

It is common to store property with friends and relatives—everything from bikes, beds, and books to washing machines, weights, and walking sticks. Sometimes this amounts to nothing more than leaving a few small objects for a short time. On other occasions, however, it means storing a household- or garage-full of goods for a year or more. In many situations involving friends and family, money isn't charged for storage, although payment certainly can be appropriate when bulky or valuable objects are stored for a considerable period of time. This is especially true when the goods are stored in a place (for example, a garage or spare room) that might otherwise be rented or used.

This form covers the basics of storing personal property, including the names of the parties (we call them "property owner" and "property custodian"); a description of the property being stored and its condition and value; storage location, term, and payment; who's responsible for theft of or damage to property during the rental period; and how the custodian will deal with abandoned property never reclaimed by the owner. This storage contract includes a dispute resolution clause that provides for negotiation, mediation, and/or arbitration as a means for the parties to resolve any disputes that may arise over the agreement. (See the Introduction for more on dispute resolution procedures.)

It is especially important that you carefully identify property and its value and condition. One common dispute involves the property owner who claims that a valuable item is missing, while the custodian says it was never present in the first place. The best way to prevent this is to make a thorough list of the items to be stored. In this age of digital cameras and camera-equipped phones, it's a good idea to take pictures and attach them to the contract. In Clause 1, you should identify each item as thoroughly as possible, including (as appropriate) the make, model, year, and color (you'll spell out the condition in Clause 12). Also, when you specify the value of the property (Clause 11), be sure to specify whether you mean the replacement value or the fair market value of the property, such as a TV set. (You'll be asked to make a choice.) Replacement value is how much it would cost for you to buy another of this item, such as the cost of a new TV set. Fair market value is how much you would get for an item, such as a TV set, if you sold it—for example, online or at a garage sale. Whichever you choose, specify the value of each item you store, to reduce the chance of a misunderstanding if any items are damaged or missing. Use Clause 12 to spell out any defects or damage in the property being stored (such as a stain on a sofa).

Clause 13 commits the property custodian to use reasonable care while storing the property, but the custodian will not be responsible for damage due to inherent flaws or the property's inherent defective condition. The optional part of the clause specifies that the property will be insured by the owner, and that the custodian will also cover the property subject to the limits and limitations of the owner's own homeowners' or other insurance policy. Homeowners' policies will generally cover damage or loss to another's property up to a certain amount, and typically will not cover automobiles.

Use Clause 18 to describe any special terms of the storage—for example, if you want the custodian to start the car at least once a week while it's in storage.

Signing Instructions

Both parties must sign this Storage Contract for it to be valid. Print out two copies of the form (or enough for each person who will be signing the form to have a separate copy). Each person should sign and date all copies of the form and keep a signed document with all original signatures.

Home Repairs and Maintenance

This chapter contains three agreements that cover home maintenance and repairs, as well as other work you plan to have done at your residence, such as painting or yard work. To get the job done right, your most important task is to find a contractor who has done excellent work for other people in your community. (Our forms use the term "contractor" for someone who does home repairs or maintenance.)

But even with a highly recommended person, serious misunderstandings between a homeowner and contractor can easily arise if the key job specifications, payment details, and work schedule haven't been carefully worked out and written down before the work begins. That's the purpose of these forms. These written agreements will help you get the work done right, on time, and within your budget.

 CAUTION

The first two forms in this chapter are not suitable for complicated jobs. You'll need a more detailed contract than the ones provided here if you're planning on remodeling a kitchen, adding a room, putting on a new roof, painting the complete exterior or interior, or doing any other similarly large project. A large firm doing major home repairs and remodeling will usually present you with its own contract. The forms in this chapter can help you analyze an agreement proposed by a contractor and make sure the basics are covered.

State Licensing and Registration Requirements for Home Repair Work

Almost all states have licensing requirements for certain categories of highly skilled home improvement and construction work. For example, most states license people who do residential electrical and plumbing work or who build new structures. By contrast, there is less uniformity among the states as to whether licensing is required for contractors who do general repair and remodeling work, such as framing, drywall installation, paneling, deck construction, siding, and painting.

License and registration requirements are often tied to the following factors:

- **Size of the project**—a license may be required for work on any job over a specified amount, such as $5,000.
- **Type of job**—some states require a license for plumbing or electrical work but not for painting, for example.
- **Location of contractor**—most states regulate contracting work of any type that is done by out-of-state contractors.

Most states that require a license for general repair and remodeling tasks require some experience and skills training, as well as some evidence of financial responsibility or effective customer recourse policy. For details, contact your state's consumer protection office or visit its website to find out whether your state regulates the type of contractor you are hiring, and if so, the name of the agency that does the regulating, such as the State Contractors' Licensing Board. Then check out the agency's website. Many let you check online whether a contractor's license is current and in good standing. Also, many state agencies publish and distribute free consumer information on home repair work, with useful advice on finding and working with a home repair contractor and legal requirements that apply in your state.

 CAUTION

Beware of unlicensed contractors.

Even where licenses are required, you can always find someone unlicensed who will do the work, usually promising a cheap price. Be wary about accepting these offers—unlicensed contractors are not bonded, meaning that their work isn't insured, and your homeowners' insurance may refuse to cover their injuries, leaving you open to personal liability. And, of course, an unlicensed contractor is almost sure to work without getting a building permit, which may cause problems later.

Some states require people who do home repair and remodeling work to register with the state. Registration usually does not require demonstrated experience or training. It is primarily designed to keep track of people offering contractor services so that homeowners can locate them if something goes wrong during or after the job.

Local Permits and Approvals for Home Repair Work

In addition to state licensing and registration rules, homeowners often must obtain a permit from a city or county agency for jobs that involve structural alterations, additions, substantial remodeling, or new electrical wiring or plumbing installations. Permits are usually not required for casual carpentry, minor plumbing and electrical repairs, or replacing a window or door.

In addition to a local permit, if the house is part of a condominium complex or planned unit development, a homeowners' association or "architectural review committee" will likely insist on formal approval of the work, especially if the work affects the home's exterior appearance. Homeowners' association approval is usually necessary for new windows, exterior painting, roofing, and room additions.

Either the homeowner or the contractor must be responsible for getting information about the necessary permits. If the job requires a permit or approval but no one obtains it, the homeowner may have to redo some or all of the work if a later inspection reveals deficiencies. Also, the value of the home may be adversely affected when it comes to resale if the buyer learns of the nonpermit work.

Independent Contractor Versus Employee

Our contracts (Clause 4 in each) assume that the person who will come to your house is an independent contractor, not your employee. As long as the contractor is doing one job or occasional work, this is legal. If a person will work for you regularly (an every-day gardener, for example), the law probably requires that you treat the individual as an employee, for whom you are legally required to pay income taxes, Social Security, and other benefits.

 RESOURCE

For more information on the difference between an independent contractor and an employee, see IRS Form SS-8, available on the IRS website at www.irs.gov, or by phone at 800-829-3676.

Dispute Resolution Clause

The two forms in this chapter do not include a dispute resolution clause mandating mediation and arbitration to resolve disputes before going to court. If you would like to include a dispute resolution clause in either of these forms, see the Introduction to this book, where this option is explained.

Form 63: Home Maintenance Agreement

This form is intended for hiring unskilled labor on a one-time job that isn't expected to last for more than a day or two and doesn't need a significant amount of materials. Typical jobs that fall into this category are hauling refuse, cleaning a garage or house, washing windows, and gardening and other yard work. Such jobs are usually performed by one person, who supplies the required tools.

This form is easy to complete. Simply spell out the details of the work and the amount, form, and schedule of payment, and any additional terms that are relevant, such as who will pay the fee for hauling refuse to the dump, or who will be responsible for obtaining and paying for any necessary permits.

Signing Instructions

You (the homeowner) and the contractor must sign this Home Maintenance Agreement for it to be valid. Print out two copies of the form and have each party sign and date both copies. Give the contractor one of the signed documents and keep the other for your own records.

Form 64: Home Repairs Agreement

This form covers home repairs done by skilled labor for a job that isn't expected to take more than a few days, such as installing new locks or windows, nonstructural carpentry repairs, touch-up painting, masonry work, or roofing repairs. Use it to spell out the who (names of the homeowner and contractor), what and how (specific details of the job, such as painting the kitchen or installing new bathroom flooring), how much (dollar amount and details of payment), when (beginning and ending dates) of the work, and any additional terms, such as who will be paying for and picking up materials and supplies, such as paint.

> ### TIP
> **Don't pay too much up front—just enough to let the contractor purchase the materials needed to get started.** It is usually best to agree to make periodic payments that are tied to measurable, easy-to-define goals. Clause 2 is

the place to spell out the details of your payment arrangement. For example, you may decide to pay one lump sum at the end of the work, or pay in increments (such as half at the beginning of work and half at the end), or pay an hourly rate for work done.

Simple home repairs probably won't require a contractor's license or permit, but if they do, Clauses 4 and 5 of the Home Repairs Agreement allow you to spell out the details regarding licenses and permits. If you don't need them, follow the instructions in the Introduction for deleting unnecessary contract clauses.

Clause 6 specifies that the contractor must carry insurance and accept responsibility for injuries that occur during the course of the work.

Signing Instructions

You (the homeowner) and the contractor must sign this Home Repairs Agreement for it to be valid. Print out two copies and have each party sign and date both. Give the contractor one of the signed documents and keep the other for your own records.

Form 65: Contractor Mid-Job Worksheet

If you've hired a contractor to perform home or business repair or maintenance, you probably have a good idea of what work will be done and what it's going to cost. For extensive jobs, you may have a full-blown contract, which you've accepted by signing it; or, you may have a written bid that you've orally agreed to. Or, you may have only an oral bid and acceptance—basically, you and the contractor had a conversation and came to an understanding of the work and the cost. All of these methods for recording the scope of the work and the cost are legal and enforceable—although, of course, a written understanding is always preferable.

Having a clear understanding of the extent and cost of the work does not mean, however, that events will always turn out as planned. In fact, anyone who has done even modest remodeling will tell you that you will always have surprises as work progresses. For all but the simplest of jobs, you're likely to have lots of questions, which will pop up as you arrive home at night to survey the day's work or, more likely, as you lie in bed at night. You'll be wondering, "Will it look like this when it's done?" "Is this the final color?" "Can I change the placement of that fixture?" "Should we do this while we're at it?" and so on. Most importantly, if the scope of the work changes or the time needed to do it increases, you'll want to know how, if at all, these changes will affect the cost of the job.

It's important that you and your contractor have continuing, clear communication about the progress of your repair or remodeling job. Don't let important questions go unanswered during the brief exchange you typically have with your contractor each morning. Write questions down as they occur to you and go over the list with your contractor on a daily basis. Even the busiest contractor will pause as you approach with clipboard in hand, and will take a few minutes to go over your questions.

Our Contractor Mid-Job Worksheet, which you'll date as of the day of your discussion, provides a place for you to list your issues and gives you room to record the answer and, possibly, the plan. You'll be able to note whether the intended resolution will vary the bid and, if so, by how much. (To be extra careful, after deciding whether the bid will be affected, you can ask your contractor to initial or sign the form.) You'll also be able to record whether the work or variation was actually done and whether it's satisfactory.

This worksheet is valuable primarily as a way to preserve and present your questions, but it has other uses, as well. If there is uncertainty later about what you agreed to—and whether it would cost additional money—you'll have a record of the discussion and the plan. If worst come to worst and you and the contractor get into a legal squabble, your notes will be valuable evidence as well.

Use our Contractor Mid-Job Worksheet on a daily basis if your project is multifaceted and moving quickly; or use it weekly if progress is slow.

Be sure to keep all worksheets in a safe place (in a folder or binder, along with the original contract), and keep all documents for at least ten years (the typical time period in which you can sue for most construction defects).

Signing Instructions

For each issue you discuss with your contractor, fill in a row on the Contractor Mid-Job Worksheet. Once you reach agreement on a given issue, have your contractor initial the last column, and place your initials next to the contractor's.

Handling Personal Finances

You may not think too much about monthly budgets, credit reports, or stopping payment on a check unless you are having financial problems. But by being proactive—reviewing your finances in advance and knowing your legal rights—you can often avoid legal and money problems. The forms in this chapter are designed to help you get a handle on your personal finances—budgeting, dealing with debts and debt collectors, and reviewing your credit report—whether you're trying to avoid problems or are in the midst of a crisis.

RESOURCE

Detailed information and forms on dealing with debts, planning a budget, rebuilding your credit, and other similar topics can be found in *Solve Your Money Troubles: Strategies to Get Out of Debt and Stay That Way* and *Credit Repair: Make a Plan, Improve Your Credit, Avoid Scams*, both by Robin Leonard (Nolo).

Form 66: Daily Expenses

Creating a budget—comparing your average monthly expenses to your total monthly income—is the most effective way to start putting your financial house in order. Although it's not hard to do, budgeting is a three-step process. Step one is to get a clear picture of how you spend your money. You can do that using this form (Daily Expenses), on which you record everything you spend over the course of a week. Step two is to total up your income using the Monthly Income form. The final step is comparing the two and figuring out where you might need to make some changes. For that you can use the Monthly Budget form.

Here's how to use the Daily Expenses form:

1. Make ten copies of the Daily Expenses form (if you're using the tear-out form)

or print a new copy each week. You will use nine copies of the form to record your expenses for about two months. By using your expense figures for two months, you'll avoid creating a budget based on a week or a month of unusually high or low expenses. If you and another adult (such as a spouse or partner) share finances, make nine copies for each of you. You will use the tenth copy to record other expenses.

2. Begin recording your expenses on the first of the month; record that date in the blank at the top of one copy of the form.

3. Record every expense you pay by cash or cash equivalent—check, ATM, debit card, or automatic bank withdrawal—on that week's form. Include deposits into savings accounts, certificates of deposit, or money market accounts, and purchases of investments. Do not record credit card charges. When you make a payment on a credit card bill, however, list the amount of your payment and the items it covers.

4. At the end of the week, total your weekly expenses. Put away the completed Daily Expenses form, take out another copy, and fill it out according to Step 3. Repeat until you have two full months of expenses recorded.

5. At the end of the two months, take out the tenth sheet. Anywhere on it, list seasonal, annual, semiannual, or quarterly expenses that you incur each year but that did not come due during your two-month recording period. Common examples are property taxes, car registration, charitable gifts, tax preparation fees, and auto and house insurance payments. Divide the annual cost of these items by 12 to figure out the monthly amount.

6. Total up all expenses for the two months you tracked, including two months' worth of the expenses described in Step 5. Divide the total by two to calculate your average monthly expenses.

Signing Instructions

There are no signing instructions for this form. Simply fill it out and use it to evaluate your spending patterns and prepare a budget.

Form 67: Monthly Income

Use this form together with the Daily Expenses form to help you create a budget. On this form, total up your monthly income. Be sure to include income information for both people if you and another adult share finances.

Part A is for jobs for which you receive a salary or wages. Part B is for self-employment income, including sales commissions. Part C is for investment income, and Part D is for other sources of income, such as bonus pay, alimony or child support, pension or retirement income, and public assistance.

When you are done listing all sources of income, add them all up for your total monthly income. If your income varies each month, repeat this process for two or three months to determine your average monthly income.

 TIP

Don't include income that is automatically reinvested. As you list your income, you may be inclined to include interest and dividends that are automatically reinvested, such as retirement plan income and stock dividends, to get a true sense of your earnings. But the purpose of creating a budget is to keep track of your actual expenses and the income you have available to pay those expenses. By listing income you don't actually receive, you will be left with the impression that you have more income to cover your expenses each month than you actually have available.

Signing Instructions

There are no signing instructions for the Monthly Income form. Simply fill it out and use it to prepare a monthly budget.

Form 68: Monthly Budget

After you've kept track of your expenses and income for a couple of months, you're ready to create a budget using this form. Follow these steps:

1. Using your actual expenses, project your monthly expenses for the categories relevant to you on this Monthly Budget form. Be sure to include the monthly equivalent of any quarterly, semiannual, or annual expenses that you noted on your tenth sheet of the Daily Expenses form.
2. Enter your projected monthly expenses into the projected (Proj.) column on this Monthly Budget. Remember, this is just an estimate based on two months of record keeping. Enter the total at the end of the form, near the bottom of the column.
3. Enter your projected monthly income (bottom line of your Monthly Income form) below your total projected expenses on this Monthly Budget.
4. Figure out the difference. If your expenses exceed your income, you may have to cut your projected expenses or increase your income to make ends meet.
5. During each month, write down your actual expenses in each category. Do this as accurately as possible—remember, creating a budget is really designed to help you adopt a sound spending plan, not to

fill in the "correct" numbers. Check your actual monthly expenditures periodically to help you keep an eye on how you're doing. Are you keeping close to your projected figures? If you are not, you will need to change the projected amount for those categories.

TIP

When a large payment comes due. While you have included one-twelfth of your quarterly, semiannual, and annual expenses in each month's projection, those expenses and other unanticipated ones don't arise every month. Ideally, your budget provides for a cushion each month—that is, your income exceeds your expenses—so you'll be able to handle the large payments when they come due by using that month's cushion or the savings you've built up from the excess each month. If you don't have the cash on hand to pay the large payment, you will have to cut back in other expense categories.

Signing Instructions

There are no signing instructions for this Monthly Budget form. Simply fill it out and use it to balance your income and expenses.

Form 69: Statement of Assets and Liabilities

Subtracting what you owe (liabilities) from what you own (assets) reveals your net worth. A net worth statement can help you and a lender analyze your eligibility for a loan.

To find your net worth, use this Statement of Assets and Liabilities form. Fill in as much information as you can. Don't worry about listing every asset or debt; the information on this form changes daily as your assets change value and the balances on your debts rise or

fall. You can estimate the date of purchase, or write "N/A" in this column if you don't know.

What values should you use for your assets? As best you can, you will want to include an asset's current market value—the amount you could get if you sold the item on the open market. This means you are not looking at what you could get in a forced sale—such as a house repossession or foreclosure, or if you had to sell all your personal belongings at a garage sale. Instead, you're looking at what your home could bring in under normal selling conditions, how much you could get for your car by selling it through the paper or to a dealer, and how much your household goods are worth, considering they generally depreciate about 20% a year.

RELATED TOPIC

For a related form, specifically geared toward determining eligibility for a home loan, see the Family Financial Statement in Chapter 6.

Signing Instructions

There are no signing instructions for this Statement of Assets and Liabilities. Simply fill this form out and update it from time to time. Use it to determine your net worth, information that will be useful should you apply for a loan.

Form 70: Assignment of Rights

You can use this form to transfer property or money that you are entitled to receive (for example, under a contract or promissory note) to another person. This is called "assigning" your right to receive the property or money. In legal terms, you are the "assignor": the person transferring a right to property or money to another person, who is the "assignee." For example, if Bette signed a promissory note owing you money and you owe Roger money, you might assign your right to Bette's money to Roger. You are the assignor and Roger is the assignee. Or, you might assign your right to receive income from a book contract to your teenage son so that the money would be taxed in his bracket, not yours. (See a tax adviser before you do this, though.)

This Assignment of Rights form provides for one or two assignors and one or two assignees. There may be situations in which two people have the right to receive money or property and jointly transfer that right, or in which two people are granted the right to receive money or property. This typically, but not exclusively, arises when a husband and wife jointly have the right to money or property or are jointly granted such a right. (Chapter 5 includes a discussion of marital property.)

Often the assignment covers a set period, especially when you assign the right to receive payments. This form (Clauses 3 and 4) allows you to specify the beginning and ending dates of the assignment; if you don't have an exact end date in mind, you can simply say that the assignment will end when a specific event occurs or you revoke the assignment.

Here are some questions to ask when considering an assignment:

- **If you are assigning rights based on a previously existing contract, does the contract allow the assignment?** Be sure to read the contract carefully and make sure you can assign your rights under it. For example, leases and installment purchase contracts for motor vehicles typically prohibit assignment without the lessor's or lender's advance written consent. Mortgages and deeds of trust also typically cannot be assigned.

- **Are there tax implications of the assignment?** If you assign money to another person and receive something of equal value in return, there should be no tax implications. If, however, you assign your right to receive money to another person as a gift and the IRS learns of the assignment, the IRS will treat the assignment as a taxable transaction. For many assignments, this won't be a problem because you can make a tax-free gift of up to $14,000 per individual per year (2016 figure). But if you are assigning more than that, you should get tax advice.

- **Does the assignment substantially change the obligations of the person with whom you signed a contract?** If the contractual obligations will become more onerous, you may not be allowed to make the assignment. For example, if you have signed a contract with Happy Housekeepers to clean your house once a week for $150, you may not assign this obligation to a neighbor whose house would require a lot more time and effort to clean.

Signing Instructions

You must sign the Assignment of Rights form for it to be valid. Print out two copies of the form (or enough for each person who will be signing the form to have a separate copy). Each person (assignor and assignee) should sign and date all copies of the form and keep a signed document with all original signatures.

Form 71: Notice to Terminate Joint Account

If you are separating from or divorcing a spouse or partner, you will want to close any joint credit cards or accounts immediately.

This involves notifying all creditors of your request to close joint accounts so that no new charges can be made. You should send this notice to every creditor, including credit card issuers, banks, department stores, and other retailers, with whom you and your spouse or partner hold a joint credit account. Send it to the customer service address on the back of a billing statement, not to the address where you send payments. You must complete a separate Notice to Terminate Joint Account for each credit card account you want to close. Be sure you enter the full names of the joint account holders exactly as they appear on the account, and include the correct account number.

The only way to make sure that an account is truly closed is to insist, as this notice does, that the creditor do a "hard close," so that no new charges can be made. (You can close your account even if you haven't paid off the balance. In that case, the account will remain active only for the purpose of paying off the balance.) This notice states that if a "hard close" is not done, you will not be responsible for any charges made on the account. While such a letter may not fully protect you, it is better than doing nothing and puts the burden on the creditor to show why the account wasn't closed as you requested.

If time is of the essence, call the creditor and request a hard close. Follow up by sending a signed copy of this form, along with a cover letter referring to your earlier phone call. You might also be able to close accounts on the card issuer's website.

Signing Instructions

Print out a copy of the Notice to Terminate Joint Account form and sign it in the space provided. Make two copies of the signed form and mail the original and one of the copies to the creditor you wish to notify of the joint account termination. Include a stamped, self-addressed envelope. The creditor will sign the copy and return it to you in the self-addressed envelope as a receipt.

Send the form by certified mail, return receipt requested, and keep a copy of the form and receipt for your records. You may later need it as proof that you properly notified the creditor of your intent to close the joint account.

TIP

Don't overlook home equity lines of credit. You and your ex may have applied for a home equity line of credit a while ago and forgotten about it. Equity credit lines that supply a checkbook can be used just like a joint checking account. Because the risk of leaving an equity line of credit open is so great (you could lose your home if your ex is irresponsible with the funds), we recommend closing it in person. Pay a visit to your banker to request that the account be closed or frozen. Even if you have the checkbook, request that the account be closed so that your ex can't request more checks. Get a written record that the bank has closed the account.

Form 72: Notice to Stop Payment of Check

It's not unusual to write a check, hand it over or mail it to the recipient, and then change your mind and want to stop payment. For example, you might not notice that delivered goods were defective until after the delivery person was paid and left. Many other situations give rise to the need to put a stop payment on a check.

The first thing to do is call the bank, savings and loan, credit union, or other financial institution where your account is located to make an oral request to stop payment. Ask how much the charge is, if any, for this service.

Then immediately send or, better yet, drop off a written confirmation of your stop payment notice (this form). Include payment for any required charge with your notice.

In many situations, the stop payment notice lasts only six months or a year. If you fear the person to whom you wrote the check will try to cash it much later, you may need to renew your stop payment notice. Banks, savings and loans, credit unions, and other financial institutions have the option of rejecting checks they deem too old, often six months or older, but they usually don't exercise this right. In fact, most people who work in a bank or other financial institution never look at the date of the check. They simply post it to the account. If the money is there to cover it, the check is paid.

Signing Instructions

Print out three copies of the Notice to Stop Payment of Check form. Sign the copies and mail or give two of them to the appropriate bank or financial institution along with a stamped, self-addressed envelope. As requested in this form, the financial institution should then sign and return one of the copies, acknowledging receipt of your letter. Keep a copy for your records.

Form 73: Request for Credit Report

If you want to repair your credit, establish credit, or apply for a loan, your first step is to get a copy of your credit report. This is a file maintained by credit reporting agencies that sell information to banks, lenders, landlords, and others who routinely evaluate customers' creditworthiness. Credit reports contain personal information about you, including your current and past use of credit cards; loans (home, car, student, and the like); any defaults

on bills, such as utility payments or doctor's bills; public records, such as lawsuits; and inquiries by creditors.

The federal Fair Credit Reporting Act (FCRA) now requires each major national credit reporting agency—Equifax, Experian, and TransUnion—to provide you one free copy of your credit report each year.

You can request your free report by one of these means:

- Telephone—877-322-8228
- Internet—www.annualcreditreport.com
- Mail—Annual Credit Report Request Service, P.O. Box 105281, Atlanta, GA 30348-5281

You must provide your name, address, Social Security number, and date of birth when you order. You also may be required to provide information that only you would know, such as the amount of your monthly mortgage payment.

If you already received your free annual credit reports from the nationwide reporting agencies within the last 12 months, use this form (Request for Credit Report) to get an additional copy and send it to one or all of the three major national credit bureaus:

- Equifax, 800-685-1111; www.equifax.com
- Experian, 888-397-3742; www.experian.com
- TransUnion, 800-888-4213; www. transunion.com

Additional copies of your credit report usually cost less than than $15 (and are free in some cases, listed below), but check first for the exact amount.

You are entitled to an additional copy of your credit report at no charge or at a reduced fee if:

- One of the following happened because of information in your credit file: you were denied credit; you were granted credit, but not nearly the amount or on the terms you requested; your credit account was terminated; the creditor made unfavorable changes to your account (but did not change the terms of all, or substantially all of other consumer accounts of the same type); or the creditor took an action or made a determination in connection with an application or transaction you initiated that is adverse to your interests. The creditor must tell you the name and address of the credit reporting agency reporting the information that led to the denial of credit or other adverse action. You must request your report from that particular credit reporting agency within 60 days from the denial of credit or adverse action.

- You are unemployed and planning to apply for a job within 60 days following your request for your credit report. It's a good idea to include documents verifying your unemployment (such as a recent unemployment check or layoff notice). You must also provide a statement swearing that the information is true. You are entitled to one free report in a 12-month period.

- You receive public assistance. Enclose a statement swearing that this is true and provide a copy of your most recent public assistance check as verification. You are entitled to one free report in any 12-month period.

- You reasonably believe your credit file contains errors due to someone's fraud, such as using your credit card, name, or Social Security number. Here, too, you will need to enclose a statement swearing that this is true. You are entitled to one free report in any 12-month period.

- You are a victim of identity theft or fraud, or think that you may be. The FCRA gives consumers the right to request free credit reports in connection with fraud alerts.

  - If you suspect in good faith that you are, or may be, a victim of identity theft or another fraud, you can instruct the major bureaus to add a "fraud alert" to your file. You can request a free copy of your report from each bureau once it places the fraud alert in your file.
  - If you are a victim of identity theft, you can send the major bureaus an identity theft report and instruct them to add an extended fraud alert to your file. You can request two free copies of your credit report from each bureau during the next 12 months once it places the extended fraud alert in your file.

Signing Instructions

Sign your Request for Credit Report and mail it certified mail, return receipt requested, to the credit bureau. Keep a copy of the letter for your files. Include payment and any supporting documentation required, as noted above.

Form 74: Request Reinvestigation of Credit Report Entry

Under the federal Fair Credit Reporting Act, you have the right to dispute all incorrect or incomplete information in your credit file, such as an incorrect name, employer, account, or tax history, a lawsuit older than seven years or one you weren't involved in, or a bankruptcy older than ten years. You can use this form to request a reinvestigation of an item you dispute ("reinvestigation" is what the credit reporting agencies call this process).

Once the credit reporting agency receives your letter, it must either reinvestigate the items you dispute or delete them from your credit report within three business days after receiving your dispute.

If the agency does not delete the information within three business days, it must:

- complete its investigation within 45 days if you disputed the information after receiving your free annual credit report (otherwise it has only 30 days, which can be extended up to 45 days if you send the agency additional relevant information during the 30-day period)
- contact the creditor reporting the information you dispute within five business days of receiving your dispute
- review and consider all relevant information you submit and forward this information to the creditor that provided the information, and
- provide you with the results of its reinvestigation within five business days of completion, including a revised credit report if any changes were made.

If the credit reporting agency cannot verify that the disputed information is correct (or agrees that it is incorrect), in addition to either removing it or correcting it, the agency must also notify the creditor that furnished the information that it has been deleted or modified. This lets the creditor know that it must correct the information in its records as well.

If you let an agency know that you're trying to obtain a mortgage or car loan, it can often do a "rush" reinvestigation. Requesting a reinvestigation won't cost you anything.

The credit reporting agency is not required to investigate any dispute that it determines to be frivolous or irrelevant. It might make this determination if, for example, you don't provide enough information to investigate the dispute, or your dispute appears to be a blanket dispute of almost everything in your credit file either generated by a credit repair company service or prepared by you using a credit repair service's forms. Once the agency determines that the dispute is frivolous, it has five business days to notify you of the decision and its reasons for the decision.

To make sure your dispute is not dismissed as frivolous, dispute only those items in your report that you believe are incorrect or incomplete, explain why you believe they are incorrect or incomplete, and if you have documentation, include it. When using this form, be sure to delete any paragraphs that don't apply to you. For more information, see *Credit Repair: Make a Plan, Improve Your Credit, Avoid Scams*, by Robin Leonard (Nolo).

You can also dispute inaccurate or incomplete items of information online by going to the credit report agency's website (contact information appears in the instructions for the Request for Credit Report). Look for the button or link for submitting disputes online. (If you have documents that support your position, it's better to use this reinvestigation request form and enclose copies of the documents.)

Signing Instructions

Sign your Request Reinvestigation of Credit Report Entry form and mail it certified mail, return receipt requested, to the credit bureau that prepared the report you are disputing. Include copies of any documents supporting your claim. Keep a copy of the letter for your files.

Form 75: Dispute Credit Card Charge

If you use a credit or charge card but don't receive the product you purchased, or you received a defective item, you can legally refuse to pay if you meet certain criteria:

- **Dispute concerning a purchase made with a credit card issued by the seller, such as department store or gas station.** You can legally refuse to pay if you first attempt in good faith to resolve the dispute with the merchant who refuses to replace, repair, or otherwise correct the problem.

- **Dispute concerning a purchase made with a credit card, such as Visa or MasterCard, not issued by the seller.** You can legally refuse to pay if you first attempt in good faith to resolve the dispute with the merchant who refuses to replace, repair, or otherwise correct the problem. But, you can withhold payment only if the purchase was for more than $50 and was made within the state in which you live or was within 100 miles of your home.

You may withhold only the balance on the disputed item or service that is unpaid when you first notify the seller or card issuer of the problem. (To cover yourself as fully as possible, make sure that the card issuer receives your dispute within 60 days after the date of the first credit card statement showing the disputed purchase.)

If you are entitled to withhold payment, complete and mail this form to the credit card company at the address for disputed charges (not the billing address) and explain why you aren't paying. Explain how you tried to resolve the problem with the merchant. Attach a copy of the credit card bill showing the disputed item, along with any additional documentation of your attempt to resolve the dispute, such as a letter you sent to a merchant regarding a defective item.

The card issuer cannot tell a credit reporting agency that the amount you withheld is delinquent until the dispute has been settled, provided that you do not withhold more than you are entitled. Nor can the issuer "freeze" or place a hold on any funds that you may have on deposit with it. However, the issuer can tell a credit reporting agency that your failure to pay is "disputed," so it's important not to abuse this right.

For more information on credit card problems, check the Federal Trade Commission website, at www.ftc.gov.

TIP

Do not use this form if the problem is unauthorized use of your credit card—for example, charges made by someone who stole your card. In this situation, promptly report your loss to the police and the credit card issuer to limit your liability for unauthorized charges. Then call the three major credit reporting agencies to report fraud (contact information appears in the instructions for the Request for Credit Report form).

Signing Instructions

Sign your Dispute Credit Card Charge letter and mail it to the credit card issuer, along with copies of any documents supporting your claim. Keep a copy of the letter and your original supporting documentation for your files.

Form 76: Demand Collection Agency Cease Contact

If you owe money and your debt has been passed along to a collection agency, you will no doubt be contacted by a collector working for the agency. Many people don't understand that they have the legal right under federal law (the Fair Debt Collection Practices Act, 15 U.S.C. § 1692 and following) to tell a bill collector who works for a collection agency to leave them alone. (This does not apply to in-house collectors—for example, at a bank, department store, or hospital—unless your state has enacted a similar restriction on in-house collectors.) To pursue this right, you must put your demand in writing (that's the purpose of this form) and send it to the collection agency. By law, all collectors from the agency must then cease all phone calls, letters, and other communications with you, unless they are contacting you to notify you that:

- collection efforts against you have ended, or
- the collection agency or the creditor will invoke a specific remedy against you, such as suing you.

Alternatively, you can inform the collector that you are represented by an attorney and instruct that all communications be directed to the attorney (you must provide the attorney's name and address).

 TIP

It's usually best not to ignore the debt or try to hide from the collector. Usually, the longer you put off resolving the issue, the worse the situation and consequences will become. Whether you negotiate directly with the collector or obtain a lawyer's assistance, many counselors feel the best strategy almost always is to engage the collector, at least initially.

Signing Instructions

Sign your Demand Collection Agency Cease Contact letter and mail it to the collection agency, along with copies of any documents supporting your demand. It's best to send this letter by certified mail and request a return receipt. Keep a copy of the letter and your original documents for your files.

Dealing With Junk Mail and Telemarketing Calls

Many consumers have made the digital leap to smartphones (although plenty of good old-fashioned landlines are still around too) and, unfortunately, telemarketers have followed suit. The good news is that, for mobile devices and fixed phone lines alike, there are two federal laws—the Telephone Consumer Protection Act (47 U.S.C. § 227) and the Telemarketing and Consumer Fraud and Abuse Prevention Act (15 U.S.C. § 6101)—that put some limits on how telemarketers must act. Most states also have laws to curb abusive telemarketing. Some provisions are part of an effort to curb telemarketing fraud; others are aimed at reducing annoyance to consumers. For example, before you pay (usually by credit card) for something purchased from a telemarketer, the seller must accurately state the total cost, quantity of goods or services, and all other important conditions and restrictions. A seller must also explain its refund policy or state that it doesn't allow a refund, exchange, or cancellation.

Even more common than telemarketing fraud are legitimate but incredibly annoying phone calls that we most often get at dinner time. It may be some consolation that federal law at least prohibits telemarketers from making these calls before 8 a.m. and after 9 p.m. (local time) unless they have your permission to call. Telemarketers also must put you on a "do not call list" if you so request (see "Do Not Call Registries," below). And that's where the forms in this chapter come in—we show you how to tell a company to stop calling you and what to do if it doesn't.

Sometimes, your mailbox can become just as irritating as your phone. For most of us, catalogs, credit card offers, and all kinds of other junk mail take up more space than our first-class mail. Moreover, this never-read junk mail is an incredible waste of environmental resources. Again, fortunately, some federal laws can help you get off various mailing lists. In this chapter, we provide you with the easy-to-use forms to accomplish this.

RESOURCE
The Privacy Rights Clearinghouse is a nonprofit consumer organization with extensive information and advice on consumer rights regarding junk mail, telemarketing, and related privacy issues. For more information, see their website at www.privacyrights.org or call 619-298-3396.

What About "Spam" Email and Text Messages?

If you're receiving unwanted commercial email or text messages on your mobile device or your computer, you may be able to take action under the Telephone Consumer Protection Act or the "CAN-SPAM" Act (formally known as the Controlling the Assault of Non-Solicited Pornography and Marketing Act).

Depending on the nature of the communication, a commercial text or email usually needs to include an easy way for you to "opt-out" of receiving future messages from the sender. In some situations, you may have unwittingly given your "consent" to receive certain commercial messages, so watch what you're signing up for when you give your email address to certain companies and organizations. But when your consent was given, you still have the right to "opt out" of future messages in most situations.

To learn more about federal laws and your rights when it comes to spam, check out the following resources:

- Federal Communications Commission (FCC) guide to handling unwanted text messages and emails at www.fcc.gov/node/180572
- OnguardOnline.gov resources on spam at www.onguardonline.gov/articles/0038-spam.

"Do Not Call" Registries

The federal government created a National Do Not Call Registry to make it easier for you to stop getting telemarketing sales calls you don't want. You can register online at www.donotcall.gov or call toll-free, 888-382-1222, from the number you wish to register (mobile device or landline). Registration is free. You can verify that your phone number is on the Registry by going to www.donotcall.gov/confirm/conf.aspx.

Your number stays on the list permanently; the registration does not expire. You can ask to have your number taken off the Registry at any time. Telemarketers must update their "do not call" lists with names from the National Do Not Call Registry at least once every 31 days. The FTC can fine telemarketers that call a number on the Registry.

Placing your number on the National Do Not Call Registry will stop most, but not all, unwelcome calls. For example, you may still be called by nonprofits, political campaigns, reseachers, or by companies you've recently contacted or with which you've done business (although a business may only contact you for up to 18 months after your last transaction.)

Before the federal Do Not Call Registry opened, more than half the states started their own registries of telephone subscribers who do not want to receive telemarketing calls. These state laws continue to be valid if they impose more restrictions on intrastate telemarketing (calls made and completed within the state) than the federal law. In order to do business in these states, telemarketers must buy the "do not call" list and abide by the wishes of the persons named on the list. Violators are subject to fines. Some state registries are free; others charge a small fee to put your name on the list.

How to Complain to Government Agencies

In addition to taking all of the steps suggested in this chapter, it is also a good idea to complain to government enforcement agencies about abusive phone calls and letters. You can simply send a copy of the written notice, such as the Demand for Damages for Excessive Calls, to one or more of the following agencies:

- **State Attorneys General.** You can find contact information for your state Attorney General's office from the National Association of Attorneys General at www.naag.org. This is also a good resource to find out more about your state telemarketing laws.
- **State Consumer Protection Office.** To find the consumer protection office in your state, visit the Federal Consumer Information website at www.usa.gov/directory/stateconsumer/index.shtml.
- **Federal Trade Commission.** Consumer Response Center, 600 Pennsylvania Avenue, NW, Washington, DC 20580; toll-free 877-382-4357; www.ftc.gov. The FTC strongly encourages consumers to file complaints online, or to print out and mail an FTC form.
- **Federal Communications Commission.** Consumer Inquiries and Complaints Division, 445 12th Street, SW, Washington, DC 20554; 888-225-5322 (voice); 888-835-5322 (TTY); www.fcc.gov.

All registries exempt some categories of callers (as does the National Do Not Call Registry). For example, many states allow charities, companies seeking payment of debts, and those calling on behalf of political candidates to continue to call you. If an organization is exempt from whichever registry you participate in, you can still follow the procedures outlined below to get on that organization's "do not call" list. (See the instructions on the Telemarketing Phone Call Log.)

Some, but not all, of the states are transferring their "do not call" registries to the National Do Not Call Registry. If you want to know whether your state has a separate registry, contact your state attorney general or consumer protection agency.

If your number is listed on a "do not call" registry and you get a call from a telemarketer, report the call to the appropriate agency, either state or national. For a violation of the national registry, file a complaint at www. donotcall.gov. Most state registries also provide complaint forms online. You can also check with your local consumer protection office or state Attorney General (see "How to Complain to Government Agencies," above, for information on contacting these agencies).

Form 77: Telemarketing Phone Call Log

A federal law, the Telephone Consumer Protection Act, requires every telemarketer to keep a list of consumers who say that they do not want to be called again. If you tell a telemarketer not to call you and it calls you within 12 months, you can sue the company on whose behalf the call is made for the actual amount of money you lost (actual damages), or $500, whichever is greater. (The telemarketer is allowed up to 30 days to put your number on its "do not call" list.) If the court finds that the telemarketer willfully or knowingly violated the law, the court can award you up to three times your actual damages, or $1,500, whichever is greater. Most states' small claims courts allow claims of at least $1,500 (but range up to $12,000 or more), so you can sue on your own, without hiring a lawyer.

Some states also have telemarketing laws. Often, those laws are even stricter than federal law. Contact your state consumer protection office to find out more about your state's telemarketing laws (see "How to Complain to Government Agencies," above, for information on contacting these agencies).

Use this Telemarketing Phone Call Log to keep a record of telemarketing calls you have received. You will need to note the date, the time of the call, the company on whose behalf the call is being made, the telemarketer's name (probably a fake, but write it down anyway), the product being sold, and the fact that you stated "put me on a 'do not call' list." Telemarketers may not block their phone numbers from being identified, so check your call history or use caller ID and write down the caller's name and phone number whenever possible and include it on the form. This information will help you recognize repeat callers, and will provide a form of identification if the caller refuses to give a name. You will need this evidence to prove that you received more than one call from the same telemarketing company.

If you follow up with a letter, such as the Notice to Put Name on Company's "Do Not Call" List, note this on the call log, too.

Suing a company whose telemarketer violates the Telephone Consumer Protection Act presents at least two practical problems. First, you must be able to locate the company (see the instructions for the next form for suggestions). Second, the court in your state must be able to assert jurisdiction over the company. This is difficult (and practically speaking, often impossible) if it's located in another state.

Signing Instructions

There are no signing instructions for the Telemarketing Phone Call Log. Simply fill it out every time you get a call from a telemarketer.

Form 78: Notice to Put Name on Company's "Do Not Call" List

Proving that a telemarketer willfully violated the law by calling you more than once may be difficult. One way you can generate evidence of a company's willful act is to *always* end your phone call by stating "Put me on your 'do not call' list," and follow up with a letter stating the same. Include all of your telephone numbers in the letter. You can use this form for this purpose.

You can also use this form to stop calls that are not prohibited by the "do not call" list—for example, calls from companies that you do business with.

You will need to find out the mailing address of the company on whose behalf the call is made in order to send your letter. Here are a few suggestions:

- Ask the telemarketer who calls you for the company's address. Telemarketers are required by law to give you the telephone number or the address of the company. Despite the law, many telemarketers will claim they don't know the information or can't tell you. If that happens, contact your state consumer protection office (see "How to Complain to Government Agencies," above).
- If it's a local company, or you know the city in which the company is located, see if you can find the address online or in your phone book; if you find a phone number, but not the address, call and ask for the mailing address.
- Consult *Hoover's Handbook of American Business: Profiles of Major U.S. Companies.* Your local library should have a copy, or you can visit the website at www.hoovers.com and browse the directory of companies.
- Try doing an online search, to locate the company's address.

This form also may be used to eliminate telemarketing calls from one or more specific companies if you'd rather not eliminate all calls by registering with the National Do Not Call Registry.

Signing Instructions

Sign and date your Notice to Put Name on Company's "Do Not Call" List and mail it to the company whose telemarketer has called you. Keep a copy of the notice for your own records. You may need this if you end up suing the company for excessive calls (more on this below).

Form 79: Demand for Damages for Excessive Calls

You can use this form after you receive a second (or third or fourth) telemarketing call on behalf of the same company. (Remember, it can take up to 30 days for your number to get on the "do not call" list.) It details the history of telemarketing phone calls you have received on behalf of the company and your requests to be put on the "do not call" list. This form spells out your right to monetary compensation for a violation of the federal Telephone Consumer Protection Act, as explained in the discussion of the Telemarketing Phone Call Log, above. It specifies that you will seek all appropriate remedies in court if you do not get the requested compensation within 30 days. You will need to find out the mailing address of the company in order to send your letter. See the discussion under Notice to Put Name on Company's "Do Not Call" List for some suggestions on obtaining the address.

In addition to locating the company on whose behalf the calls were made, the court in your state must be able to assert jurisdiction over it. This is difficult (and practically speaking, often impossible) if the company is located in another state.

Signing Instructions

Sign your Demand for Damages for Excessive Calls letter and mail it to the company on whose behalf the telemarketing calls were made. Keep a copy for your files.

Form 80: Notice to Remove Name From List

If you want to receive some catalogs, promotional mailings, or telemarketing phone calls, but not others, you must use a two-step approach.

First, send this Notice to all companies that collect names in order to sell them to direct marketers and telemarketers, telling them to remove your name. On the form, provide all spellings of your name, and the names of any other household members on the mailing label. If you're receiving junk mail for previous occupants at your address, provide their names, too.

The second step is to send the Notice to Add or Retain Name but Not Sell or Trade It (which we discuss below) to those businesses whose materials or phone calls you want to receive. If you don't want to receive any unsolicited mail, just follow step one of this process.

The tricky part of this two-step process is stopping the mail you don't want to receive. Dozens of companies gather names and addresses to sell to direct marketers and telemarketers. It's nearly impossible to get off all direct marketing and telemarketing lists, but to get off many, do the following:

Prescreened offers. To stop receiving most prescreened credit card and insurance offers, you can participate in the three major credit reporting agencies' opt-out program. Visit www.optoutprescreen.com to opt-out online, or call 888-5OPTOUT. You can choose to opt out for five years or permanently. To opt-out permanently, you must print and fill out the form on the website and mail it to the address provided.

Other junk mail. To reduce the amount of other types of junk mail, you can participate in the Direct Marketing Association's (DMA) Mail Preference Service (MPS) opt-out program. This program gets you off the lists of all DMA subscribers, which include many national direct marketing companies. The DMA opt out lasts for five years. There are two ways to register:

- Register online at www.dmachoice. org/register.php (it's free if you register online).
- Send the Notice to Remove Name From List to DMAchoice, P.O. Box 643, Carmel, NY 10512. Include a check or money order in the amount of $1.

Catalogs. To reduce the amount of mail order catalogs you receive, you can opt out of the Abacus Cooperative database. This database compiles customer information from catalog companies and retailers. Abacus subscribes to the DMA, so registering for the DMA Mail Preference Service should reduce mail order catalogs as well. However if you want to stop receiving catalogs, but still receive other types of unsolicited mail, you can register for Abacus and not the DMA program. To register for the Abacus program, send an email to abacusoptout@epsilon.com and include your full name (including middle initial), current address, and previous address if you have been at your current address less than six months.

Individual businesses. To stop junk mail from companies that aren't on lists maintained by the major credit reporting agencies, the DMA, and the Abacus Cooperative, you'll have to contact the company individually. Send this Notice to Remove Name From List to the customer service department of each company that sends you catalogs or other unwanted mail.

Privacy notices from your financial institution. You can cut down on offers and solicitations from your financial institution, and prevent it from providing your information to other companies, by completing and returning the opt out portion of your financial institution's privacy notice. These institutions must send you a privacy notice when you open a new account, and once a year after that. But you can opt out at any time. Usually, the privacy notice comes with a detachable opt out form. If not, look for an 800 number in the notice to call and register your opt out preference. Or, get a sample opt out letter from www.privacyrights.org (click on "Banking & Finance" and look in the FAQ for a link to the sample letter).

Signing Instructions

Sign and date your Notice to Remove Name From List, and mail it to some or all of the companies listed above that sell lists of names to direct marketers and telemarketers. Keep a copy of the notice for your files.

Form 81: Notice to Add or Retain Name but Not Sell or Trade It

After sending the Notice to Remove Name to get your name off the lists of all businesses that sell names to direct marketers and telemarketers, use the Notice to Add or Retain Name to get onto (or keep yourself on) the lists maintained by businesses whose mailings and/or phone calls you do want to receive. This notice states that you do not want your name sold, traded, or shared with any other company or business. Also, you can specify whether or not you want to accept telemarketing phone calls from the company.

Signing Instructions

Sign and date your Notice to Add or Retain Name and mail it to the companies whose mailings and/or phone calls you do want to receive. Keep a copy of the notice for your files.

Hiring Child Care, Elder Care, or Household Help

Many people hire others to work regularly in their homes—for example, to take care of children during the workday, care for elderly parents, or clean the house. These relationships are often set up informally, with no written agreement. But informal arrangements can be fraught with problems. If you don't have a written agreement clearly defining responsibilities and benefits, you and those helping you are all too likely to have different expectations about the job. This can lead to serious disputes—even to one or both parties bitterly backing out of the arrangement. Far better to draft a clear written understanding of what the job entails.

The agreements in this chapter are for hiring care providers and other household workers who are employees, not independent contractors. When you hire an employee, you set the hours, responsibilities, and pay rate of the worker. Legally, most babysitters and household workers who work for you on a regular basis are considered employees for whom you are required to pay taxes, Social Security, and other benefits described below. In contrast, independent contractors typically own their own businesses and work for you only occasionally.

This chapter also includes a Child Care Instructions form you can use for either a full-time child care provider or an occasional babysitter.

 RESOURCE

For detailed information on hiring child care, see *Nannies & Au Pairs: Hiring In-Home Child Care*, by Ilona Bray (Nolo). For more information on hiring independent contractors, see *Working With Independent Contractors*, by Stephen Fishman (Nolo).

Legal Obligations for Employees

Assuming your child care worker, elder care worker, or housecleaner is your employee,

you have legal obligations to that person, obligations that include a certain amount of paperwork and record keeping. You do not have to put this information in your child care, elder care, or housekeeping agreement, but you need to be aware of your responsibilities.

Social Security and income taxes. If you pay a child care or elder care worker $2,000 or more in a calendar year, you must make Social Security (FICA) payments on those wages and withhold the employee's share of FICA. You do not have to deduct income taxes from wages paid to an employee for working in your home unless the employee requests it and you agree to do so. You make these payments by attaching Schedule H, *Household Employment Taxes*, to your annual Form 1040.

Your state government may also impose separate tax withholding requirements. Contact your state taxing authority, or ask your payroll service (if you use one).

Unemployment compensation. If you pay a household employee $1,000 or more in a three-month period, you must pay quarterly taxes under the Federal Unemployment Tax Act (FUTA), using IRS Form 940 or 940-EZ. As with FICA, you pay this amount by attaching Schedule H, *Household Employment Taxes*, to your annual Form 1040.

Workers' compensation. Your state may require you to provide workers' compensation insurance against job-related injuries or illnesses suffered by your employees. Check with your state department of labor or employment.

Minimum wage and overtime. The federal minimum hourly wage is $7.25 (2016). Your child care or elder care worker may be entitled to minimum wage, depending upon their particular hours and earnings. If your state minimum wage is higher, you will need to pay the state wage. In addition, under federal law, most domestic workers (other than live-in workers) qualify for overtime pay. Workers must be paid overtime at a rate one-and-a-half times the regular rate for all hours worked beyond a 40-hour workweek. You can check the U.S. Department of Labor website, www.dol.gov, for current information about federal and state minimum wage laws.

New Hire Reporting Form. Within a short time after you hire someone—20 days or less, depending on your state's rules—you must file a New Hire Reporting Form with a designated state agency. The information on the form becomes part of the National Directory of New Hires, used primarily to locate parents to collect child support.

Federal ID number. If you hire a household employee, you must obtain a federal employer identification number (EIN), required by the IRS of all employers for tax filing and reporting purposes. The form you need is IRS Form SS-4, *Application for Employer Identification Number.*

IRS Resources

The IRS has a number of publications and forms that might help you. Call the IRS at 800-424-FORM or visit its website at www.irs.gov to download these forms and publications. Start with Publication 926, *Household Employer's Tax Guide*, which describes the major tax responsibilities of employers. You may also want to look at:

- Form SS-8, which contains IRS definitions of independent contractor and employee, and
- Form SS-4, *Application for Employer Identification Number.*

Reality Check

Many families don't comply with the law that requires them to pay taxes or Social Security for certain household workers, some of whom are undocumented aliens. This chapter is not intended to preach about the law, but to alert you to the rules that affect your relationships with care providers and housekeeping workers. No question, if you fail to pay Social Security and to meet your other legal obligations as an employer, there may be several negative consequences.

- You may be assessed substantial financial penalties. For example, if your full-time elder care provider files for Social Security five years from now and can prove prior earnings, but no Social Security has been paid, the IRS could back-bill you at high interest rates.
- If you don't meet a state requirement to provide workers' compensation insurance and your child care worker is injured while on the job and can't work for a few months, you may be in hot water if the worker files for workers' compensation. You will probably be held liable for the worker's medical costs and a portion of any lost wages, as well as be fined for not having the insurance in the first place.
- You will not be able to take a child care tax credit on your federal income taxes. The credit is based on your work-related expenses and income, but can actually offset the amount you might save by paying under the table.

 RESOURCE

For more about sharing care for children, elders, and disabled family members, as well as dozens of other ideas, see *The Sharing Solution: How to Save Money, Simplify Your Life & Build Community*, by Janelle Orsi and Emily Doskow (Nolo).

Form 82: Child Care Agreement

A child care provider who takes care of your children in your house, either part time or full time, may live out (often called a caregiver or babysitter) or live in (a nanny). The responsibilities of the position may vary widely, from performing a whole range of housekeeping services to only taking care of the children.

CAUTION

Do not use this form if you hire a care provider or house cleaner through a placement agency. If you use an agency that sets and collects the worker's fee from you, pays the worker, and controls the terms of the work, the agency will have its own contract for you to complete. People you hire through an agency are not your employees—they are the employees of their agencies.

CAUTION

Special rules govern hiring of au pairs. If you hire an au pair from another country (on a cultural exchange visa), you'll need to comply with federal laws governing the au pair's responsibilities, working hours, rate of pay, and more. An au pair agency will help you with this process. For these reasons, we don't recommend using the child care agreement provided here if you're hiring an au pair from another country.

Use this form to spell out your agreement about the child care worker's responsibilities, hours, benefits, amount and schedule of payment, and other important aspects of the job. The best approach is to be as detailed as possible.

Start by filling in your name, address, phone numbers, and other contact information for yourself (and a second parent if another parent will be signing the Child Care Agreement) and your child care provider. List your children's names and birth dates.

Here's some advice on filling in various sections of the Child Care Agreement:

Location and Schedule of Care (Clause 4). Provide the address where child care will be provided (typically your home) and the days and hours of care, such as 8 a.m. to 6 p.m. weekdays. Live-in nannies often work some weeknights and weekends.

Beginning Date (Clause 5) and **Training or Probation Period (Clause 6).** Specify the date employment will begin and the length of any training or probation period, such as the first 15 or 30 days of child care. This is the time to make sure that the relationship will work for everyone involved. A training period helps your child care provider get to know your home and neighborhood and the exact way you want things done. If there will be no training or probation period, you can skip this clause.

Responsibilities (Clause 7). The responsibilities of the child care position may vary depending on many factors, including the number and age of your children; whether the child care worker lives in or out; the hours worked; your family situation and needs; and the skills and background of the child care provider. In some households, particularly with infants and toddlers, the babysitter only takes care of the children and does not do housework, except for doing the children's laundry. In other families, especially with older children, the employee may function more as a housekeeper, cook, and chauffeur. You should specify the child care worker's responsibilities in as much detail as possible, including cooking, bathing, and personal care for your children, social and recreational activities (such as arranging the children's play dates), transportation (driving kids to and from school or practices), shopping and errands for the family, housecleaning, ironing, and laundry.

EXAMPLE: Here's an example of responsibilities for a live-in nanny taking care of an infant (Kate), and preschooler (Tom):

> The child care provider's primary responsibility is to provide loving care of Kate and Tom. This includes playing with and reading to them, taking them to the park as weather permits, making sure they have naps as needed, and preparing their meals and snacks. The care provider will bathe Kate and Tom every other day, more frequently if necessary. Other responsibilities include driving Tom to "Baby Gym" twice a week, doing the children's laundry, and keeping their rooms tidy.

Wage or Salary (Clause 8). You should specify exactly how the child care provider will be paid, such as an hourly rate or weekly salary. How much you pay depends on many factors. These include the number and ages of your children; the type of care provided and responsibilities; the number of hours, time of day, and regularity of the schedule; the experience and training of the employee; benefits such as room and board; and the going rate in your community. Check local sources to find out what similar workers are being paid—neighborhood websites and social media groups are a great source for this type of information. Before you fill in this section, be sure you understand your legal obligations when hiring an employee, such as minimum wage and overtime rules, as described above.

Payment Schedule (Clause 9). You can decide to pay your child care provider weekly (say, on Friday), twice per month (such as on the 15th and on the last day of the month), or once per month.

Benefits (Clause 10). In addition to payment, you may offer the child care provider any benefits you wish, such as paid vacations and holidays, health insurance, or sick leave. Spell out the rules for using these benefits, such as how much advance notice you need of planned vacation time, and what happens if the child care provider gets sick after having used up all his or her sick leave.

Termination Policy (Clause 11). If things don't work out, the Child Care Agreement provides a termination policy that allows either the parents or the child care provider the right to terminate the agreement at any time, for any reason, and without notice.

Confidentiality (Clause 12). This protects your privacy, and potentially, that of your friends, coworkers, and clients.

Additional Provisions (Clause 13). Describe any additional terms of this agreement, such as a schedule for salary reviews, house rules, such as a no-smoking and no personal visitors policy, or a requirement that the child care provider take a first aid course.

Modifications (Clause 14). This agreement provides that any changes to it must be made in writing and signed by all parties to the agreement. This protects both the parents and the child care provider against misunderstandings over major issues that were agreed to verbally.

Signing Instructions

To make the Child Care Agreement valid, the parent(s) and the child care provider must sign it. (If you and your children's other parent are living in the same home and raising your kids together, it's best if both of you sign this document.) Print out two copies of the form. You, your children's other parent (if signing the form), and the caregiver must sign and date the form where indicated. Give one of the signed originals to the child care provider and keep the other for your records.

Shared In-Home Care

Some families pool their resources and share an in-home child care provider. These arrangements are ideal for neighbors or coworkers with children who are close in age. Just as a written agreement between a family and a child care worker can clarify expectations and prevent conflicts, a written understanding between the two families who are sharing a child care provider can accomplish the same objectives. If you share in-home care with another family, be sure you agree on the key issues before drafting your contract with the child care worker, including location of the care, splitting expenses, termination procedures, and supervision. The other parents should make their own child care arrangements with the care provider.

Form 83: Child Care Instructions

Use this form to provide important information for babysitters and child care providers (including au pairs), such as phone numbers of doctors, instructions about meals and naps, and other details of your child's care, including any allergies or health conditions your child has.

This form has space for you to fill in the names, addresses, and phone numbers of people that your babysitter or child care provider can contact if they can't reach you in an emergency. We suggest that you list at least two or three friends, relatives, or neighbors who live nearby and are well known to your children and family. The form will print out with a reminder to call 911 in case of emergency. If you wish to list another emergency number for the police, fire department, or poison control, you may do so.

Finally, the Child Care Instructions form has space to provide additional important information your family or home, such as the location of first aid supplies, the phone number of a local taxi service, or the fact that you have a rule against smoking, drinking alcohol, or entertaining personal visitors in the house.

 RELATED TOPIC
Use a separate form to authorize medical care. While these Child Care Instructions provide important medical information about your child, such as any medications or allergies, this form does not authorize your babysitter or child care provider to arrange medical care for your child. For that, you will need to use the Authorization for Minor's Medical Treatment (see Chapter 1).

Signing Instructions

There is no need to sign the Child Care Instructions. Simply fill in the information and print out the form after reading it carefully to make sure all information is complete and correct. Give the babysitter or child care provider a copy and keep one posted in a prominent place, such as on your refrigerator. Be sure to review and update your Child Care Instructions from time to time.

Form 84: Elder Care Agreement

Many older people remain at home or live with relatives rather than enter a residential facility for extended recovery or long-term care. Often this requires hiring someone (an elder care provider) to help with their personal and medical care, cooking, housekeeping, and other services.

An elder care provider (sometimes called a home health aide) can either live out or live in, and work full or part time. The responsibilities of this position may vary, from performing a wide range of housekeeping services to attending to the personal and health care needs of the older adult (or adults, in case the elder care worker is taking care of two people, such as both of your parents). Responsibilities may range from dispensing medicine to helping with bathing to driving to doctor's appointments, activities, or social functions.

Use this form to spell out your written agreement about the elder care worker's responsibilities, hours, benefits, amount and schedule of payment, and other important aspects of the job. The best approach is to be as detailed as possible. Follow the directions for the Child Care Agreement when completing this form.

Signing Instructions

To make the Elder Care Agreement valid, the employer(s) and the elder care provider must sign it. Start by printing out two copies of the form. You (the employer) and the caregiver must sign and date the form where indicated. Give one of the signed originals to the elder care provider and keep the other for your records.

 RESOURCE
For more about sharing care for children, elders, and disabled family members, as well as dozens of other ideas, see *The Sharing Solution: How to Save Money, Simplify Your Life & Build Community*, by Emily Doskow and Janelle Orsi (Nolo).

Form 85: Housekeeping Services Agreement

If you hire the same person every week to clean your house, a written contract can be a valuable way to define the worker's responsibilities and benefits. If your housecleaner will be your employee, use this form to spell out the housecleaner's hours, benefits, amount and schedule of payment, termination policy, and other aspects of the job. Your agreement should cover regular weekly cleaning tasks (Clause 5)—for example, cleaning the bathroom and mopping the kitchen floor—as well as occasional projects, such as washing blinds. Be sure to spell out other responsibilities as well (Clause 6), such as cooking, laundry, ironing, shopping, gardening, and yard work. The best approach is to be as detailed as possible. Follow the directions for the Child Care Agreement when completing this form.

Signing Instructions

To make the Housekeeping Services Agreement valid, the employer(s) and the housekeeper must sign it. Finalizing your housekeeping services agreement is easy. Start by printing out two copies of the form. You (the employer) and the housekeeper must sign and date the form where indicated. Give one of the signed originals to the housekeeper and keep the other for your records.

Living Together

A contract is no more than an agreement to do (or not to do) something. It contains promises made by one person in exchange for another's actions. Marriage is a contractual relationship, even though the "terms" of the contract are rarely stated explicitly, or even necessarily known by the marrying couple. Saying "I do" commits a couple to a well-established set of state laws and rules governing, among other things, the couple's property rights should one spouse die or the couple split up. (Prenuptial agreements are a way people who plan to marry can modify the contract imposed on married people by state law.)

On the other hand, unmarried couples do not automatically agree to any state-imposed contractual agreement when they begin living together. Nor does simply living together for a certain period of time automatically entitle you to a property settlement (or inheritance) should you split up (or one of you die) as it would if you were married.

Fortunately, when it comes to financial and property concerns, unmarried couples have the right to create whatever kind of living together contract they want. Sometimes these agreements are made in anticipation of ending a relationship. But more often, the purpose is to record the couple's needs and expectations as to money and property—either at the start of the relationship or when the couple makes a major purchase.

This chapter includes some basic property ownership agreement forms for unmarried couples. It also includes a basic name change form.

RESOURCE

Nolo's *Living Together: A Legal Guide for Unmarried Couples*, by Ralph Warner, Toni Ihara, and Frederick Hertz, and *A Legal Guide for Lesbian & Gay Couples*, by Denis Clifford, Frederick Hertz, and Emily Doskow, cover the main legal issues affecting unmarried couples in areas of property and money, estate planning, children, house ownership, medical decisions, and separation. And if you're a same-sex couple considering marriage or registration, see *Making It Legal: A Guide to Same-Sex Marriage, Domestic Partnership & Civil Unions*, by Frederick Hertz with Emily Doskow (Nolo).

Form 86: Agreement to Keep Property Separate

Especially in the first year or two after getting together, most unmarried couples keep all or most of their money and property separate—with the occasional exception of a joint account to pay household bills or an agreement to purchase one or more items jointly.

You may think at first that a decision to keep your property ownership separate is so simple there is no need for a written agreement. Think again. Because most states recognize oral contracts between unmarried couples, the lack of a written agreement can be an invitation for one partner to later claim the existence of an oral property-sharing agreement. This is just what commonly occurs in the so-called "palimony cases" that regularly hit the headlines.

To avoid the possibility of future misunderstandings about property ownership, use the Agreement to Keep Property Separate to confirm that each of you plans to keep your property and income separate unless you have a specific written agreement that says otherwise—for example, to purchase a piece of furniture together. This form keeps all of your property separate, including property you brought into the relationship as well as property you purchased or received by gift or inheritance while living together.

Here are a few things to keep in mind when you're using this form:

- Clause 2 states that you will attach a separate list of major items you own to the agreement and includes Attachments A and B for this purpose. Be very specific in describing the items you list.

- Clause 4 specifies that if you register under a domestic partnership program that makes you responsible for each other's basic living expenses, you agree to only the minimal level of reciprocal financial responsibility for living expenses. Without this type of disclaimer, registering as domestic partners may imply that you intend to share ownership of property—and if you are part of a same-sex couple and you register as domestic partners or enter a civil union in one of the states that still allows it, the law may impose property sharing on you. If you register as domestic partners or form a civil union, and you do not want to share property, you should create a new, more specific agreement to keep property separate. Of course, if you do not register as domestic partners, you can simply delete this sentence of Clause 4.

- Clause 5 provides that you will share expenses for household items and services equally. If you have a different arrangement, or want to spell out how you will split expenses on nonhousehold items, such as insurance or car repairs, you can edit Clause 5 accordingly.

- Clause 6 refers to a joint ownership agreement that you may prepare from time to time relating to a specific item—for example, if you purchase a television or computer together. (You can use the Agreement for a Joint Purchase, which we'll discuss next, for this purpose.)

- Clause 9 provides for mediation if a dispute arises out of this agreement. "Resolving Disputes," in the Introduction, discusses mediation and dispute resolution procedures.

Signing Instructions

You and your partner must sign this Agreement to Keep Property Separate for it to be valid. Print out two copies of the form, so you'll each have your own copy. Each person should sign and date both copies of the agreement and keep a signed document for their own records. Keep your agreement in a safe place along with other important documents, such as insurance and financial papers, lease, copies of wills, and the like.

 FORM

Optional: Using a notary public. To have a form notarized, you must go to the notary before signing it. (See the Introduction for general advice on having a form notarized.) Notarization will add a measure of legal credibility, but it is not legally required.

Form 87: Agreement for a Joint Purchase

Many couples make purchases item by item, with the understanding that whoever makes the purchase owns the property. George buys the kitchen table and chairs, and Edna buys the lamp and stereo. If they split up, each keeps the property that person bought. In this situation, George and Edna would use the Agreement to Keep Property Separate. Couples can also pool money for their purchases. Edna and George can jointly own everything bought during the relationship, and divide it all 50-50 if they separate. In this case, the Agreement to Share Property would be appropriate.

While these types of consistent approaches to property ownership may simplify things, they are not required by either law or logic. Edna and George could choose a combination of the two methods. Some items may be separately owned, some pooled 50-50, and some shared in proportion to how much money each contributed toward the purchase price or how much labor each put into upkeep.

Many unmarried couples opt for a basic keeping-things-separate approach, at least when they first get together. Despite this, however, an unmarried couple will often want to own one or more major items together, as would be the case if they pool income to buy a new bed and an expensive sound system. Clause 6 in the Agreement to Keep Property Separate allows you to do this.

Whatever type of property is purchased, it is important that your joint ownership agreement be written down. This is especially true if you have previously signed a form like the Agreement to Keep Property Separate. This Agreement for a Joint Purchase allows you to record your joint ownership agreement for a specific purchase quickly and easily. Simply fill in the details of your joint purchase, including the item or property bought, the percentage of ownership (such as 50-50 or 60-40) each of you has, and how you will deal with the property should you split up. For example, you may specify that one person automatically has the right (of first refusal) to buy out the other's share, or you may agree to do a simple coin toss or come up with your own approach depending upon the particular property.

Signing Instructions

You and your partner must sign this Agreement for a Joint Purchase for it to be valid. Print out two copies of the form, so you'll each have your own copy. Each person should sign and date both copies of the agreement and keep a signed document for their own records. Keep your agreement in a safe place along with other important documents, such as insurance and financial papers, lease, copies of wills, and the like.

 CAUTION
Don't use the Agreement for a Joint Purchase if you're buying a car or house together. Check with your state's motor vehicles department for rules regarding the language that should be used to establish joint ownership of a motor vehicle. Also, houses and other real property will have their own specialized rules for ownership and taking title.

Form 88: Agreement to Share Property

Especially if you have been together several years or more and have begun to purchase property jointly (a new car or bed, for example), you may want to do what a fair number of unmarried couples do—abandon your agreement to keep property separate, and instead treat property either of you purchases as jointly owned. If this is your understanding, write it down. Use this form to establish that all property acquired after a certain date—except that given to or inherited by one partner, or that which is clearly specified in writing as separate property, is to be jointly owned by both, and equally divided should you separate.

Note that Clause 3 states that you will attach a list of the property each of you owned prior to the date of your agreement, as well as a list of jointly owned property, and includes Attachments A, B, and C for this purpose. You may be as detailed as you want in preparing these separate property lists, but at least include major items (valued at $100 or more).

Clause 6 provides for mediation if a dispute arises out of this agreement. The Introduction discusses mediation and dispute resolution procedures.

Signing Instructions

You and your partner must sign this Agreement to Share Property for it to be valid. Print out two copies of the form, so you'll each have your own copy. Each person should sign and date both copies of the agreement and keep a signed document for their own records. Keep your agreement in a safe place along with other important documents, such as insurance and financial papers, lease, copies of wills, and the like.

FORM

Optional: Using a notary public. To have a form notarized, you must go to the notary before signing it. (See the Introduction for general advice on having a form notarized.) Notarization will add a measure of legal credibility, but it is not legally required.

CAUTION

Giving or receiving property for the purpose of evading creditors is illegal. A contract agreeing to keep all property separate will protect you from your partner's creditors and avoid any suggestion of impropriety.

Form 89: Declaration of Legal Name Change

Committed unmarried partners occasionally prefer to use the same last name, or a hyphenated version of both last names. But doing this means that one or both partners must change their existing name.

The best way to change your name is by court order. This is usually fairly simple—you fill out and file a short petition (legal paperwork) at the courthouse, publish legal notice of your intention to change your name in a local legal newspaper, and attend a routine court hearing. This is the foolproof way to change your name. Although it used to be more common to change one's name simply by using the new name for a period of time, it is more and more difficult to find agencies that will honor this way of changing your name, called a "usage method name change." After you change your legal name, you will need to notify the relevant agencies. That's the purpose of the Declaration of Legal Name Change, which officially states that you have changed to a new name. Use it to change your personal records, identity cards, and documents. Getting official agencies such as the Department of Motor Vehicles and Social Security Administration to accept your name change is particularly important to getting your new name accepted. Once you follow those agencies' procedures and actually get official documents in your new name, it will be easy to switch over other accounts and documents.

CAUTION

Illegal reasons to change your name. You cannot change your name to defraud creditors, for any illegal purpose, to benefit economically by the use of another person's name, or to invade someone's privacy (don't name yourself Madonna or George Bush). Otherwise, you can change your name for any reason and assume any name you wish.

RESOURCE

If you live in California, you can get all the forms and instructions you need to do your own legal name change in *How to Change Your Name in California*, by Lisa Sedano and Emily Doskow (Nolo).

Signing Instructions

You must sign this Declaration of Legal Name Change form for it to be valid. Print out enough copies for every agency and organization you wish to notify of your name change. Keep a signed copy for your own records.

Settling Legal Disputes

Becoming involved in any legal dispute can be harrowing. Many people lose time, money, and sleep trying to right their wrongs, even informally. Then, take it to the next step—the prospect of facing an unpredictable court trial can intimidate even the bravest soul. That's why it's so easy to appreciate the curse that says, "May you have a lawsuit in which you know you are right."

Fortunately, most legal disputes are resolved long before anyone sees the inside of a court-room—one person demands a settlement, the other person counters, and the negotiations continue from there. If settlement still proves elusive, it's common to turn for assistance to a mediator who will attempt to help the parties come to an agreement. ("Resolving Disputes," in the Introduction, discusses mediation and other means of resolving disputes.)

This chapter presents useful tools to help you resolve your dispute. And if you do settle, it also provides several releases that you or the other party should sign so neither of you risks being hauled into court after you write or receive the check you believe settles the matter.

RESOURCE

Additional information and sample forms for settling disputes can be found in *Everybody's Guide to Small Claims Court*, by Ralph Warner, and *Mediate, Don't Litigate: Strategies for Successful Mediation*, by Peter Lovenheim and Lisa Guerin (available only as an eBook at www.nolo.com). Sample forms for settling a claim with an insurance company can be found in *How to Win Your Personal Injury Claim*, by Joseph Matthews. For a detailed discussion of representing yourself in a lawsuit, see *Represent Yourself in Court: How to Prepare & Try a Winning Case*, by Paul Bergman and Sarah Berman. All titles are published by Nolo.

Form 90: Demand Letter

Assuming your dispute has escalated to the point where you and the other party can no longer civilly discuss a compromise, your next step in trying to resolve it is to send a demand letter clearly stating what you want. That's the purpose of this form. Studies show that in as many as one-third of all disputes, your demand letter will serve as a catalyst to arriving at a settlement. It is fair to ask why demand letters work so frequently to resolve disputes that couldn't simply be talked out. The answer seems to be that a written document often serves as a wake-up call, convincing the other party you really are serious about going to court if you can't settle the matter. Your demand letter also gives you a chance to organize the facts of your case, so if you wind up in mediation, arbitration, or court (such as small claims court), you will have already done much of your preparation.

When writing your demand letter, here are some suggestions:

- Be polite. Avoid personally attacking your adversary.
- Concisely review the main facts of the dispute—including who, what, where, and when. (See "How to Word a Demand," below.) Even though your adversary knows this information, a judge, mediator, or other third party may eventually see your letter.
- Ask for exactly what you want—the return of property, a specific amount of money, or whatever.
- Conclude by stating that if the problem isn't resolved within a set period of time (seven to ten days is often good), you will take further action, such as filing a court case.

The demand letter included here indicates that you are willing to try mediation. Mediation, a nonadversarial process involving a neutral person (a mediator) is usually a great way for people to resolve differences. If you are not willing to try mediation (that is, you plan to sue if your demands aren't met), delete the mediation language in the demand letter.

How to Word a Demand

When writing a demand letter, describe in your own words exactly what happened. Specify dates, names of people with whom you dealt, and the damages you have suffered. Here's an example:

> On September 21, 20xx, I took my car to your garage for service. Shortly after I picked it up the next day, the engine caught fire because of your failure to connect the fuel line to the fuel injector properly. Fortunately, I was able to douse the fire without injury. As a direct result of the engine fire, I paid ABC Garage $1,281 for necessary repair work. I enclose a copy of the invoice. Also, I was without the use of my car for three days and had to rent a car to get to work. I enclose a copy of an invoice showing the rental cost of $145. In total, I was out $1,426.

Signing Instructions

Sign the Demand Letter and send it certified mail (return receipt requested) to the person with whom you're having a dispute. Keep a copy of the letter. You may need it later if you end up filing a lawsuit.

Form 91: Online Auction Buyer Demand Letter

Not everyone who buys goods via an online auction has a satisfactory experience. If you have a dispute with an online auction seller (on eBay or elsewhere), use this demand letter to alert the seller of your complaint and to establish your claim.

This demand letter gives you the option of proposing to the seller that the two of you use an online dispute resolution service to resolve your claim. Make sure to research these services (suggested sites are listed on this form) first to understand how they work before proposing this option to the seller.

Online Auctions: Think Before You Bid

Are you a novice buyer, unfamiliar with how auction sites work? If so, review the auction site's rules and find out what the company does if a problem occurs. Also, compare the price of the item elsewhere—not every item for sale at an online auction is a bargain.

Most important, learn as much as you can about the seller. Use common sense. Possible danger signs are if the seller:

- has a history of negative feedback
- is using a post office box
- wants payment in cash
- is outside the United States, or
- wants your Social Security or driver's license number.

For more advice on how to protect yourself, check out Fraud.org's Fake Merchandise Scams page at www.fraud.org/fake_merchandise.

Signing Instructions

If you have the seller's physical address, sign the Online Auction Buyer Demand Letter and send it via certified mail, return receipt requested. If not, send it by email. Keep a copy of the letter. You may need it later if you wind up filing a lawsuit.

Form 92: Request for Refund or Repair of Goods Under Warranty

Use this form to request compensation when an item you purchased, such as a Blu-ray player or bicycle, is defective. Most new products you buy (and even some used ones) come with a warranty that offers protection if the product fails during the warranty period. Here are the basic rules regarding warranties:

- If a product comes with a written warranty from either the seller or the manufacturer, you have the right to rely on it.
- If a seller makes a statement describing a product's feature—for example, "This sleeping bag will keep you warm at 25 degrees below zero"—and you make your purchase because of the statement, then the statement is an express warranty that you have a right to rely on.
- For most purchases, you automatically have an implied warranty of merchantability, meaning that the item will work for its intended use—for example, a lawnmower will cut grass. If the item doesn't work, you should be able to return it for a refund or replacement.

If a warranty is breached—for example, a plasma TV with a one-year warranty breaks after two weeks—ask the seller for redress. Simply call or visit the store, explain the problem, and ask for a refund or replacement

of the defective TV. If the seller refuses, use this form to notify the seller and manufacturer of your demand for them to make good under the warranty. Give them a reasonable chance—such as 30 days—to make necessary repairs, replace the defective product, or refund the purchase price. Most reputable sellers and manufacturers will. This form states that you may take further action, such as filing a court action, if your request is unmet.

TIP

If you are using this form to request warranty coverage, make sure the product warranty covers your situation. Read the warranty to see how long it lasts; whom you contact for warranty service (seller or manufacturer); your options if the product fails (refund, replacement, or repair); what parts and problems are covered (some warranties cover replacement of parts but not labor, or cover only problems due to faulty material or workmanship); and any conditions (such as registration) or limitations that may apply.

Here's how to prepare a Request for Refund or Repair of Goods form:

Start by filling in the name(s) and address(es) of the seller or manufacturer (depending upon the particular warranty and your complaint). If you have a written manufacturer's warranty, check it for the appropriate address to send requests for warranty coverage; this may be the seller/dealer or the manufacturer. If you are not sure, ask the seller from whom you purchased the item. This may be a retail store or website. In many cases, you will need to mail or deliver the product along with your request for warranty coverage to either the seller/dealer or the manufacturer.

If you do not have a written manufacturer's warranty and the dispute is with the seller, send this form to the seller. It shouldn't be too hard for you to determine the name and address of the seller, if you made an in-person purchase. For online purchases, you may have to search the seller's website to locate an address. If you can't find this on the site, look for a phone number to call for the address. If all else fails, ask your local reference librarian for suggestions on how to get the seller's address.

Fill in the item name or description. If possible, include the model number—for example, Tasty Toaster Model 9333.

Next, fill in the purchase price, date, and place of purchase.

Describe the problem (reason you are demanding redress) and why you are dissatisfied with your purchase. Provide as much detail as possible, including what your written warranty (if any) says; what you were told (and by whom) when you made the purchase; how you have used the product; what has gone wrong; and what efforts you have made to obtain a new item or refund. For example, if you called the seller, provide the date and details of the phone conversation. If you have already sent the seller an informal note about the problem, mention that and attach a copy of the note to this form. If you are enclosing anything, such as a copy of the purchase receipt as proof of purchase or a copy of the written warranty, be sure to say so in this section of the form. (See "How to Complain About a Defective Product," below.)

Indicate whether or not the item is enclosed. Whether you are seeking redress by mail or in person, you may need to return the item, such as a broken toaster or punctured tires. This will not always be feasible—for example, in the case of a shattered mirror.

Specify what type of compensation you want. Read your warranty (if any) to find out what kind of redress may be available and to make sure that the warranty covers your situation.

How to Complain About a Defective Product

Here are a couple of examples of how to explain your dissatisfaction with a product you've purchased and why you're seeking redress:

Complaint about manufacturer's warranty.

> On May 21, 20xx, I purchased a Tasty Toaster (Model 9333) from the Toaster Store, 195 Main Street, Columbus, Ohio. This toaster came with a one-year warranty (copy enclosed). Last week, the toaster coils overheated and the toaster simply does not work. I have owned the toaster only four months, used it only occasionally, and have not subjected it to any extraordinary usage.

Complaint about store's warranty.

> On April 16, 20xx, I purchased an UpHill Bicycle (model number 12345ht) from CycLeader, 3300 Sharper Avenue, Denver, Colorado. In the presence of my friend, Randy Jacobs, I explained to the store clerk, "Mark," that I planned to use the bicycle for off-road mountain cycling throughout Colorado. The clerk assured me that the tires on this particular UpHill bicycle could "handle any surface." Just last week, less than a month after I purchased the bike, both tires punctured while I was cycling on a much-used mountain bike trail near Greeley. When I asked for a partial refund so as to purchase new tires, the store manager claimed that no one named Mark currently works at CycLeader and claimed that this model UpHill bicycle would never have been sold for off-road use.

Some manufacturer warranties promise only to repair or replace a defective item; others will give you the additional choice of seeking a full or partial refund of your purchase price. If you don't care, or don't have a written warranty, ask for either a refund or a replacement item.

Indicate when you want to receive the requested compensation. We suggest 30 days, after which you will take further action such as filing a lawsuit.

Signing Instructions

Sign the Request for Refund or Repair of Goods form and include any relevant material, such as a copy of the written warranty (often part of the owner's manual that came with the item from the manufacturer), the advertisement that you relied on when making your purchase, your receipt, previous correspondence with the seller, or the item itself. If you are addressing this form to the manufacturer, send a copy to the seller, too. You may also want to send a copy of this letter to a state or local consumer agency or the Better Business Bureau. (See "How to Complain to Government Agencies," in the instructions for the Complaint Letter in Chapter 15.)

Keep a copy of your form and any attached materials for your records. You may need this if you end up filing a small claims court case.

Form 93: Accident Claim Worksheet

Many legal disputes involve claims against a person, business, or insurance company arising out of an accident where a person was injured or property was damaged (or both). This includes both car accidents and "slip and fall incidents." Use the Accident Claim Worksheet, to keep track of the names, addresses, and phone numbers of parties and witnesses involved if you are injured, along with communications with them, dates of relevant events and conversations, details from insurance companies, and other information you will need to process an accident claim. This worksheet is for your personal reference and is not intended to become part of your claim.

> **CAUTION**
> **Get witness statements in writing as soon as possible.** Don't count on an eyewitness's memory for too long, especially given the fact that the witness is likely to be contacted by the other party. Ask the witness to make and sign a note about what happened as soon after the accident as possible.

Signing Instructions

There are no signing instructions for the Accident Claim Worksheet. Simply fill it in for use in preparing a claim after an accident.

> **RELATED TOPIC**
> **Use the Notice of Insurance Claim,** to notify the appropriate insurance company of the accident.

Forms 94–99: Releases

A common means of settling minor disputes (such as an argument about an unpaid loan, a minor fender bender, or a golf ball crashing through a window) is for one party to pay the other a sum of money in exchange for giving up any legal claim related to the incident. Another way to settle a claim is for the person who was in the wrong to do something of benefit for the other. For example, if your neighbor's dog destroys your garden, you might agree to take no further action if your neighbor agrees to replace your most valuable plants and build a fence.

In either situation, you'll want to write out your agreement in the form of a contract, commonly called a release. A release usually consists of no more than one party saying, "I'll pay a certain amount or do a certain thing," and the other party saying that, "In exchange, I'll forever give up my legal claim against you."

What Makes a Release Legally Enforceable?

To be legally enforceable, a release must satisfy two contract law requirements:

- **The release must be voluntary.** Each side must enter into the agreement voluntarily. If a party was coerced into signing an agreement because of the other's threats or intimidation, a court may consider it involuntary and therefore unenforceable. Courts are quite leery about tossing out a release for this reason, however. For example, in a dispute involving the repair of a bicycle, one party telling the other "I'll sue for $100,000 tomorrow if you don't agree to this release" is not the kind of threat that will make a release unenforceable. The threat or coercion must be both significant and within the realm of possibility.

- **The agreement must be arrived at fairly.** Judges are usually unwilling to enforce any agreement that is the product of deceit or the result of one side taking undue advantage of the other. For example, if a person is persuaded to sign a release two hours after an accident that left her groggy, or doesn't understand the meaning of the document or the rights being waived because of limited English, a court will likely not uphold it.

Releases are powerful documents. If you sign one forever giving up a legal claim in exchange for $500, and learn six months later that the extent of what you lost is much greater than you realized when you signed the release, you are out of luck unless a court declares the release unenforceable for one of the above reasons.

Questions to Ask Before Signing a Release

In most situations where both sides understand the dispute and the consequences of various settlement options, you can confidently sign a release, knowing that the dispute will finally be put to rest. But it is always wise for you and the other party to answer the following questions before signing on the dotted line:

- Do you both understand the issues that underlie the dispute?
- Do you both understand what the release accomplishes?

If the answer to these questions is yes, it's wise to ask another three additional questions, but this time just of yourself:

- Do I understand the alternative to a settlement—the legal result I am likely to obtain (and the time and dollars I am likely to spend to get it) if I go to court rather than accepting the release and settling the matter?
- Have I discussed my decision to sign the release with someone who has good business sense and is not emotionally involved with the issue or parties?
- If a lot of money is involved, have I consulted an attorney with practical experience in this field?

If big bucks are at stake and the answer to either of the last three questions is "no," or even a waffling "maybe," do the necessary homework before agreeing to release the other party.

This chapter contains several release forms, including a General Release (to settle a dispute when only one party is alleged to have been injured or suffered damages), and a General

Mutual Release (to settle a dispute when both parties claim the other is at fault and that each has suffered injury or damage). We also include specific releases for damage to real estate, property damage in an automobile accident, personal injury, and contract claims. Review them all to see which one is most appropriate to your situation.

Note on Legal Terminology

The person with the claim who releases the other is called the "releasor." The "releasee" is the person responsible for the injury or the claim who agrees to pay money or promises to do something of value (or not to do anything) in exchange for the release. This is called "paying consideration." To be binding, all contracts, including releases, require an exchange of consideration. The exchange of consideration (such as payment of a specific sum of money) should ideally occur before the release is signed. If this is not possible or feasible, the release should specify when the payment or consideration will be provided.

Making the Release Binding on Others

If one of the parties dies, you want the release to be binding on that person's heirs. Our release forms include language about "successors, assigns, and heirs." In addition, in all community property states (and in some non–community-property states), one spouse is generally liable for the debts of the other spouse, and is entitled to recover monies owed to the other—even if the first spouse had nothing to do with the event leading up to the liability. For this reason, our release forms are binding on spouses and require the spouse's signature signifying consent to the deal. The discussion of promissory notes, in Chapter 5, explains the basics of the community property system.

Signing Instructions for Release Forms

You must sign the Release for it to be valid. Print out two copies of the form. All parties to the release, including spouses (if any) should sign and date both copies of the document in the appropriate spaces. Print the name(s) of the spouse(s) in the blank line provided; if one or both of the parties is not married, write "N/A" on the blank line. Each party should keep one copy of the release, signed by all parties.

 FORM
Notarization of these release forms is optional. You can choose to have any of these release forms notarized. While notarization will add a measure of legal credibility to the release, it's not required to make the agreement enforceable. (See the Introduction for general advice on having a form notarized.) If you do decide to sign your release in front of a licensed notary public, attach the notary certificate where indicated on the form.

Form 94: General Release

A General Release is appropriate for settling personal disputes over a contract, debt, or minor personal injury when only one party is alleged to have been injured or suffered damage. (This form is not appropriate, however, if both parties claim the other is at fault and that each has suffered damage or injury as a result. This requires a mutual release, in which case you would use the General Mutual Release, below.)

 TIP
You can't release what you don't own. If you've assigned your rights to someone else, that person becomes the releasor, not you. Paragraph 4 of the General Release form represents your promise that you own the right that is the subject of the release.

Form 95: General Mutual Release

This form is appropriate for settling disputes—for example, over a debt or minor personal injury—where both parties say the other is at fault and each claims damage or injury as a result. Here the main point is often to trade legal releases—in which case the value or consideration is each person's relinquishment of the legal rights involved in the dispute (Clause 3 of this form). It is not unusual, however, for the person who has suffered the more serious loss (or who was less at fault) to receive additional consideration (Clause 4 of this form). This may be a cash payment or other benefit—for example, free use of a spa facility owned by one of the parties.

If the dispute concerns an oral or written contract, use the Mutual Release of Contract Claims, below.

Form 96: Release for Damage to Real Estate

This form is appropriate for settling disputes between landowners that arise when one owner's property is damaged by another's action or inaction. Common examples include one person's tree overhanging another's yard or pool, or an uphill neighbor digging a ditch that diverts rain runoff onto a downhill neighbor's property. And, of course, walls, fences, view-blocking trees, and noise can all lead to serious disagreements between neighbors.

 RESOURCE

Before you settle a neighbor dispute, it will help if you understand the legal issues—for example, if a tree grows on a property line, which neighbor owns it? For answers to this and similar questions, see *Neighbor Law: Fences, Trees, Boundaries & Noise*, by Emily Doskow and Lina Guillen (Nolo).

Form 97: Release for Property Damage in Auto Accident

Use this form to settle claims over minor property damage from an auto accident. Do not use it if personal injuries are involved. In that case, use the Release for Personal Injury, below.

Form 98: Release for Personal Injury

Use this form when one party has suffered a relatively minor personal injury because of another's actions.

 CAUTION

Don't sign a release involving personal injuries unless the parties are sure that the scope of the injury is fully known. For example, be sure that an injury has completely healed and your doctor has examined you, clearly established the scope of your injury, and unequivocally stated that you have fully recovered and that there will be no further problem. It is almost never wise to sign very soon after an injury—you never know what problems may develop later.

Here are a few examples of language describing an injury for use in Clause 2:
- Cat scratches sustained on both arms after Releasor was attacked by Releasee's cat, Roscoe.
- Cuts Releasor sustained from a shattered window when a baseball hit by Releasee's son broke a window in Releasor's house.

RESOURCE

For detailed advice on filing a personal injury claim, see *How to Win Your Personal Injury Claim*, by Joseph Matthews (Nolo).

Form 99: Mutual Release of Contract Claims

This final release can be used to settle a disagreement that arises from the breach of a written or oral contract. Unlike the General Release or the General Mutual Release, this release is useful only for dealing with contract disputes.

What If One of the Parties to a Release Doesn't Follow Through?

If either of the people signing the release doesn't pay the money or do the promised deed, the other has a choice. The wronged party can take the appropriate legal steps concerning the original dispute as though no release had been signed. Or, either person could go to court and ask a judge to enforce the release (after all, it's a contract). A judge will consider whether the release was voluntary and whether the agreement was arrived at fairly.

You can use small claims court to enforce the release if the amount is within the jurisdictional limits of the court. This is a good option, especially if money is the basis for the dispute.

Miscellaneous Forms for Personal Use

The forms in this chapter are designed to help with various consumer issues, including writing a complaint letter to a government agency, asking your school to evaluate your child's eligibility for special education services, and dealing with identity theft.

Form 100: Complaint Letter

In every state, and at the federal level, unfair or deceptive trade acts or practices are prohibited by law. This means that it is illegal for a seller to deceive, abuse, mislead, defraud, or otherwise cheat you. If you think you've been cheated by someone selling a service or product, start by contacting the company directly. USA.gov has useful advice on how to draft a complaint letter or email to a company. (See the "Complaints" section of the Consumer Protection topic (www.usa.gov/consumer).)

If you have been unable to resolve the problem directly, you should let the appropriate federal, state, and local government offices know. Although law enforcement in the area of consumer fraud is not uniformly great, many hardworking investigators do their jobs well. The more agencies you notify, the more likely it is that someone will take notice of your complaint and act on it—especially if more than one consumer has registered a complaint about the same company.

Your first step is to draft a complaint letter to the relevant government agencies, using this form. Be as detailed as possible regarding your complaint, including the name and title of the person you dealt with, the dates and details of the service or product problem, and any follow-up communication. Keep your language neutral and state the facts of the situation. (See "How to Word a Complaint," below, for sample language.) To back up your complaint, attach copies (never the originals) of all purchase receipts, contracts, warranties, advertisements, and other written documents relating to your complaint.

Finally, your letter will be more persuasive if you suggest a solution, such as a refund, or at least request a reply from the person investigating your complaint.

How to Word a Complaint

Here's an example of language to include in a complaint letter to a government agency:

I wish to complain about a business called Celebrity Cards located in your state. About three months ago, I received a package of cards from this company, unsolicited. I received a second package two months ago. Last month I received a bill from the company for $50 plus shipping and handling. I never ordered these cards and I wrote to the company to say so. (A copy of my letter is attached.) I also stated that I considered the unsolicited items sent to my home to be a gift. Just this week, I received a second bill and a threat to send this debt to a collection agency and report it to a credit bureau.

Compile a list of agencies and their addresses where you will send your complaint letter. Start by checking www.usa.gov for information about federal, state, and local agencies. This will help you identify the appropriate federal agency to receive your complaint, depending on the nature of your problem. For example, a complaint about an online auction would go to the Federal Trade Commission (www.ftc.gov). (See "How to Complain to Government Agencies," below, for a list of resources.)

Many government agencies have their own online complaint form, but it doesn't hurt to follow up with a written complaint letter, such as the one included in this book.

Be sure to send a copy of your letter to the company you are complaining about.

How to Complain to Government Agencies

Depending on the problem, you can send a copy of your complaint letter to one or more of the following agencies:

- **Local district attorney's consumer fraud division.** Ask about local consumer protection services available, including mediation.
- **Local Better Business Bureau.** Find yours at www.bbb.org.
- **State Attorneys General.** You can find contact information for your state Attorney General's office from the National Association of Attorneys General at www.naag.org.
- **State Consumer Protection Office.** Your state consumer protection office can also provide advice, including the name of the appropriate licensing board that handles consumer complaints (for example, if your complaint concerns a licensed professional, such as a contractor or lawyer). Find your state consumer protection agency at www.usa.gov/state-consumer. (This website also has information on other useful government offices and consumer organizations.)
- **Federal Trade Commission.** The FTC handles fraudulent, deceptive, and unfair business practices, but does not resolve individual complaints. It enters all complaints into an online database used by law enforcement agencies. For details, see the "File a Consumer Complaint" section, at www.ftc.gov.

Signing Instructions

There are no specific signing instructions for this Complaint Letter. Simply sign the form and send it to the appropriate government agencies with a copy to the company you're complaining about. Be sure to include copies of any relevant material such as previous correspondence with the seller or service provider. Keep a copy of your complaint letter and attached materials for your records. You may need this if you end up filing a small claims court case or taking other legal action.

 RELATED TOPIC

If your complaint involves a defective product under warranty, use the Request for Refund or Repair of Goods Under Warranty, discussed in Chapter 14.

Form 101: Notice of Insurance Claim

If you're planning to make a claim against an insurance company—because you were injured in a car accident, slip and fall, dog bite, or similar incident—you can use this form to notify the appropriate company or companies. Depending on the circumstances, send your letter to the insurance company of the individual or business you believe was at fault. If you were in a car accident, send your insurance claim notice to the insurance company of the owner and the driver of the vehicle involved in the accident. If you were in a slip and fall, such as at a store, send your notice to the insurance company of the owner of the building where the accident occurred and of the owner of the store where you fell. You will need to get the name and address of the insurance company from the appropriate party—for example, the person driving the car involved in the accident.

If you are covered by your own auto, home-owners', business, or other policy, be sure to notify your own insurer. You can begin by contacting your agent or broker by phone, but it's a good idea to mail in or submit a claim online as well, keeping a copy for yourself.

Your Notice of Insurance Claim should be a simple letter giving only basic information and asking for a written response. It should not discuss fault, responsibility, or the details of your injuries. Make sure your notice includes the following:

- Your name, address, and phone number.
- The date, approximate time of day, and general location of the accident or incident.
- The type of accident (such as motor vehicle or animal bite) and an indication of whether you were injured or suffered property damage in the accident.
- If a vehicle was involved: details on the driver's car (such as make, model, and license plate number) and driver's license number.

If you completed the Accident Claim Worksheet discussed in Chapter 14, you should already have this information at hand.

This Notice of Insurance Claim includes a request that the insurance company confirm by return letter whom it represents, liability coverage of the insured, and whether the company is aware of anyone else who might be responsible for the accident. If the insurance company does not feel you provided sufficient information, it may send you its own form to complete.

Signing Instructions

There are no specific signing instructions for the Notice of Insurance Claim form. Simply sign the form and send it to the other party's company with a copy to your own insurance company. Keep a copy of your insurance claim notice for your records. You may need this if you end up filing a small claims court case or taking other legal action.

RESOURCE

For more about personal injury claims, see *How to Win Your Personal Injury Claim,* by Joseph Matthews (Nolo).

Form 102: Notice to Cancel Certain Contracts

Under the Federal Trade Commission (FTC) "cooling-off rule," consumers have the right to cancel certain types of consumer contracts within three days of signing. This right-to-cancel law applies to door-to-door sales contracts for $25 or more and contracts for $130 or more made anywhere other than the seller's normal place of business—for instance, at a sales presentation at a friend's house, hotel or restaurant, outdoor exhibit, computer show, or trade show. (Real estate, insurance, public car auctions, and craft fairs are exempted from coverage.)

The cooling-off rule applies only to goods or services primarily intended for personal, family, or household purposes. It does not apply to sales made entirely by mail, telephone, or online. The cooling-off rule also does not apply to sales made as part of a request for a seller to do home repairs or maintenance (but purchases made beyond the maintenance or repair request are covered).

To take advantage of this right to cancel, you have until midnight of the third business day following the day you signed the contract to cancel the contract either in person or by mail. If you were not given notice of this right and a cancellation form when you signed the contract, simply use this form.

After canceling, the seller must refund your money within ten business days. Then, the seller must either pick up the items purchased or reimburse you within 20 days for your expense of mailing the goods back to the seller. If the seller doesn't come for the goods or make an arrangement for you to mail them back, you can keep them.

 RESOURCE

For more information on the federal cooling-off rule, see www.ftc.gov or call 877-FTC-HELP. Also, contact your state consumer protection office to see if your state law gives you more rights than the FTC's cooling-off rule. (See "How to Complain to Government Agencies," above, for contact information.)

Consumer Rights to Cancel Other Types of Contracts

Federal law (the Truth in Lending Act) lets you cancel a home improvement loan, second mortgage, or other loan where you pledge your home as security (except for a first mortgage or first deed of trust). Again, you have until midnight of the third business day after you signed the contract to cancel it. Contact the FTC for more information on the Truth in Lending Act. In addition, contact your state office of consumer protection regarding state laws that allow consumers to cancel contracts for other types of goods and services (such as a health club membership) within a few days of signing. You can find your state agency at www.usa.gov/state-consumer.

Signing Instructions

To cancel a contract under the FTC cooling-off rule, fill in the number of days the seller has to refund you money (ten under the FTC rule, or perhaps less under state rule), and the number of days the seller has to reimburse you for any mailing expenses (20 under the FTC rule, or perhaps less under state rules.) Sign

and date one copy of the Notice to Cancel Certain Contracts. Mail it to the seller or the address given for cancellation (if different from the place of purchase). Keep a copy of the notice for your own file. Be sure your envelope is postmarked before midnight of the third business day after the contract date. (Saturday is considered a business day, while Sundays and federal holidays are not.) It is a good idea to send this form by certified mail so you can get a return receipt. You may need this later as proof that you properly canceled the contract.

Form 103: Cancel Membership or Subscription Notice

Use this form to provide written confirmation that you wish to cancel membership in a club or organization, or that you wish to cancel your subscription to a magazine, newspaper, or other periodical. Many organizations and publications make it easy to cancel a subscription online, but it's a good idea to follow up in writing.

Look in the front of the publication for the address of the department that handles subscriptions (or find this information on the publication website). Check mailings from membership groups for similar information. If there is not a separate membership or subscription department, send your Cancel Membership or Subscription Notice to the main address.

Fill in the requested information, specifically your name, address, and identifying information as listed on mailing labels on the magazine or on printed materials you receive from the membership organization. If there is a business name or second name listed on the subscription or membership materials, fill in both names.

State the date you want to cancel the particular subscription or membership, such as "effective May 1, 20xx." If you want, you may specify the reason you are canceling a magazine subscription or other periodical, or no longer want to receive mailings from a membership organization. You may also request a refund for the remainder of the subscription or membership period if you think it is appropriate.

SAMPLE INSERT 1:

> I want to cancel my subscription to *Beef Roundup* because I have recently become a vegetarian.

EXAMPLE 2:

> I want to cancel my subscription to *Beef Roundup* because I am offended by your recent series on the lifestyles of vegetarians. Please refund the value of my remaining issues.

Signing Instructions

Sign the Cancel Membership or Subscription Notice in the space provided. Make a copy of the form and mail the original to the publisher or organization whose periodical or membership you wish to cancel. If applicable, attach a copy of the mailing label or payment invoice to your notice. Keep a copy of the form for your records.

Form 104: Request to Begin Special Education Process

This form can be used by parents who believe their child is in need of special help from their school district. A federal law—the Individuals with Disabilities Education Act (IDEA)—gives parents and guardians the right to request

evaluations (assessments) of their children for physical or psychological disabilities that may affect their ability to learn. Upon your request, the school must present you with an assessment plan, listing all testing to be done on your child. Assessments usually include objective tests of your child's abilities in all areas of suspected disability (for example, reading, memory, motor skills, or vision). In addition to formal tests, assessments often include subjective information relating to your child's educational status, such as comments by teachers, the school psychologist, or a classroom aide.

The IDEA requires the school to provide special services (an Individualized Education Program, or IEP) to a child found to have disabilities. "Special education" is the broad term used to describe the educational system for children who have disabilities, such as mental retardation; autism; specific learning disabilities; hearing, speech, language, orthopedic or visual impairment; or serious emotional disturbance.

Your child's eligibility for special education will depend on the results of the assessment. This letter starts the formal process by requesting an initial assessment of your child's eligibility for special education, an assessment plan, and general information on the IEP process.

This letter also asks the school district to provide a copy of your child's school file, including all tests, report cards, disciplinary records, and teacher notes about your child, so you can learn everything they already know about your child at school. This information is crucial as you assess your child's difficulties and the need for special education services. You have a legal right to inspect and review any educational record relating to your child. If your child has not yet been found eligible for services under the IDEA, you have the right to a copy of the school's file under the Family

Educational Rights and Privacy Act (FERPA) (20 U.S.C. § 1232[g]). State laws also may give you a right to your child's file. Rules vary in different states, but you should be entitled to obtain the file without unnecessary delay. You may be charged for the copies as long as the fee "does not effectively prevent you from exercising your right to inspect and review the records" (34 C.F.R. § 300.617).

Once you send this letter, the school district is required by federal law to inform you of the regulations, guidelines, and procedures that apply to special education services and to begin the process of evaluation (assessment).

Send this Request to Begin Special Education Process to the special education administrator at your child's school. Ask your child's teacher or the school principal for this person's name and address. Be sure to include a brief summary of your child's difficulties at school, such as developmental delays in language or reading problems, that you have noticed or have been told about by teachers, doctors, friends, or anyone who has spent time with your child.

RESOURCE

For a comprehensive and thorough guide to special education laws and services, see *The Complete IEP Guide,* by Lawrence Siegel (Nolo). If you know or suspect that your child has a learning disability, check out *Nolo's IEP Guide: Learning Disabilities,* also by Lawrence Siegel (Nolo).

Signing Instructions

There are no specific signing instructions for the Request to Begin Special Education Process. Simply sign the form and keep a copy for your records.

Describing Your Child's Special Needs

It is very common for parents to recognize that their child has problems with school and simply not know what to do about them. It may be that your child's difficulties can be isolated and addressed very specifically, or the problems may be more wide-ranging. Following are some examples of difficulties your child may be experiencing in school that you should mention in your letter to the special education administrator:

- academic problems in reading, spelling, or math
- delays in developmental areas, such as language or fine motor skills
- difficulties processing or retaining information, such as understanding simple instructions or problems with short- or long-term memory
- social or emotional problems
- trouble sleeping, eating, or getting along with family
- sustained difficulties in paying attention or staying focused
- inappropriate or hyperactive behavior, or
- delays in physical milestones, or other physiological difficulties, such as hearing loss, sight problems, difficulties with mobility, or handwriting problems.

Be as specific as possible in describing your child's difficulties, but do not worry about listing everything. Don't get bogged down in things such as special classes or eligibility. Just write down what you have observed about your child's behavior, focusing on specific patterns. Keep in mind that this is just the beginning of the process. Trained professionals and assessments will help determine whether your intuition is correct.

Form 105: Identity Theft Worksheet

Identity theft has become an epidemic, affecting millions of Americans. Despite the mounting number of victims of identity theft, many people don't know what to do if it happens to them. If you believe that you are a victim of identity theft or fear that you may soon become one— for example, if you lost your wallet, had your home burglarized, or divulged your financial information because of an email scam—take these simple steps immediately. The order in which you take these steps will depend on your situation. For instance, if someone stole your wallet, you would likely want to start by contacting the relevant authorities and canceling all the accounts that are tied to the stolen cards.

This form will help you keep track of what you've done, whom you've spoken to, and what else you'll need to do to protect your personal information.

Regardless of your situation, be sure to follow every step.

1. **Start a log.** Keep notes of your conversations and correspondence with authorities and financial institutions, including dates, names, and phone numbers. Also keep track of all time spent and expenses you incur; you can deduct theft-related expenses on your income tax return if you itemize deductions, and you may be able to seek compensation if you ever sue the thief.

2. **Check your homeowners' insurance policy.** Many now include coverage for certain administrative costs of dealing with identity theft, including attorneys' fees. Give your carrier a call to find out how it can help and what you'll need to keep track of. Unfortunately, the insurance typically won't cover any amounts that were actually stolen.

3. **Contact the credit bureaus to place a fraud alert.** Contact one of the three major credit bureaus (Equifax, Experian, or TransUnion), and ask to have a free credit report sent to you, and to have your account flagged with an initial 90-day fraud alert. Activating a fraud alert (also called a security alert) removes you from all preapproved credit and insurance offers, and requests that creditors contact you before opening any new accounts or making any changes to your existing accounts. When activating a fraud alert, whichever one of three main credit bureaus you contact is required to notify the other two (but follow up to make sure this happens). You can request 90-day extensions or, with proof that you're an actual victim of identity theft, get an extended seven-year fraud alert. If you make additional calls to the credit bureaus on other subjects, be sure to contact all three, as they are not required to communicate with each other after your initial fraud-alert call. Here are the places to contact:
   - Equifax: www.equifax.com
   - Experian: 888-397-3742 or www.experian.com, and
   - TransUnion: 800-680-7289 or www.transunion.com

4. **Review your credit reports.** After you receive your credit reports from the three credit bureaus, review them thoroughly. Make sure that all your personal information, including name, address, and Social Security number, is correct and that there are no fraudulent accounts or inquiries. Immediately report any suspicious information or activity to

the credit bureau that issued the credit report. And in two to three months, order another report to ensure that no new fraudulent activity has occurred. Depending on where you live, a nominal fee may apply when you order a follow-up credit report.

5. **Close any accounts that have been accessed fraudulently:** Contact all creditors, including banks, credit card companies, and other service providers, with whom there has been fraudulent activity. Close all accounts the thief opened or used fraudulently. Request that creditors notate closed accounts as "account closed at consumer's request," because a mark of "card lost or stolen" can reflect poorly on your credit report.

TIP

If your ATM or debit card was stolen, do not use your old PIN for your new card. Choose a password that is obscure but that you will remember. Do not use obvious numbers, such as your or your spouse's birth date.

If a thief stole checks or opened bank accounts in your name, contact one of the major check verification companies (such as ChexSystems) to report the fraudulent activity and to stop payment on stolen checks.

6. **Call the police.** File a report of the crime with your local police department. Provide as much evidence as you can, and ask the officer to list all fraudulently accessed accounts on the police report. Be sure to ask for a copy of the police report, because creditors will probably ask to see it. Remember to log the phone numbers and names of all the law enforcement agents with whom you speak; creditors

may want this information. It's also recommended that you file a police report in the community where the crime occurred.

7. **Report the fraud to the Federal Trade Commission (FTC).** Go to www.identity theft.gov, the agency's dedicated site for reporting identity theft and getting a recovery plan. Start by answering a few questions about your situation. The information you provide will be used to generate a personalized recovery plan, and you'll get step-by-step help with putting that plan into action. The FTC also uses identity theft claims to assist law enforcement agencies in finding and arresting identity thieves.

Further Steps

Depending on the severity of your identity theft case, there are several other actions you may wish to pursue.

- **Contact the postal inspector.** If you believe that someone has changed your address through the post office or has committed mail fraud, contact the U.S. Postal Inspection Service at https://postalinspectors.uspis.gov. If you discover that mail in your name is being sent to an address other than your own, ask the local postmaster to forward all mail in your name to your own address.

- **Contact the Social Security Administration (SSA).** If you believe that your Social Security number (SSN) has been used to fraudulently obtain welfare or Social Security benefits and you wish to get a new SSN, visit www.ssa.gov/ssnumber.

- **Deal with debt collectors.** While you are handling your identity theft case, debt collectors may ask you to pay outstanding bills from fraudulently activated credit accounts. Inform the debt collector by phone and in writing that you are a victim of identity theft and that you are not responsible for the unpaid bill. In your letter, be sure to include copies of documents, such as a police report, that demonstrate that you are the victim of identity theft. With some exceptions, the company is legally prohibited from contacting you once it receives your letter. Request all pertinent information (e.g., name, phone number, address, account number) relating to both the debt collector and the referring credit issuer, and ask whether they want you to fill out the FTC's Identity Theft Victim's Complaint and Affidavit (available at www.consumer. ftc.gov/articles/pdf-0094-identity-theft-affidavit.pdf). Finally, ask the debt collector to confirm in writing that you are not responsible for the outstanding debt and that the account has been closed.

- **Contact the U.S. State Department.** If your passport was stolen or if you believe someone may be fraudulently ordering a passport in your name, contact the U.S. State Department at 877-487-2778 or visit https://travel.state.gov/content/passports/en/passports/lost-stolen.html.

- **Contact the Department of Motor Vehicles (DMV).** If your driver's license was stolen or if someone is using the number to facilitate fraud, contact your state's DMV. Most states will put a fraud alert on your license if you ask for one. You should also request a new license number and fill out the DMV's complaint form.

RESOURCE

Where to go for more information. For a one-stop resource on reporting and recovering from identity theft, visit the federal government's dedicated identity theft site at www.identitytheft.gov.

Signing Instructions

There are no specific signing instructions for the Identity Theft Worksheet. Simply use the form to keep track of what you've done to follow up on an identity theft.

Using the Interactive Forms

The forms in this book are available for instant download at:

www.nolo.com/back-of-book/SPOT.html

You can open, edit, save, and print the RTF files provided by this book using most word processing programs such as Microsoft Word.

Each word processing program uses different commands to open, format, save, and print documents, so refer to your software's help documents for help using your program. Nolo cannot provide technical support for questions about how to use your computer or your software.

Editing RTFs

Here are some general instructions about editing RTF forms in your word processing program. Refer to the book's instructions for help on what should go in each blank.

- **Underlines.** Underlines indicate where to enter information. After filling in the needed text, delete the underline. In most word processing programs you can do this by highlighting the underlined portion and typing CTRL-U.
- **Bracketed and italicized text.** Bracketed and italicized text indicates instructions. Be sure to remove all instructional text before you finalize your document.
- **Optional text.** Optional text gives you the choice to include or exclude text. Delete any optional text you don't want to use. Renumber numbered items, if necessary.

- **Alternative text.** Alternative text gives you the choice between two or more text options. Delete those options you don't want to use. Renumber numbered items, if necessary.

Using PDFs

You can view these files with Adobe Acrobat *Reader*, free software available for download at https://get.adobe.com/reader. Most PDFs are designed to be printed out and completed by hand.

Signature Lines

If your form or letter is more than one page long, be sure that both the signature (including any signature declaration, "I declare…") and signature block are not the only words on the final page. The final page should have some text preceding this material. To force the text to the last page, on the next to the last page, use double hash marks (//) on each line of the lower few inches of the page, then resume your form or letter on the final page.

CAUTION
In accordance with U.S. copyright laws, the forms provided by this book are for your personal use only.

List of Forms

All forms are available for download at: **www.nolo.com/back-of-book/SPOT.html**

Form No.	Title	File Name
1	Temporary Guardianship Authorization for Care of Minor	Form1.rtf
2	Authorization for Minor's Medical Treatment	Form2.rtf
3	Authorization for Foreign Travel With Minor	Form3.rtf
4	House-Sitting Instructions	Form4.rtf
5	Children's Carpool Agreement	Form5.rtf
6	Pet Care Agreement	Form6.rtf
7	Authorization to Drive a Motor Vehicle	Form7.rtf
8	Power of Attorney for Finances (Limited Power)	Form8.rtf
8NY	New York Power of Attorney for Finances (Limited Power)	Form8NY.rtf
8PA	Pennsylvania Power of Attorney for Finances (Limited Power)	Form8PA.rtf
9	Power of Attorney for Real Estate	Form9.rtf
9NY	New York Power of Attorney for Real Estate	Form9NY.rtf
9PA	Pennsylvania Power of Attorney for Real Estate	Form9PA.rtf
10	Notice of Revocation of Power of Attorney	Form10.rtf
11	Property Worksheet	Form11.rtf
12	Beneficiary Worksheet	Form12.rtf
13	Will for Adult With No Children	Form13.rtf
14	Will for Adult With Child(ren)	Form14.rtf
15	Will Codicil	Form15.rtf
16	Request for Death Certificate	Form16.rtf
17	Notice to Creditor of Death	Form17.rtf
18	Executor's Checklist	Form18.pdf
19	General Notice of Death	Form19.rtf
20	Obituary Information Fact Sheet	Form20.rtf
21	Notice to Deceased's Homeowners' Insurance Company	Form21.rtf
22	Notice to Deceased's Vehicle Insurance Company	Form22.rtf

Form No.	Title	File Name
23	Rental Application	Form23.rtf
24	Tenant References	Form24.rtf
25	Landlord-Tenant Checklist	Form25.rtf
26	Move-In Letter	Form26.rtf
27	Notice of Needed Repairs	Form27.rtf
28	Semiannual Safety and Maintenance Update	Form28.rtf
29	Landlord-Tenant Agreement to Terminate Lease	Form29.rtf
30	Consent to Assignment of Lease	Form30.rtf
31	Tenant's Notice of Intent to Move Out	Form31.rtf
32	Demand for Return of Security Deposit	Form32.rtf
33	Loan Comparison Worksheet	Form33.rtf
34	Authorization to Check Credit and Employment References	Form34.rtf
35	Monthly Payment Record	Form35.rtf
36	Promissory Note—Installment Payments With Interest	Form36.rtf
37	Promissory Note—Installment Payments With Interest and Balloon Payment	Form37.rtf
38	Promissory Note—Installment Payments Without Interest	Form38.rtf
39	Promissory Note—Lump Sum Payment With Interest	Form39.rtf
40	Promissory Note—Lump Sum Payment Without Interest	Form40.rtf
41	Cosigner Provision	Form41.rtf
42	Security Agreement Provision for Promissory Note	Form42.rtf
43	Security Agreement for Borrowing Money	Form43.rtf
44	U.C.C. Financing Statement	Form44.rtf
45	Release of U.C.C. Financing Statement	Form45.rtf
46	Agreement to Modify Promissory Note	Form46.rtf
47	Overdue Payment Demand	Form47.rtf
48	Demand to Make Good on Bad Check	Form48.rtf
49	Ideal House Profile	Form49.rtf
50	House Priorities Worksheet	Form50.rtf

Form No.	Title	File Name
51	House Comparison Worksheet	Form51.rtf
52	Family Financial Statement	Form52.rtf
53	Monthly Carrying Costs Worksheet	Form53.rtf
54	Mortgage Rates and Terms Worksheet	Form54.rtf
55	Moving Checklist	Form55.rtf
56	Motor Vehicle Bill of Sale	Form56.rtf
57	Boat Bill of Sale	Form57.rtf
58	General Bill of Sale	Form58.rtf
59	Bill of Sale for Dog	Form59.rtf
60	Personal Property Rental Agreement	Form60.rtf
61	Notice of Termination of Personal Property Rental Agreement	Form61.rtf
62	Storage Contract	Form62.rtf
63	Home Maintenance Agreement	Form63.rtf
64	Home Repairs Agreement	Form64.rtf
65	Contractor Mid-job Worksheet	Form65.rtf
66	Daily Expenses	Form66.rtf
67	Monthly Income	Form67.rtf
68	Monthly Budget	Form68.rtf
69	Statement of Assets and Liabilities	Form69.rtf
70	Assignment of Rights	Form70.rtf
71	Notice to Terminate Joint Account	Form71.rtf
72	Notice to Stop Payment of Check	Form72.rtf
73	Request for Credit Report	Form73.rtf
74	Request Reinvestigation of Credit Report Entry	Form74.rtf
75	Dispute Credit Card Charge	Form75.rtf
76	Demand Collection Agency Cease Contact	Form76.rtf
77	Telemarketing Phone Call Log	Form77.rtf
78	Notice to Put Name on Company's "Do Not Call" List	Form78.rtf

Form No.	Title	File Name
79	Demand for Damages for Excessive Calls	Form79.rtf
80	Notice to Remove Name from List	Form80.rtf
81	Notice to Add or Retain Name But Not Sell or Trade it	Form81.rtf
82	Child Care Agreement	Form82.rtf
83	Child Care Instructions	Form83.rtf
84	Elder Care Agreement	Form84.rtf
85	Housekeeping Services Agreement	Form85.rtf
86	Agreement to Keep Property Separate	Form86.rtf
87	Agreement for a Joint Purchase	Form87.rtf
88	Agreement to Share Property	Form88.rtf
89	Declaration of Legal Name Change	Form89.rtf
90	Demand Letter	Form90.rtf
91	Online Auction Buyer Demand Letter	Form91.rtf
92	Request for Refund or Repair of Goods Under Warranty	Form92.rtf
93	Accident Claim Worksheet	Form93.rtf
94	General Release	Form94.rtf
95	General Mutual Release	Form95.rtf
96	Release for Damage to Real Estate	Form96.rtf
97	Release for Property Damage in Auto Accident	Form97.rtf
98	Release for Personal Injury	Form98.rtf
99	Mutual Release of Contract Claims	Form99.rtf
100	Complaint Letter	Form100.rtf
101	Notice of Insurance Claim	Form101.rtf
102	Notice to Cancel Certain Contracts	Form102.rtf
103	Cancel Membership or Subscription Notice	Form103.rtf
104	Request to Begin Special Education Process	Form104.rtf
105	Identity Theft Worksheet	Form105.rtf
N/A	Dispute Resolution Clause	Disputes.rtf

Forms

Temporary Guardianship Authorization for Care of Minor

Child

Name: _____

Permanent address: _____

Phone: _____ Birthdate: _____

Child's School or Day Care

(Leave this section blank if your child is not in school or any type of child care program.)

School or day care program: _____

Teacher or day care provider: _____ Grade (if in school): _____

School or day care address: _____

_____ Phone: _____

Child's Doctor, Dentist, and Insurance

Doctor (or HMO): _____

Address: _____

_____ Phone: _____

Name of medical insurer/health plan: _____

Policy or medical records number: _____

Phone: _____

Dentist: _____

Address: _____

_____ Phone: _____

Name of dental insurer/dental plan: _____

Policy number: _____ Phone: _____

Parents (or Legal Guardians)

Parent 1

Name: _____

Address: _____

_____

Home phone: _____ Work phone: _____

Cell phone: _____ Email: _____

Parent 2

Name: _____

Address: _____

_____

Home phone: _____ Work phone: _____

Cell phone: _____ Email: _____

Temporary Guardian

Name: _____

Address: _____

_____

Home phone: _____ Work phone: _____

Cell phone: _____ Email: _____

Emergency Contact Information

In case of emergency, if a parent, guardian, or temporary guardian cannot be reached, contact:

Name: _____

Phone: _____ Email: _____

Additional contact information: _____

_____

_____

Authorization and Consent of Parent(s) or Legal Guardian(s)

1. I am the parent or legal guardian of, and have legal custody of, the minor child named above. I authorize my child to live with and travel with the temporary guardian. I give the temporary guardian permission to care for my child in my place and make decisions pertaining to my child's care, including educational, recreational, and religious activities.

2. I give the temporary guardian permission to authorize medical and dental care for my child, including but not limited to medical examinations, X-rays, tests, anesthesia, surgical operations, hospital care, or other treatments that, in the temporary guardian's sole opinion, are needed or useful for my child. Such medical treatment shall be provided only upon the advice of and supervision by a physician, surgeon, dentist, or other medical practitioner licensed to practice in the United States.

3. This authorization shall cover the period from _____ to _____ .

4. While the temporary guardian cares for my child, the costs of my child's upkeep, living expenses, and medical and dental expenses shall be paid as follows: _____

_____

Parent 1's signature: _____

Date: _____

Parent 2's signature: _____ Date: _____

Consent of Temporary Guardian

I solemnly affirm that I will assume full responsibility for the minor who will live with me during the period designated above.

Temporary guardian's signature: _____

Date: _____

[OPTIONAL: ATTACH NOTARY CERTIFICATE]

Authorization for Minor's Medical Treatment

Child

Name: _____

Birthdate: _____ Age: _____ Grade in school: _____

Doctor (or HMO): _____

Address: _____

_____ Phone: _____

Name of medical insurer/health plan: _____

Policy number: _____ Phone: _____

Allergies (medications): _____

Allergies (other): _____

Medications the child is currently taking: _____

_____

Other important medical information: _____

_____

Dentist: _____

Address: _____

_____ Phone: _____

Name of dental insurer/dental plan: _____

Policy number: _____ Phone: _____

Parents (or Legal Guardians)

Parent 1

Name: _____

Address: _____

_____

Home phone: _____ Work phone: _____

Cell phone: _____ Email: _____

Additional contact information: _____

Parent 2

Name: _____

Address: _____

_____

Home phone: _____ Work phone: _____

Cell phone: _____ Email: _____

Additional contact information: _____

Emergency Contact

Name: _____

Address: _____

_____

Home phone: _____ Work phone: _____

Cell phone: _____ Email: _____

Authorization and Consent of Parent(s) or Legal Guardian(s)

I am the parent or legal guardian of, and have legal custody of, the minor child named above. If I cannot
be reached to give consent to medical or dental care for my child, I authorize _____

_____ [*name of the person to whom
you want to give authority to get medical care for your child*] to give consent to such care in my place.

This authorization includes permission to consent to medical and dental care for my child, including
but not limited to medical examinations, X-rays, tests, anesthesia, surgical operations, hospital care, or
other treatments that in the opinion of _____
[*name of the person to whom you want to give authority to get medical care for your child*] are needed
or useful for my child. Such medical treatment shall be provided only upon the advice of and shall be
supervised by a physician, surgeon, dentist, or other medical practitioner licensed to practice in the
United States.

Parent 1's signature: _____ Date: _____

Parent 2's signature: _____ Date: _____

[OPTIONAL: ATTACH NOTARY CERTIFICATE]

Authorization for Foreign Travel With Minor

To Whom It May Concern:

This letter concerns my child, _____ [*name of child*],

a United States citizen and a minor born on _____ , _____ , [*child's date of birth*],

who has been issued a United States passport with the number _____ .

I affirm that I have legal custody of my child, and that there are no pending divorce or child custody

proceedings that involve my child. I give my full authorization and consent for my child to travel outside

of the United States with _____ [*name of adult*

with whom child will travel], who is the _____ [*state adult's*

relationship with child] of my child. The purpose of the travel is _____

_____ [*specify vacation, touring, to visit relatives, to accompany adult*

on business trip, or other reason].

I have approved the following travel plans:

Dates of travel	Destinations/Accommodations
_____	_____
_____	_____
_____	_____
_____	_____
_____	_____
_____	_____

Furthermore, I hereby authorize _____ [*name of adult with whom child*

will travel] to modify the travel plans specified above as he/she deems necessary.

I declare under penalty of perjury under the laws of the state of _____

that the foregoing is true and correct.

Parent 1's signature: _____ Date: _____

Printed name: _____

Address: _____

_____

Home phone: _____ Work phone: _____

Cell phone: _____ Email: _____

Parent 2's signature: _____ Date: _____

Printed name: _____

Address: _____

_____

Home phone: _____ Work phone: _____

Cell phone: _____ Email: _____

[OPTIONAL: ATTACH NOTARY CERTIFICATE]

House-Sitting Instructions

Home Owner(s)

Name(s): _____

Home address: _____

_____ Home phone: _____

Temporary address(es) and phone numbers while housesitter is staying at home (or attach schedule):

_____

Plants and Garden. [*What to water, when.*] _____

_____

Newspapers and Mail. [*What to do about mail and newspapers; what to save, what to throw out.*]

_____

Garbage and Recycling. [*Details of garbage pickup and recycling—what, where, when.*] _____

_____

Appliances. [*Where to find manuals/booklets on major and minor appliances, plus odds and ends of information as to location and operation of vacuum cleaner, stove, etc.*] _____

_____

Lights. [*Any special details on lights, timers, automatic night light, and external motion-sensitive lights.*]

_____

Windows, Doors, Security Systems, and Keys. [*Details on how locks and security system work, and who has extra keys.*] _____

_____

Smoke Detectors and Fire Extinguishers. [*Details on location and functioning of smoke detectors and fire extinguishers.*] _____

_____

Utilities. [*Details on location and use of thermostat, gas and water shut-off valves, fuse box, and spare fuses.*]

_____

_____

Tools and Supplies. [*Location of house supplies, such as tools, lightbulbs, batteries, iron, cleaning supplies, and first aid kit.*] _____

_____

Vehicles. [*Details on cars, whether they need to be started once a week, etc.*] _____

_____

_____

Neighbors and Friends. [*Names and phone numbers of neighbors and friends who can help with any*
questions.] _____

_____

Repair People and Service Contacts. [*Names and phone numbers of repairperson, plumber, insurance*
agent, etc.] _____

_____

Miscellaneous. [*Anything else you want the housesitter to know.*] _____

_____

Signature: _____ Date: _____

Children's Carpool Agreement

1. The purpose of this carpool is to transport children to _____ [*name of activity*], located at _____ [*address*].

2. The carpool will begin on _____ [*date*] and end on _____ [*date*].

3. Inbound trip: The carpool will pick up _____ [*the first child to be picked up*] at _____ [*time*] and pick up the rest of the children in this order: _____ _____ [*list the pickup order*].

4. Return trip: The carpool will meet the children at _____ [*time*] and deliver the children to the addresses listed below in this order: _____ _____ [*list the drop-off order*].

5. Special agreements (waiting time, alternate drop-off sites, etc.): _____ _____ .

6. The members of the carpool and the riders are:

Child 1

Child's name: _____

Inbound pickup address: _____

Outbound drop-off address: _____

Parents'/guardians' name(s): _____

Parents'/guardians' home address: _____

Parents'/guardians' work address: _____

Parents'/guardians' contact information:

Home phone: _____ Work phone: _____

Cell phone: _____ Email: _____

Names, phone numbers, and relationship to you/child of two people, other than those listed above, to call in an emergency: _____ _____

Name and phone number of child's physician: _____

Driver's name: _____

Driver's license number: _____

Driver's address, if different from above: _____

Driver's phone, if different from above: _____

Model, make, and license number of vehicle(s) driver expects to use: _____ _____

Name of insurance company: _____

Child 2

Child's name: _____

Inbound pickup address: _____

Outbound drop-off address: _____

Parents'/guardians' name(s): _____

Parents'/guardians' home address: _____

Parents'/guardians' work address: _____

Parents'/guardians' contact information:

Home phone: _____ Work phone: _____

Cell phone: _____ Email: _____

Names, phone numbers, and relationship to you/child of two people, other than those listed above, to call in an emergency: _____

_____

Name and phone number of child's physician: _____

Driver's name: _____

Driver's license number: _____

Driver's address, if different from above: _____

Driver's phone, if different from above: _____

Model, make, and license number of vehicle(s) driver expects to use: _____

_____

Name of insurance company: _____

Child 3

Child's name: _____

Inbound pickup address: _____

Outbound drop-off address: _____

Parents'/guardians' name(s): _____

Parents'/guardians' home address: _____

Parents'/guardians' work address: _____

Parents'/guardians' contact information:

Home phone: _____ Work phone: _____

Cell phone: _____ Email: _____

Names, phone numbers, and relationship to you/child of two people, other than those listed above, to call in an emergency: _____

_____

Name and phone number of child's physician: _____

Driver's name: _____

Driver's license number: _____

Driver's address, if different from above: _____

Driver's phone, if different from above: _____

Model, make, and license number of vehicle(s) driver expects to use: _____

_____

Name of insurance company: _____

Child 4

Child's name: _____

Inbound pickup address: _____

Outbound drop-off address: _____

Parents'/guardians' name(s): _____

Parents'/guardians' home address: _____

Parents'/guardians' work address: _____

Parents'/guardians' contact information:

Home phone: _____ Work phone: _____

Cell phone: _____ Email: _____

Names, phone numbers, and relationship to you/child of two people, other than those listed above, to call in an emergency: _____

_____

Name and phone number of child's physician: _____

Driver's name: _____

Driver's license number: _____

Driver's address, if different from above: _____

Driver's phone, if different from above: _____

Model, make, and license number of vehicle(s) driver expects to use: _____

_____

Name of insurance company: _____

7. By signing this Agreement, I agree to abide by its terms to the best of my ability. I understand that any member of the carpool can stop participating without notice but agree to give as much notice as is possible under the circumstances. I understand that if a member is not fulfilling his or her responsibilities, that member may be asked to leave. I understand that this document is not a legally binding agreement and is entered into in a spirit of cooperation and a shared desire to make the carpool work well for the benefit of the children and their parents or guardians.

Parent or Guardian Signature: _____ Date: _____

Parent or Guardian Signature: _____ Date: _____

Parent or Guardian Signature: _____ Date: _____

Parent or Guardian Signature: _____ Date: _____

Pet Care Agreement

Pet Owner

Name: _____

Home address: _____

_____

Home phone: _____ Work phone: _____

Cell phone: _____ Email: _____

Temporary address while pet is in Caregiver's care: _____

_____ Phone: _____

Cell phone: _____ Email: _____

[*if more than one temporary address, attach itinerary*]

Caregiver

Name: _____

Home address: _____

_____

Home phone: _____ Work phone: _____

Cell phone: _____ Email: _____

Temporary address while pet is in Caregiver's care: _____

_____ Phone: _____

Cell phone: _____ Email: _____

Pet(s)

Caregiver will take care of: [*list name, species, breed, age, and, if necessary, any distinguishing characteristics*]

_____

_____

_____

_____

Dates of Care

Caregiver will care for the animal(s) at _____

[*location, either caregiver's home or your home*] from _____ [*beginning date*] until

_____ [*ending date*].

Reimbursement and Compensation

Owner will reimburse Caregiver for reasonable out-of-pocket expenses, including veterinary bills incurred while caring for the animal(s). Owner will also compensate Caregiver as follows:

☐ no compensation

☐ payment of $_____

☐ other: _____

Care Instructions

Caregiver will exercise reasonable care to protect the animal(s) from sickness, injury, and theft, and will follow these instructions:

Food

Type of food: _____

Amount: _____

Frequency: _____

Special instructions: _____

_____

Medication

1. Name: _____ Dosage: _____

   Special instructions: _____

2. Name: _____ Dosage: _____

   Special instructions: _____

Exercise

Frequency and type: _____

Special instructions: _____

Grooming

Frequency and type: _____

Special instructions: _____

Veterinary Care

Name: _____

Address: _____

_____ Phone: _____

Veterinary insurance company and policy no.: _____

Special instructions: _____

Emergency Contact

If Caregiver becomes unable to care for the pet(s), Caregiver will contact _____

_____ [name] at _____ [phone number]

to try to make substitute arrangements for care of the pet(s) and will promptly notify Owner. If arrange-ments cannot be made, Caregiver will turn the pet(s) over to _____

_____ [name] at _____ [phone number]

and promptly notify Owner.

Disputes

If any dispute arises under this agreement, the parties agree to select a mutually agreeable third party to help them mediate it, and to share equally any costs of mediation.

Additional Terms

_____

_____

_____

_____

_____

_____

_____

_____

Entire Agreement

This agreement contains the entire agreement between Owner and Caregiver. Any modifications must be in writing.

Signatures

Pet owner's name: _____

Signature: _____ Date: _____

Caregiver's name: _____

Signature: _____ Date: _____

Authorization to Drive a Motor Vehicle

Vehicle Owner ("Owner")

Name: _____

Address: _____

_____

Home phone: _____ Work phone: _____

Cell phone: _____ Email: _____

Vehicle

Make, model, and year of vehicle: _____

Vehicle license plate number: _____ State of registration: _____

Vehicle identification number (VIN): _____

Insurance company: _____

Insurance policy number: _____

Odometer reading when authorization begins: _____

Person Authorized to Drive ("Borrower")

Name: _____

Address: _____

_____

Home phone: _____ Work phone: _____

Cell phone: _____ Email: _____

Driver's license number: _____

Motor vehicle insurance company (if any): _____

Insurance policy number (if any): _____

Authorization and Consent of Vehicle Owner

I am the lawful owner of the vehicle indicated above. I give my authorization and consent for Borrower
to use this vehicle as follows:

Dates of use: _____

Area in which vehicle may be used: _____

Any restrictions or conditions on use: _____

I declare under penalty of perjury under the laws of the state of _____

that the foregoing is true and correct.

Owner's signature: _____ Date: _____

Power of Attorney for Finances (Limited Power)

I, _____ [*your name*] (principal),

of _____ [*your city and state*],

appoint _____ [*name of your*

attorney-in-fact] to act in my place for the purposes of: _____

_____

_____ .

This power of attorney takes effect on _____ ,

and shall continue until terminated in writing, or until _____ ,

whichever comes first. In the event of my incapacity or death, this power of attorney shall terminate immediately.

I grant my attorney-in-fact full authority to act in any manner both proper and necessary to the exercise of the foregoing powers, and I ratify every act that my attorney-in-fact may lawfully perform in exercising those powers.

I agree that any third party who receives a copy of this document may act under it. Revocation of the power of attorney is not effective as to a third party until the third party has actual knowledge of the revocation. I agree to indemnify the third party for any claims that arise against the third party because of reliance on this power of attorney.

Signed: This _____ day of _____ , _____

State of: _____ County of: _____

Signature: _____ , Principal

Witnesses

[*Witnesses are required in some states, optional in others*]

On the date written above, the principal declared to me that this instrument is his or her financial power of attorney, and that he or she willingly executed it as a free and voluntary act. The principal signed this instrument in my presence.

Witness 1

Signature: _____

Name: _____

Address: _____

_____

Witness 2

Signature: _____

Name: _____

Address: _____

_____

Acknowledgment of Attorney-in-Fact

By accepting or acting under the appointment, I assume the fiduciary and other legal responsibilities and liabilities of an agent. I understand that I owe a duty of loyalty and good faith to the principal and must use the powers granted to me only for the benefit of the principal. I acknowledge that my authority to act on behalf of the principal ceases at the death of the principal.

Name of Attorney-in-Fact: _____

Signature of Attorney-in-Fact: _____

[ATTACH NOTARY CERTIFICATE]

New York Power of Attorney for Finances (Limited Power)

CAUTION TO THE PRINCIPAL: Your Power of Attorney is an important document. As the "principal," you give the person whom you choose (your "agent") authority to spend your money and sell or dispose of your property during your lifetime without telling you. You do not lose your authority to act even though you have given your agent similar authority.

When your agent exercises this authority, he or she must act according to any instructions you have provided or, where there are no specific instructions, in your best interest. "Important Information for the Agent" at the end of this document describes your agent's responsibilities.

Your agent can act on your behalf only after signing the Power of Attorney before a notary public.

You can request information from your agent at any time. If you are revoking a prior Power of Attorney, you should provide written notice of the revocation to your prior agent(s) and to any third parties who may have acted upon it, including the financial institutions where your accounts are located.

You can revoke or terminate your Power of Attorney at any time for any reason as long as you are of sound mind. If you are no longer of sound mind, a court can remove an agent for acting improperly.

Your agent cannot make health care decisions for you. You may execute a "Health Care Proxy" to do this.

The law governing Powers of Attorney is contained in the New York General Obligations Law, Article 5, Title 15. This law is available at a law library, or online through the New York State Senate or Assembly websites, nysenate.gov or www.assembly.state.ny.us.

If there is anything about this document that you do not understand, you should ask a lawyer of your own choosing to explain it to you.

I, _____ [*your name*],

of _____ [*your city and state*],

appoint _____ [*name of your agent*]

to act in my place for the purposes of: _____ .

This power of attorney takes effect on _____ and shall continue until

terminated in writing or until _____ , whichever comes first.

I grant my agent full authority to act in any manner both proper and necessary to the exercise of the foregoing powers, and I ratify every act that my agent may lawfully perform in exercising those powers.

I agree that any third party who receives a copy of this document may act under it. Revocation of the power of attorney is not effective as to a third party until the third party has actual knowledge of the revocation. I agree to indemnify the third party for any claims that arise against the third party because of reliance on this power of attorney.

Signed: This _____ day of _____ , _____

State of: _____ County of: _____

Signature: _____ , Principal

STATE OF NEW YORK)
) ss:

COUNTY OF _____)

On the _____ day of _____ , 20_____ , before me, the undersigned,

personally appeared _____ , personally

known to me or proved to me on the basis of satisfactory evidence to be the individual whose name is subscribed to the within instrument and acknowledged to me that he/she executed the same in his/her capacity, and that by his/her signature on the instrument, the individual, or the person upon behalf of which the individual acted, executed the instrument.

Notary Public: _____

IMPORTANT INFORMATION FOR THE AGENT:

When you accept the authority granted under this Power of Attorney, a special legal relationship is created between you and the principal. This relationship imposes on you legal responsibilities that continue until you resign or the Power of Attorney is terminated or revoked. You must:

(1) act according to any instructions from the principal, or, where there are no instructions, in the principal's best interest;

(2) avoid conflicts that would impair your ability to act in the principal's best interest;

(3) keep the principal's property separate and distinct from any assets you own or control, unless otherwise permitted by law;

(4) keep a record of all receipts, payments, and transactions conducted for the principal; and

(5) disclose your identity as an agent whenever you act for the principal by writing or printing the principal's name and signing your own name as "agent" in either of the following manners: (Principal's Name) by (Your Signature) as Agent, or (your signature) as Agent for (Principal's Name).

You may not use the principal's assets to benefit yourself or anyone else or make gifts to yourself or anyone else unless the principal has specifically granted you that authority in this document, which is either a Statutory Gifts Rider attached to a Statutory Short Form Power of Attorney or a Non-Statutory Power of Attorney. If you have that authority, you must act according to any instructions of the principal or, where there are no such instructions, in the principal's best interest.

You may resign by giving written notice to the principal and to any co-agent, successor agent, monitor if one has been named in this document, or the principal's guardian if one has been appointed. If there is anything about this document or your responsibilities that you do not understand, you should seek legal advice.

Liability of agent: The meaning of the authority given to you is defined in New York's General Obligations Law, Article 5, Title 15. If it is found that you have violated the law or acted outside the authority granted to you in the Power of Attorney, you may be liable under the law for your violation.

AGENT'S SIGNATURE AND ACKNOWLEDGMENT OF APPOINTMENT:

It is not required that the principal and the agent(s) sign at the same time, nor that multiple agents sign at the same time.

I, _____ , have read the foregoing Power of Attorney. I am the person identified therein as agent for the principal named therein.

I acknowledge my legal responsibilities.

Agent(s) sign(s) here: ==> _____

STATE OF NEW YORK   )

) ss:

COUNTY OF _____)

On the _____ day of _____ , 20_____ , before me, the undersigned, personally appeared _____ , personally known to me or proved to me on the basis of satisfactory evidence to be the individual whose name is subscribed to the within instrument and acknowledged to me that he/she executed the same in his/her capacity, and that by his/her signature on the instrument, the individual, or the person upon behalf of which the individual acted, executed the instrument.

Notary Public: _____

Pennsylvania Power of Attorney for Finances (Limited Power)

NOTICE

THE PURPOSE OF THIS POWER OF ATTORNEY IS TO GIVE THE PERSON YOU DESIGNATE (YOUR "AGENT") BROAD POWERS TO HANDLE YOUR PROPERTY, WHICH MAY INCLUDE POWERS TO SELL OR OTHERWISE DISPOSE OF ANY REAL OR PERSONAL PROPERTY WITHOUT ADVANCE NOTICE TO YOU OR APPROVAL BY YOU.

THIS POWER OF ATTORNEY DOES NOT IMPOSE A DUTY ON YOUR AGENT TO EXERCISE GRANTED POWERS, BUT WHEN POWERS ARE EXERCISED, YOUR AGENT MUST USE DUE CARE TO ACT FOR YOUR BENEFIT AND IN ACCORDANCE WITH THIS POWER OF ATTORNEY.

YOUR AGENT MAY EXERCISE THE POWERS GIVEN HERE THROUGHOUT YOUR LIFETIME, EVEN AFTER YOU BECOME INCAPACITATED, UNLESS YOU EXPRESSLY LIMIT THE DURATION OF THESE POWERS OR YOU REVOKE THESE POWERS OR A COURT ACTING ON YOUR BEHALF TERMINATES YOUR AGENT'S AUTHORITY.

YOUR AGENT MUST ACT IN ACCORDANCE WITH YOUR REASONABLE EXPECTATIONS TO THE EXTENT ACTUALLY KNOWN BY YOUR AGENT AND, OTHERWISE, IN YOUR BEST INTEREST, ACT IN GOOD FAITH AND ACT ONLY WITHIN THE SCOPE OF AUTHORITY GRANTED BY YOU IN THE POWER OF ATTORNEY.

THE LAW PERMITS YOU, IF YOU CHOOSE, TO GRANT BROAD AUTHORITY TO AN AGENT UNDER POWER OF ATTORNEY, INCLUDING THE ABILITY TO GIVE AWAY ALL OF YOUR PROPERTY WHILE YOU ARE ALIVE OR TO SUBSTANTIALLY CHANGE HOW YOUR PROPERTY IS DISTRIBUTED AT YOUR DEATH. BEFORE SIGNING THIS DOCUMENT, YOU SHOULD SEEK THE ADVICE OF AN ATTORNEY AT LAW TO MAKE SURE YOU UNDERSTAND IT.

A COURT CAN TAKE AWAY THE POWERS OF YOUR AGENT IF IT FINDS YOUR AGENT IS NOT ACTING PROPERLY.

THE POWERS AND DUTIES OF AN AGENT UNDER A POWER OF ATTORNEY ARE EXPLAINED MORE FULLY IN 20 PA.C.S. CH. 56.

IF THERE IS ANYTHING ABOUT THIS FORM THAT YOU DO NOT UNDERSTAND, YOU SHOULD ASK A LAWYER OF YOUR OWN CHOOSING TO EXPLAIN IT TO YOU.

I have read or had explained to me this notice and I understand its contents.

Signature: _____, Principal

Date: _____

I, _____ [*your name*], (principal) of _____ [*your city and state*], appoint [*name of your agent*] _____ to act in my place for the purposes of:

_____ .

This power of attorney takes effect on _____ and shall continue until terminated in writing or until _____, whichever comes first. In the event of my incapacity or death, this power of attorney shall terminate immediately.

I grant my agent full authority to act in any manner both proper and necessary to the exercise of the foregoing powers, and I ratify every act that my agent may lawfully perform in exercising those powers.

I agree that any third party who receives a copy of this document may act under it. Revocation of the power of attorney is not effective as to a third party until the third party has actual knowledge of the revocation. I agree to indemnify the third party for any claims that arise against the third party because of reliance on this power of attorney.

[Special instructions for signatures]

To ensure that the validity of your document will not be challenged, it is important that the signature clause does not begin a new page. Because pages will vary from user to user, it is your responsibility to make sure that there is at least one line of text preceding the signature clause on this page. If after printing out your document, you discover that there is no text preceding the signature clause, you will need to edit this document (perhaps by adding some paragraph returns to the previous page) so that the signature clause no longer begins the page.

Delete these instructions so they do not appear in your final document.

[End of instructions]

Signed: This _____ day of _____ , _____

State of Pennsylvania, County of_____

Signature: _____ , Principal

Witnesses

On the date written above, the principal declared to me that this instrument is his or her financial power of attorney, and that he or she willingly executed it as a free and voluntary act. The principal signed this instrument in my presence.

Witness 1

Signature: _____

Name: _____

Address: _____

Witness 2

Signature: _____

Name: _____

Address: _____

Certificate of Acknowledgment of Notary Public

State of Pennsylvania_____

County of _____ $\Big\}$ ss

This record was acknowledged before me on (date) _____ , by (name(s)
of individual(s)), _____
_____ , and_____ .

[NOTARIAL SEAL]

Signature of Notarial Officer: _____
Title of Office: _____
My commission expires: _____

Acknowledgment of Agent

I, _____, have read the attached power of attorney
and am the person identified as the agent for the principal. I hereby acknowledge that when I act as agent
I shall act in accordance with the principal's reasonable expectations to the extent actually known by me
and, otherwise, in the principal's best interest, act in good faith and act only within the scope of authority
granted to me by the principal in the power of attorney.

Name of Agent: _____
Signature of Agent: _____
Date: _____

Power of Attorney for Real Estate

RECORDING REQUESTED BY
AND WHEN RECORDED MAIL TO

_____

_____

_____

Power of Attorney for Real Estate

I, _____ [name of principal],

of _____ [city], _____ [county],

_____ [state], appoint _____

_____ [name of attorney-in-fact], of _____ [city],

_____ [county] _____ [state]

to act in my place with respect to the real property described as follows:

_____

_____

_____

_____

_____

_____

_____

_____

_____

_____

_____

_____

_____

_____

_____

_____

_____

_____

_____

My attorney-in-fact may act for me in any manner to deal with all or any part of any interest in the real property described in this document, under such terms, conditions, and covenants as my attorney-in-fact deems proper. My attorney-in-fact's powers include but are not limited to the power to:

1. Accept as a gift or as security for a loan, reject, demand, buy, lease, receive, or otherwise acquire ownership or possession of any estate or interest in real property.

2. Sell, exchange, convey with or without covenants, quitclaim, release, surrender, mortgage, encumber, partition or consent to the partitioning of, grant options concerning, lease, sublet, or otherwise dispose of any interest in the real property described in this document.

3. Maintain, repair, improve, insure, rent, lease, and pay or contest taxes or assessments on any estate or interest in the real property described in this document.

4. Prosecute, defend, intervene in, submit to arbitration, settle, and propose or accept a compromise with respect to any claim in favor of or against me based on or involving the real property described in this document.

However, my attorney-in-fact shall not have the power to:

_____

_____

_____

_____

_____

_____

_____

_____

_____

_____

_____

_____

_____

_____

_____

_____

_____

_____

I further grant to my attorney-in-fact full authority to act in any manner both proper and necessary to the exercise of the foregoing powers, including _____

_____

and I ratify every act that my attorney-in-fact may lawfully perform in exercising those powers.

This power of attorney takes effect on _____ , and shall continue until terminated in writing, or until _____ , whichever comes first. In the event of my incapacity or death, this power of attorney shall terminate immediately.

I agree that any third party who receives a copy of this document may act under it. Revocation of the power of attorney is not effective as to a third party until the third party has actual knowledge of the revocation. I agree to indemnify the third party for any claims that arise against the third party because of reliance on this power of attorney.

Signed this _____ day of _____ , _____

State of _____ , County of _____

Signature: _____

Witness

On the date written above, the principal declared to me that this instrument is his or her power of attorney for real estate, and that he or she willingly executed it as a free and voluntary act. The principal signed this instrument in my presence.

Name: _____

Address: _____

County: _____

Preparation Statement

This document was prepared by:

Print Name: _____

Signature: _____

Address: _____

Signature of Attorney-in-Fact

By accepting or acting under the appointment, the attorney-in-fact assumes the fiduciary and other legal responsibilities of an agent.

Signature of attorney-in-fact: _____

[ATTACH NOTARY CERTIFICATE]

I agree that any third party who receives a copy of this document may act under it. Revocation of the power of attorney is not effective as to a third party until the third party has actual knowledge of the revocation. I agree to indemnify the third party for any claims that arise against the third party because of reliance on this power of attorney.

Signed this _____ day of _____ , _____

State of _____ , County of _____

Signature: _____

Witnesses

On the date written above, the principal declared to me that this instrument is his or her power of attorney for real estate, and that he or she willingly executed it as a free and voluntary act. The principal signed this instrument in my presence.

Name: _____ Name: _____

Address: _____ Address: _____

County: _____ County: _____

Preparation Statement

This document was prepared by:

Print Name: _____

Signature: _____

Address: _____

Signature of Attorney-in-Fact

By accepting or acting under the appointment, the attorney-in-fact assumes the fiduciary and other legal responsibilities of an agent.

Signature of attorney-in-fact: _____

[ATTACH NOTARY CERTIFICATE]

I agree that any third party who receives a copy of this document may act under it. Revocation of the power of attorney is not effective as to a third party until the third party has actual knowledge of the revocation. I agree to indemnify the third party for any claims that arise against the third party because of reliance on this power of attorney.

Signed this _____ day of _____ , _____

State of _____ , County of _____

Signature: _____

Preparation Statement

This document was prepared by:

Print Name: _____

Signature: _____

Address: _____

Signature of Attorney-in-Fact

By accepting or acting under the appointment, the attorney-in-fact assumes the fiduciary and other legal responsibilities of an agent.

Signature of attorney-in-fact: _____

[ATTACH NOTARY CERTIFICATE]

**Form
9NY**

New York Power of Attorney for Real Estate

CAUTION TO THE PRINCIPAL: Your Power of Attorney is an important document. As the "principal," you give the person whom you choose (your "agent") authority to spend your money and sell or dispose of your property during your lifetime without telling you. You do not lose your authority to act even though you have given your agent similar authority.

When your agent exercises this authority, he or she must act according to any instructions you have provided or, where there are no specific instructions, in your best interest. "Important Information for the Agent" at the end of this document describes your agent's responsibilities.

Your agent can act on your behalf only after signing the Power of Attorney before a notary public.

You can request information from your agent at any time. If you are revoking a prior Power of Attorney, you should provide written notice of the revocation to your prior agent(s) and to any third parties who may have acted upon it, including the financial institutions where your accounts are located.

You can revoke or terminate your Power of Attorney at any time for any reason as long as you are of sound mind. If you are no longer of sound mind, a court can remove an agent for acting improperly.

Your agent cannot make health care decisions for you. You may execute a "Health Care Proxy" to do this.

The law governing Powers of Attorney is contained in the New York General Obligations Law, Article 5, Title 15. This law is available at a law library, or online through the New York State Senate or Assembly websites, www.nysenate.gov or www.assembly.state.ny.us.

If there is anything about this document that you do not understand, you should ask a lawyer of your own choosing to explain it to you.

I, _____ [name of principal], of
_____ [city] , _____ [county],
_____ [state], appoint _____
_____ [name of agent], of _____ [city],
_____ [county], _____ [state],
to act in my place with respect to the real property described as follows:_____
_____ .

    My agent may act for me in any manner to deal with all or any part of any interest in the real property described in this document, under such terms, conditions, and covenants as my agent deems proper. My agent's powers include but are not limited to the power to:

    1. Accept as a gift or as security for a loan, reject, demand, buy, lease, receive, or otherwise acquire ownership or possession of any estate or interest in real property.

2. Sell, exchange, convey with or without covenants, quitclaim, release, surrender, mortgage, encumber, partition or consent to the partitioning of, grant options concerning, lease, sublet, or otherwise dispose of any interest in the real property described in this document.

3. Maintain, repair, improve, insure, rent, lease, and pay or contest taxes or assessments on any estate or interest in the real property described in this document.

4. Prosecute, defend, intervene in, submit to arbitration, settle, and propose or accept a compromise with respect to any claim in favor of or against me based on or involving the real property described in this document.

However, my attorney-in-fact shall not have the power to: _____

_____

_____ .

I further grant to my agent full authority to act in any manner both proper and necessary to the exercise of the foregoing powers, including _____

_____ and I ratify every act that my agent may lawfully perform in exercising those powers.

This power of attorney takes effect on _____ , and shall continue until terminated in writing, or until _____ , whichever comes first. In the event of my incapacity or death, this power of attorney shall terminate immediately.

I agree that any third party who receives a copy of this document may act under it.

Revocation of the power of attorney is not effective as to a third party until the third party has actual knowledge of the revocation. I agree to indemnify the third party for any claims that arise against the third party because of reliance on this power of attorney.

Signed: This _____ day of _____ , _____

State of: _____ County of: _____

Signature: _____ , Principal

STATE OF NEW YORK   )
) ss:
COUNTY OF _____)

On the _____ day of _____ , 20_____ , before me, the undersigned, personally appeared _____ , personally known to me or proved to me on the basis of satisfactory evidence to be the individual whose name is subscribed to the within instrument and acknowledged to me that he/she executed the same in his/her capacity, and that by his/her signature on the instrument, the individual, or the person upon behalf of which the individual acted, executed the instrument.

Notary Public: _____

IMPORTANT INFORMATION FOR THE AGENT:

When you accept the authority granted under this Power of Attorney, a special legal relationship is created between you and the principal. This relationship imposes on you legal responsibilities that continue until you resign or the Power of Attorney is terminated or revoked. You must:

(1) act according to any instructions from the principal, or, where there are no instructions, in the principal's best interest;

(2) avoid conflicts that would impair your ability to act in the principal's best interest;

(3) keep the principal's property separate and distinct from any assets you own or control, unless otherwise permitted by law;

(4) keep a record of all receipts, payments, and transactions conducted for the principal; and

(5) disclose your identity as an agent whenever you act for the principal by writing or printing the principal's name and signing your own name as "agent" in either of the following manners: (Principal's Name) by (Your Signature) as Agent, or (your signature) as Agent for (Principal's Name).

You may not use the principal's assets to benefit yourself or anyone else or make gifts to yourself or anyone else unless the principal has specifically granted you that authority in this document, which is either a Statutory Gifts Rider attached to a Statutory Short Form Power of Attorney or a Non-Statutory Power of Attorney. If you have that authority, you must act according to any instructions of the principal or, where there are no such instructions, in the principal's best interest.

You may resign by giving written notice to the principal and to any co-agent, successor agent, monitor if one has been named in this document, or the principal's guardian if one has been appointed. If there is anything about this document or your responsibilities that you do not understand, you should seek legal advice.

Liability of agent: The meaning of the authority given to you is defined in New York's General Obligations Law, Article 5, Title 15. If it is found that you have violated the law or acted outside the authority granted to you in the Power of Attorney, you may be liable under the law for your violation.

AGENT'S SIGNATURE AND ACKNOWLEDGMENT OF APPOINTMENT:

It is not required that the principal and the agent(s) sign at the same time, nor that multiple agents sign at the same time.

I, _____ , have read the foregoing Power of Attorney. I am the person identified therein as agent for the principal named therein.

I acknowledge my legal responsibilities.

Agent(s) sign(s) here: ==> _____

STATE OF NEW YORK   )
) ss:
COUNTY OF _____)

On the _____ day of _____ , 20_____ , before me, the undersigned, personally appeared _____ , personally known to me or proved to me on the basis of satisfactory evidence to be the individual whose name is subscribed to the within instrument and acknowledged to me that he/she executed the same in his/her capacity, and that by his/her signature on the instrument, the individual, or the person upon behalf of which the individual acted, executed the instrument.

Notary Public: _____

Pennsylvania Power of Attorney for Real Estate

RECORDING REQUESTED BY _____

AND WHEN RECORDED MAIL TO _____

_____

NOTICE

THE PURPOSE OF THIS POWER OF ATTORNEY IS TO GIVE THE PERSON YOU DESIGNATE (YOUR "AGENT") BROAD POWERS TO HANDLE YOUR PROPERTY, WHICH MAY INCLUDE POWERS TO SELL OR OTHERWISE DISPOSE OF ANY REAL OR PERSONAL PROPERTY WITHOUT ADVANCE NOTICE TO YOU OR APPROVAL BY YOU.

THIS POWER OF ATTORNEY DOES NOT IMPOSE A DUTY ON YOUR AGENT TO EXERCISE GRANTED POWERS, BUT WHEN POWERS ARE EXERCISED, YOUR AGENT MUST USE DUE CARE TO ACT FOR YOUR BENEFIT AND IN ACCORDANCE WITH THIS POWER OF ATTORNEY.

YOUR AGENT MAY EXERCISE THE POWERS GIVEN HERE THROUGHOUT YOUR LIFETIME, EVEN AFTER YOU BECOME INCAPACITATED, UNLESS YOU EXPRESSLY LIMIT THE DURATION OF THESE POWERS OR YOU REVOKE THESE POWERS OR A COURT ACTING ON YOUR BEHALF TERMINATES YOUR AGENT'S AUTHORITY.

YOUR AGENT MUST ACT IN ACCORDANCE WITH YOUR REASONABLE EXPECTATIONS TO THE EXTENT ACTUALLY KNOWN BY YOUR AGENT AND, OTHERWISE, IN YOUR BEST INTEREST, ACT IN GOOD FAITH AND ACT ONLY WITHIN THE SCOPE OF AUTHORITY GRANTED BY YOU IN THE POWER OF ATTORNEY.

THE LAW PERMITS YOU, IF YOU CHOOSE, TO GRANT BROAD AUTHORITY TO AN AGENT UNDER POWER OF ATTORNEY, INCLUDING THE ABILITY TO GIVE AWAY ALL OF YOUR PROPERTY WHILE YOU ARE ALIVE OR TO SUBSTANTIALLY CHANGE HOW YOUR PROPERTY IS DISTRIBUTED AT YOUR DEATH. BEFORE SIGNING THIS DOCUMENT, YOU SHOULD SEEK THE ADVICE OF AN ATTORNEY AT LAW TO MAKE SURE YOU UNDERSTAND IT.

A COURT CAN TAKE AWAY THE POWERS OF YOUR AGENT IF IT FINDS YOUR AGENT IS NOT ACTING PROPERLY.

THE POWERS AND DUTIES OF AN AGENT UNDER A POWER OF ATTORNEY ARE EXPLAINED MORE FULLY IN 20 PA.C.S. CH. 56.

IF THERE IS ANYTHING ABOUT THIS FORM THAT YOU DO NOT UNDERSTAND, YOU SHOULD ASK A LAWYER OF YOUR OWN CHOOSING TO EXPLAIN IT TO YOU.

I have read or had explained to me this notice and I understand its contents.

Signature: _____ , Principal

Date: _____

Power of Attorney for Real Estate

I, _____ [name of principal], of _____ [city],

_____ [county], _____ [state],

appoint _____ [name of attorney-in-fact], of _____

[city], _____ [county] _____ [state] to act in

my place with respect to the real property described as follows:

_____

_____

_____

_____

_____

_____

_____

_____

_____

_____

_____

_____

My attorney-in-fact may act for me in any manner to deal with all or any part of any interest in the real property described in this document, under such terms, conditions, and covenants as my attorney-in-fact deems proper. My attorney-in-fact's powers include but are not limited to the power to:

1. Accept as a gift or as security for a loan, reject, demand, buy, lease, receive, or otherwise acquire ownership or possession of any estate or interest in real property.

2. Sell, exchange, convey with or without covenants, quitclaim, release, surrender, mortgage, encumber, partition or consent to the partitioning of, grant options concerning, lease, sublet, or otherwise dispose of any interest in the real property described in this document.

3. Maintain, repair, improve, insure, rent, lease, and pay or contest taxes or assessments on any estate or interest in the real property described in this document.

4. Prosecute, defend, intervene in, submit to arbitration, settle, and propose or accept a compromise with respect to any claim in favor of or against me based on or involving the real property described in this document.

However, my attorney-in-fact shall not have the power to:

_____

_____

_____

_____

_____

_____

_____

_____

_____

_____

I further grant to my attorney-in-fact full authority to act in any manner both proper and necessary to the exercise of the foregoing powers, including _____ and I ratify every act that my attorney-in-fact may lawfully perform in exercising those powers.

This power of attorney takes effect on _____ , and shall continue until terminated in writing, or until _____ , whichever comes first. In the event of my incapacity or death, this power of attorney shall terminate immediately.

I agree that any third party who receives a copy of this document may act under it. Revocation of the power of attorney is not effective as to a third party until the third party has actual knowledge of the revocation. I agree to indemnify the third party for any claims that arise against the third party because of reliance on this power of attorney.

[Special instructions for signatures]

To ensure that the validity of your document will not be challenged, it is important that the signature clause does not begin a new page. Because pages will vary from user to user, it is your responsibility to make sure that there is at least one line of text preceding the signature clause on this page. If after printing out your document, you discover that there is no text preceding the signature clause, you will need to edit this document (perhaps by adding some paragraph returns to the previous page) so that the signature clause no longer begins the page.

Delete these instructions so they do not appear in your final document.

[End of instructions]

Signed this _____ day of _____ ,

State of _____ , County of _____

Signature: _____

Witnesses

On the date written above, the principal declared to me that this instrument is his or her financial power of attorney, and that he or she willingly executed it as a free and voluntary act. The principal signed this instrument in my presence.

Witness 1

Signature: _____

Name: _____

Address: _____

Witness 2

Signature: _____

Name: _____

Address: _____

Certificate of Acknowledgment of Notary Public

STATE OF PENNSYLVANIA)

) ss:

COUNTY OF _____)

This record was acknowledged before me on (date) _____ , by (name(s) of individual(s)), _____ ,

_____ , and _____ .

[NOTARIAL SEAL]

Signature of Notarial Officer: _____

Title of Office: _____

My commission expires: _____

Acknowledgment of Agent

I, _____ , have read the attached power of attorney and am the person identified as the agent for the principal. I hereby acknowledge that when I act as agent I shall act in accordance with the principal's reasonable expectations to the extent actually known by me and, otherwise, in the principal's best interest, act in good faith and act only within the scope of authority granted to me by the principal in the power of attorney.

Name of Agent: _____

Signature of Agent: _____

Date: _____

Preparation Statement

This document was prepared by:

Print Name: _____

Signature: _____

Address: _____

_____

Notice of Revocation of Power of Attorney

I, _____ [*your name*],

of _____ [*your city and state*],

revoke the power of attorney dated _____ , empowering

_____ [*name of your attorney-in-fact*]

to act as my attorney-in-fact. I revoke and withdraw all power and authority granted under that power of attorney.

[*if applicable*]: That power of attorney was recorded on _____ , _____ .

The reference number is _____ .

Signed: This _____ day of _____ , _____

State of: _____ County of: _____

Signature: _____ , Principal

[*ATTACH NOTARY CERTIFICATE*]

Property Worksheet

Property	Name of Any Existing Beneficiary
Real Estate (list each piece of real estate by address)	
Cash and Other Liquid Assets	
Cash	
Checking accounts	
Savings and money market accounts	
Certificates of deposit	
Alternative currencies (Bitcoin, local currencies, barter units)	
Precious metals	
Securities (not in retirement accounts)	
Mutual funds	
Listed and unlisted stocks	
Government, corporate, and municipal bonds	

Property	Name of Any Existing Beneficiary

Securities (continued)

Annuities

_____

_____

Retirement Plan Assets (IRAs, Keoghs, Roth IRAs, 401(k) and 403(b) plans)

_____

_____

Vehicles

Automobiles, trucks, and recreational vehicles

_____

_____

Planes, boats, and other vehicles

_____

Other Personal Property

Household goods

_____

_____

_____

_____

_____

Valuable clothing, jewelry, and furs

_____

_____

_____

Collectibles, including artworks, and antiques

_____

_____

Tools and equipment

_____

_____

_____

Property	Name of Any Existing Beneficiary

Other Personal Property (continued)

Livestock or other valuable animals

Money owed you (personal loans, etc.)

Death benefits

Life insurance (other than term insurance)

Miscellaneous (any personal property not listed above)

Digital Assets

(Use this section to make notes about your digital accounts and property. If you want to provide your survivors with access to these accounts, leave usernames and passwords in a separate, secured document.)

Email accounts

Social media accounts (Facebook, Twitter)

Subscriptions (Netflix, Amazon Prime, journals)

Marketplace accounts (Ebay, Etsy, Craigslist, Amazon)

Apps (for phone or tablet)

Photos, books, music, videos (online, on your phone, computer, or external drive)

File sharing and storage accounts (Dropbox, Google Docs)

Property _____ **Name of Any Existing Beneficiary** _____

Digital Assets (continued)

Financial accounts (online banking, budget programs, trading, credit monitoring)

_____

_____

Medical accounts (HMO/doctor's portals, online pharmacies)

_____

_____

Insurance accounts (online accounts for car, home, life)

_____

_____

Blogs and websites (domain names, third party hosts)

_____

_____

Utilities (online accounts for gas and electric, phone, Internet)

_____

_____

Data stored on your computer (contact lists, tax prep or financial software)

_____

_____

_____

Business Personal Property

Business ownerships (partnerships, sole proprietorships, limited partnerships, limited liability companies, corporations)

_____   _____

_____   _____

_____   _____

Intellectual property (domain names, patents, copyrights, and trademarks—including the right to receive royalties)

_____   _____

_____   _____

_____   _____

Miscellaneous receivables (mortgages, deeds of trust, or promissory notes held by you; any rents due from income property you own; and payments due for professional or personal services or property sold by you for which you have not been fully paid by the purchaser)

_____   _____

_____   _____

_____   _____

Beneficiary Worksheet

Beneficiaries of Specific Gifts in Your Will

Item: _____

    Beneficiary(ies): _____

    Address(es): _____

    Alternate Beneficiary(ies): _____

    Address(es): _____

Item: _____

    Beneficiary(ies): _____

    Address(es): _____

    Alternate Beneficiary(ies): _____

    Address(es): _____

Item: _____

    Beneficiary(ies): _____

    Address(es): _____

    Alternate Beneficiary(ies): _____

    Address(es): _____

Item: _____

    Beneficiary(ies): _____

    Address(es): _____

    Alternate Beneficiary(ies): _____

    Address(es): _____

Item: _____

    Beneficiary(ies): _____

    Address(es): _____

    Alternate Beneficiary(ies): _____

    Address(es): _____

Item: _____

    Beneficiary(ies): _____

    Address(es): _____

    Alternate Beneficiary(ies): _____

    Address(es): _____

Item: _____

    Beneficiary(ies): _____

    Address(es): _____

    Alternate Beneficiary(ies): _____

    Address(es): _____

Item: _____

    Beneficiary(ies): _____

    Address(es): _____

    Alternate Beneficiary(ies): _____

    Address(es): _____

Item: _____

    Beneficiary(ies): _____

    Address(es): _____

    Alternate Beneficiary(ies): _____

    Address(es): _____

Debts Forgiven

    Amount Forgiven: _____ Date of loan: _____

    Debtor: _____

    Amount Forgiven: _____ Date of loan: _____

    Debtor: _____

    Amount Forgiven: _____ Date of loan: _____

    Debtor: _____

    Amount Forgiven: _____ Date of loan: _____

    Debtor: _____

Residuary Beneficiary or Beneficiaries

Residuary beneficiary(ies) and percentage each one receives:

_____ _____%

_____ _____%

_____ _____%

_____ _____%

_____ _____%

_____ _____%

_____ _____%

Alternate Residuary Beneficiary or Beneficiaries

Alternate residuary beneficiary(ies) and percentage each one receives:

_____ _____%

_____ _____%

_____ _____%

_____ _____%

_____ _____%

_____ _____%

_____ _____%

> ⚠ **Do not just fill in and sign this form.** To be legally valid, your will must be printed out (using the eForm that you can access with this book) or typed, eliminating all items that don't apply to you. You cannot just fill in the blanks of this form and try to use the completed form as your will.

Will for Adult With No Children

Will of _____

I, _____ ,

a resident of _____ [*county*], State of _____ ,

declare that this is my will.

1. **Revocation.** I revoke all wills that I have previously made.

2. **Marital Status.** I am ☐ married ☐ single ☐ in a registered domestic partnership or civil union.

3. **Specific Gifts.** I make the following specific gifts:

   I leave _____

   _____

   to _____

   or, if he/she/they do/does not survive me, to _____

   _____ .

   I leave _____

   _____

   to _____

   or, if he/she/they do/does not survive me, to _____

   _____ .

   I leave _____

   _____

   to _____

   or, if he/she/they do/does not survive me, to _____

   _____ .

   I leave _____

   _____

   to _____

   or, if he/she/they do/does not survive me, to _____

   _____ .

   I leave _____

   _____

   to _____

   or, if he/she/they do/does not survive me, to _____

   _____ .

   [*repeat as needed*]

4. **Residuary Estate.** I leave my residuary estate, that is, the rest of my property not otherwise specifically and validly disposed of by this will, including lapsed or failed gifts, to _____

_____

or, if he/she/they do/does not survive me, to _____

_____ .

5. **Beneficiary Provisions.** The following terms and conditions apply to the beneficiary clauses of this will.

   A. **45-Day Survivorship Period.** As used in this will, the phrase "survive me" means to be alive or in existence as an organization on the 45th day after my death. Any beneficiary, except any alternate residuary beneficiary, must survive me to take property under this will.

   B. **Shared Gifts.** If I leave property to be shared by two or more beneficiaries, it shall be shared equally by them unless this will provides otherwise.

   If any beneficiary of a shared specific gift left in a single paragraph of the Specific Gifts clause, above, does not survive me, the gift shall be given to the surviving beneficiaries in equal shares.

   If any beneficiary of a shared residuary gift does not survive me, the residue shall be given to the surviving residuary beneficiaries in equal shares.

   C. **Encumbrances.** All property that I leave by this will shall pass subject to any encumbrances or liens on the property.

6. **Executor.** I name _____

as executor, to serve without bond. If he/she does not qualify, or ceases to serve, I name _____

_____ as executor, also to serve without bond.

   I direct that my executor take all actions legally permissible to probate this will, including filing a petition in the appropriate court for the independent administration of my estate.

   I grant to my executor the following powers, to be exercised as the executor deems to be in the best interests of my estate:

   A. To retain property, without liability for loss or depreciation resulting from such retention.

   B. To sell, lease, or exchange property and to receive or administer the proceeds as a part of my estate.

   C. To vote stock; convert bonds, notes, stocks, or other securities belonging to my estate into other securities; and to exercise all other rights and privileges of a person owning similar property.

   D. To deal with and settle claims in favor of or against my estate.

   E. To continue, maintain, operate, or participate in any business that is a part of my estate, and to incorporate, dissolve, or otherwise change the form of organization of the business.

   F. To pay all debts and taxes that may be assessed against my estate, as provided under state law.

   G. To do all other acts, which in the executor's judgment may be necessary or appropriate for the proper and advantageous management, investment, and distribution of my estate.

   These powers, authority, and discretion are in addition to the powers, authority, and discretion vested in an executor by operation of law, and may be exercised as often as deemed necessary, without approval by any court in any jurisdiction.

Signature

I subscribe my name to this will this _____ day of _____ , _____ , at
_____ [county], State of _____ .

I declare that it is my will, that I sign it willingly, that I execute it as my free and voluntary act for the
purposes expressed, and that I am of the age of majority or otherwise legally empowered to make a will
and under no constraint or undue influence.

Signature: _____

Witnesses

On this _____ day of _____ , _____ , the testator,
_____

declared to us, the undersigned, that this instrument was ☐ his ☐ her   will and requested us to act as
witnesses to it. The testator signed this will in our presence, all of us being present at the same time. We
now, at the testator's request, in the testator's presence and in the presence of each other, subscribe our
names as witnesses and each declare that we are of sound mind and of proper age to witness a will. We
further declare that we understand this to be the testator's will, and that to the best of our knowledge
the testator is of the age of majority, or is otherwise legally empowered to make a will, and appears to be
of sound mind and under no constraint or undue influence.

We declare under penalty of perjury that the foregoing is true and correct, this _____ day of
_____ , _____ , at _____ [county],
State of _____ .

Witness 1

Signature: _____

Typed or printed name: _____

Residing at: _____

City, state, zip: _____

Witness 2

Signature: _____

Typed or printed name: _____

Residing at: _____

City, state, zip: _____

> ⚠️ ***Do not just fill in and sign this form.*** To be legally valid, your will must be printed out (using the eForm that you can access with this book) or typed, eliminating all items that don't apply to you. You cannot just fill in the blanks of this form and try to use the completed form as your will.

Will for Adult With Child(ren)

Will of _____

I, _____ ,

a resident of _____ [*county*], State of _____ ,

declare that this is my will.

1. **Revocation.** I revoke all wills that I have previously made.

2. **Marital Status.** I am ☐ married ☐ single ☐ in a registered domestic partnership or civil union.

3. **Children.** I have the following natural and legally adopted children:

Name	Date of Birth

[*repeat as needed*]

4. **Specific Gifts.** I make the following specific gifts:

I leave _____

_____

to _____

or, if he/she/they do/does not survive me, to _____

_____ .

I leave _____

_____

to _____

or, if he/she/they do/does not survive me, to _____

_____ .

I leave _____

_____

to _____

or, if he/she/they do/does not survive me, to _____

_____ .

I leave _____

_____

to _____

or, if he/she/they do/does not survive me, to _____

_____ .

I leave _____

_____

to _____

or, if he/she/they do/does not survive me, to _____

_____ .

[repeat as needed]

5. **Residuary Estate.** I leave my residuary estate, that is, the rest of my property not otherwise specifically and validly disposed of by this will, including lapsed or failed gifts, to _____

_____

or, if he/she/they do/does not survive me, to _____

_____ .

6. **Beneficiary Provisions.** The following terms and conditions apply to the beneficiary clauses of this will.

   A. 45-Day Survivorship Period. As used in this will, the phrase "survive me" means to be alive or in existence as an organization on the 45th day after my death. Any beneficiary, except any alternate residuary beneficiary, must survive me to take property under this will.

   B. Shared Gifts. If I leave property to be shared by two or more beneficiaries, it shall be shared equally by them unless this will provides otherwise.

      If any beneficiary of a shared specific gift left in a single paragraph of the Specific Gifts clause, above, does not survive me, the gift shall be given to the surviving beneficiaries in equal shares.

      If any beneficiary of a shared residuary gift does not survive me, the residue shall be given to the surviving residuary beneficiaries in equal shares.

   C. Encumbrances. All property that I leave by this will shall pass subject to any encumbrances or liens on the property.

7. **Executor.** I name _____

as executor, to serve without bond. If he/she does not qualify, or ceases to serve, I name _____

_____ as executor, also to serve without bond.

   I direct that my executor take all actions legally permissible to probate this will, including filing a petition in the appropriate court for the independent administration of my estate.

   I grant to my executor the following powers, to be exercised as the executor deems to be in the best interests of my estate:

   A. To retain property, without liability for loss or depreciation resulting from such retention.

   B. To sell, lease, or exchange property and to receive or administer the proceeds as a part of my estate.

   C. To vote stock; convert bonds, notes, stocks, or other securities belonging to my estate into other securities; and to exercise all other rights and privileges of a person owning similar property.

   D. To deal with and settle claims in favor of or against my estate.

E. To continue, maintain, operate, or participate in any business that is a part of my estate, and to incorporate, dissolve, or otherwise change the form of organization of the business.

F. To pay all debts and taxes that may be assessed against my estate, as provided under state law.

G. To do all other acts, which in the executor's judgment may be necessary or appropriate for the proper and advantageous management, investment, and distribution of my estate.

These powers, authority, and discretion are in addition to the powers, authority, and discretion vested in an executor by operation of law, and may be exercised as often as deemed necessary, without approval by any court in any jurisdiction.

8. **Personal Guardian.** If at my death any of my children are minors, and a personal guardian is needed, I nominate _____ to be appointed personal guardian of my minor children. If ☐ he ☐ she cannot serve as personal guardian, I nominate _____ to be appointed personal guardian.

   I direct that no bond be required of any personal guardian.

9. **Property Guardian.** If at my death any of my children are minors, and a property guardian is needed, I appoint _____ as the property guardian of my minor children. If ☐ he ☐ she cannot serve as property guardian, I appoint _____

   as property guardian.

   I direct that no bond be required of any property guardian.

10. **Gifts Under the Uniform Transfers to Minors Act.** All property left by this will to _____

   _____ [*name of minor*] shall be

   given _____ [*name of custodian*] as

   custodian for _____ [*name of minor*]

   under the Uniform Transfers to Minors Act of _____ [*your state*].

   If _____ [*name of custodian*]

   cannot serve as custodian, _____

   [*name of successor custodian*] shall serve as custodian. If _____

   [*your state*] allows testators to choose the age at which the custodianship ends, I choose the oldest age allowed by my state's Uniform Transfers to Minors Act.

   [*repeat as needed for each young person*]

Signature

I subscribe my name to this will this _____ day of _____ , _____ , at _____ [*county*], State of _____ .

I declare that it is my will, that I sign it willingly, that I execute it as my free and voluntary act for the purposes expressed, and that I am of the age of majority or otherwise legally empowered to make a will and under no constraint or undue influence.

Signature: _____

Witnesses

On this _____ day of _____ , _____ , the testator,

_____

declared to us, the undersigned, that this instrument was ☐ his ☐ her will and requested us to act as witnesses to it. The testator signed this will in our presence, all of us being present at the same time. We now, at the testator's request, in the testator's presence and in the presence of each other, subscribe our names as witnesses and each declare that we are of sound mind and of proper age to witness a will. We further declare that we understand this to be the testator's will, and that to the best of our knowledge the testator is of the age of majority, or is otherwise legally empowered to make a will, and appears to be of sound mind and under no constraint or undue influence.

We declare under penalty of perjury that the foregoing is true and correct, this _____ day of _____ , _____ , at _____ [county],

State of _____ .

Witness 1

Signature: _____

Typed or printed name: _____

Residing at: _____

City, state, zip: _____

Witness 2

Signature: _____

Typed or printed name: _____

Residing at: _____

City, state, zip: _____

Will Codicil

First Codicil to the Will of _____

I, _____ ,

a resident of _____ [county], State of _____ ,

declare this to be the first codicil to my will dated _____ , _____ .

FIRST: I revoke the provision of Clause _____ of my will that provided:

[*include the exact will language you wish to revoke*]

_____

_____

_____

_____

_____

_____

SECOND: I add the following provision to Clause _____ of my will:

[*add whatever is desired*]

_____

_____

_____

_____

_____

_____

THIRD: In all other respects I confirm and republish my will dated _____ , _____ .

Dated: _____ , _____ .

Signature

I subscribe my name to this codicil this _____ day of _____ , _____ , at

_____ [county], State of _____ .

I declare that it is my will, that I sign it willingly, that I execute it as my free and voluntary act for the purposes expressed, and that I am of the age of majority or otherwise legally empowered to make a codicil and under no constraint or undue influence.

Signature: _____

Witnesses

On this _____ day of _____ , _____ ,

_____ [codicil maker's name]

declared to us, the undersigned, that this instrument was a codicil to ☐ his ☐ her will and requested

us to act as witnesses to it. The testator signed this codicil in our presence, all of us being present at the

same time. We now, at the testator's request, in the testator's presence and in the presence of each other,

subscribe our names as witnesses and declare we understand this to be the testator's codicil and that

to the best of our knowledge the testator is of the age of majority, or is otherwise legally empowered to

make a codicil, and appears to be of sound mind and is under no constraint or undue influence.

We declare under penalty of perjury that the foregoing is true and correct, this _____ day of

_____ , _____ , at _____ [county],

State of _____ .

Witness 1

Signature: _____

Typed or printed name: _____

Residing at: _____

City, state, zip: _____

Witness 2

Signature: _____

Typed or printed name: _____

Residing at: _____

City, state, zip: _____

Request for Death Certificate

Date: _____

_____

_____

_____

_____

[insert address of vital statistics office]

Name of deceased: _____

Date of death: _____ Place of death: _____

Place of birth: _____ Social Security number: _____

Please send me _____ certified copies of the death certificate of the above-named person. I have enclosed a check in the amount of $_____ and a stamped, self-addressed envelope. The reason for my request is to administer the affairs of the deceased's estate.

Thank you for your assistance.

Signature: _____

Printed or typed name: _____

Relationship to deceased: _____

Address: _____

_____

Home phone: _____ Work phone: _____

Notice to Creditor of Death

Date: _____

_____

_____

_____

_____

[insert name and address of creditor]

Name of deceased: _____

Deceased's address: _____

Account number: _____ Date of death: _____

To whom it may concern:

I am the representative of the decedent. Please cancel this account at once.

Please also acknowledge that you received this notice by signing a copy of this letter and returning it to me in the enclosed stamped, self-addressed envelope.

If there is any outstanding balance on this account, please notify me promptly at the address below.

Thank you for your assistance.

Signature: _____

Printed or typed name: _____

Address: _____

_____

Home phone: _____ Work phone: _____

Receipt acknowledged by:

Signature: _____

Printed or typed name: _____

Title: _____

Date: _____

Executor's Checklist

☐ **1. Inventory and Safeguard Property**

  ☐ Find the deceased person's assets and keep them safe until you distribute them.

  ☐ Using money left by the deceased person, pay necessary continuing expenses—for example, mortgage payments, utility bills, and homeowners' insurance premiums.

  ☐ If the deceased person left enough money, pay debts. If there isn't enough money to pay them all, consult a lawyer before you pay anything. State law gives certain creditors priority.

  ☐ File the will in the local probate court. You should do this whether or not you think probate court proceedings will be required.

☐ **2. Handle Day-to-Day Details**

  ☐ Terminate leases and any other outstanding contracts.

  ☐ Notify the Social Security Administration of the death if the funeral director hasn't done so. You may also need to notify other agencies, such as the Department of Veterans Affairs or the state Medicaid agency.

  ☐ Get mail forwarded to you, if necessary.

☐ **3. Decide Whether or Not Probate Is Necessary**

  ☐ Probate isn't necessary for many common assets. No probate is necessary to:
- pass real estate and other assets owned in joint tenancy to the surviving joint tenant
- transfer property to beneficiaries named on "transfer on death" deeds or registrations, and "payable on death" accounts
- transfer funds in IRAs and other retirement plans to named beneficiaries
- transfer property left to the surviving spouse (in some states)
- claim life insurance proceeds, or
- transfer assets held in trust (such as revocable living trusts or bypass trusts) to named beneficiaries.

Most states also offer streamlined probate procedures for small estates. Whether probate is necessary commonly depends upon the value of everything in the estate, minus all the assets that can be transferred outside of probate.

☐ **4. Pay Taxes**

  ☐ You must file an income tax return for the year in which the person died. If the estate goes through probate and has a certain amount of income, you'll have to file an income tax return for it, too.

  ☐ Pay estate taxes if necessary. It's unlikely, but state and federal estate tax returns may be required. For deaths in 2016, estates worth less than $5.45 million do not owe federal estate tax. However, some states collect their own estate tax on smaller estates. And some states impose inheritance tax, which is paid by the people who inherit—though surviving spouses are exempt, and the tax rates are low for close family members. Check with your state's taxing authority for details about your state's tax laws.

☐ 5. Handle Probate Proceedings, If Necessary

If probate is necessary, you'll need to:

☐ Ask the probate court to confirm you as executor (personal representative). You may want to hire a lawyer to prepare the paperwork or to help you with the process. (See below.)

☐ Send notice of the probate proceeding to the beneficiaries named in the will and, if necessary, to certain close relatives—in most cases, a surviving spouse and children—who would have been entitled to property had there been no valid will.

☐ During the probate process, which in many places takes about nine months to a year, you must manage the deceased person's property. Depending on the contents of the will and the financial condition of the estate, you may need to sell real estate or securities owned by the deceased person.

☐ Set up an estate bank account to hold money that belonged to or is owed to the deceased person—for example, paychecks or stock dividends.

☐ Notify creditors of the probate proceeding in the manner required by state law. They then have a certain amount of time—about six months, in most states—to file a claim for payment of any bills or other obligations you haven't voluntarily paid. As executor, you decide whether or not a claim is valid.

☐ Supervise the distribution of property, such as cash, personal belongings, and real estate, to the people or organizations entitled to inherit.

☐ When debts and taxes have been paid and all the property distributed to the beneficiaries, ask the probate court to formally close the estate.

☐ 6. Decide Whether to Hire a Lawyer

Many people think that probate requires hiring a lawyer. Although this is often a sensible choice, especially for estates with lots of different types of property, significant tax liabilities, or the potential for disputes among inheritors, it is not mandatory. Many courts now provide lots of useful information and instructions online. You might decide that you can handle the paperwork yourself, particularly if you are a main (or sole) beneficiary and you don't expect any complications collecting and transferring the assets.

Handling a probate court proceeding requires shuffling a lot of papers through the court clerk's office; in the vast majority of cases, there are no disputes that require a decision by a judge. You may even be able to do everything by mail. Doing a good job requires persistence and attention to tedious detail—not necessarily a law degree.

Here are some ways to get help if you decide to handle the probate yourself:

- Find out what your probate court offers. Many give out packets of forms or publish good information and forms on their websites. Court clerks commonly answer basic questions about court procedure, but they staunchly avoid saying anything that could be construed as legal advice. Some courts, however, have lawyers on staff who look over probate documents; they may point out errors in your papers and tell you how to fix them.

- Get help from a legal document preparer. Some nonlawyers have set up shop to help people deal with probate paperwork. These document preparers do not offer legal advice; they just prepare documents as you instruct them. They can also file papers with the court for you.

To find one, search online for "legal document preparation" or similar terms, or check the yellow pages for "legal document preparers." Make sure that the person you hire has lots of probate experience and can provide you with references to check out.

- Consult books written for nonlawyers. The *Executor's Guide: Settling a Loved One's Estate or Trust*, by Mary Randolph (Nolo), is a good guide to an executor's duties, but does not provide state-specific probate court instructions. *How to Probate an Estate in California: A Step-by-Step Guide*, by Julia Nissley (Nolo), leads you through the California probate process step by step. Although the forms in the book are used only in California, the book provides information that's valuable in any state.

☐ 7. Working With a Lawyer

You may want some expert help, at least once in a while. There are two basic ways to work with a lawyer:

- Hire a lawyer to act as a coach, answering your legal questions as they come up. You might also want the lawyer to do some research for you or look over documents before you file them.
- Hire a lawyer to do everything. The lawyer will be paid out of the estate. In most states, lawyers charge either a lump sum or an hourly rate—$250 or more per hour is common, but be sure you negotiate this in advance. In a few states (California, for example), a lawyer may take a certain percentage of the gross value of the deceased person's estate unless you agree, in writing, to a different fee arrangement. You should be able to find a competent lawyer who will agree to a lower fee.

Some ways to find a good lawyer:

- Talk to friends who have small businesses to see if they have a good relationship with a lawyer. That lawyer can probably recommend someone with estate planning and probate experience.
- Ask whether a local senior center has a list of recommended probate lawyers.
- Use an online lawyer directory to search for lawyers in your area. You can find Nolo's lawyer directory at www.nolo.com/lawyers.

General Notice of Death

Date: _____

_____

_____

_____

_____

[insert name and address of organization]

This letter is to notify you that _____ *[name]*

of _____

_____ *[address]*

died on _____ *[date]*. Please let me know if you would like further information.

Signature: _____

Printed or typed name: _____

Relationship to deceased: _____

Address: _____

_____

Obituary Information Fact Sheet

Name of deceased: _____

Date of death: _____ Age at death: _____

Location of death: _____

Cause of death: _____

Birthplace: _____

Address: _____

_____ Length of time in community: _____

Religious affiliation or membership: _____

High school, college, or graduate degrees: _____

_____

Professional degrees or affiliations: _____

_____

Military service: _____

Profession: _____

Interesting personal facts: _____

_____

_____

Survived by: [*Names of survivors—spouses, siblings, in-laws, children, grandchildren, etc.—and their relationship to deceased*] _____

_____

Predeceased by: [*Names of spouses, siblings, and children who predeceased and when deaths occurred*]

_____

_____

_____

Time and location of funeral arrangements and services: [*often supplied by the funeral home*] _____

_____

_____

For further information, contact: _____

_____

_____

_____

Notice to Deceased's Homeowners' Insurance Company

Date: _____

_____

_____

_____

_____

[*insert insurance company name and address*]

Name of deceased: _____

Address: _____

_____ Date of death: _____

Homeowners' insurance policy number: _____

This letter is to notify you that your insured, _____

_____ [*deceased's name*], has died. I am

the executor of the estate and would like to be added as a named insured to this homeowners' insurance

policy. Enclosed with this letter you will find a certified death certificate, along with documentation that I

am the executor.

Please contact me so that we may discuss this matter. I can be reached using the information below.

Please sign and return the copy of this letter in the enclosed stamped and self-addressed envelope.

Thank you for your assistance.

Signature: _____

Printed or typed name: _____

Relationship to deceased: _____

Address: _____

_____ Home phone: _____

Work phone: _____ Email: _____

Receipt acknowledged by:

Signature: _____

Printed or typed name: _____

Title: _____

Date of receipt of notice: _____

Notice to Deceased's Vehicle Insurance Company

Date: _____

_____

_____

_____

_____

[insert insurance company name and address]

Name of deceased: _____

Address: _____

Date of death: _____

Vehicle insurance policy number: _____

Make, model, and year of vehicle: _____

This letter is to notify you that your insured, _____

_____ *[deceased's name]*, has died.

I am the executor of the estate and would like to be added as a named insured to this insurance policy. Enclosed with this letter you will find a certified death certificate for _____

_____ *[deceased's name]*, documentation of my

status as executor, and a state-certified copy of my driving record.

Please contact me so that we may discuss this matter. I can be reached using the information below. Please sign and return the second copy of this letter in the enclosed stamped and self-addressed envelope.

Thank you for your assistance.

Signature: _____

Printed or typed name: _____

Relationship to deceased: _____

Address: _____

_____ Home phone: _____

Work phone: _____ Email: _____

Receipt acknowledged by:

Signature: _____

Printed or typed name: _____

Title: _____

Date of receipt of notice: _____

Rental Application

Separate application required from each applicant age 18 or older.

Date and time received by landlord _____

Credit check fee _____ Received _____

THIS SECTION TO BE COMPLETED BY LANDLORD

Address of Property to Be Rented: _____

Rental Term: ☐ month-to-month ☐ lease from _____ to _____

Amounts Due Prior to Occupancy

First month's rent .... $_____

Security deposit .... $_____

Other (specify): _____ $_____

TOTAL... $_____

Applicant

Full Name—include all names you use(d): _____

Home Phone: _____ Work Phone: _____

Cell Phone: _____ Email: _____

Fax:* _____ Social Security Number: _____

Driver's License Number/State: _____

Other Identifying Information: _____

Vehicle Make: _____ Model: _____ Color: _____

Year: _____ License Plate Number/State: _____

Additional Occupants

List everyone, including minor children, who will live with you:

Full Name	**Relationship to Applicant**

Rental History

FIRST-TIME RENTERS: ATTACH A DESCRIPTION OF YOUR HOUSING SITUATION FOR THE PAST FIVE YEARS.

Current Address: _____

Dates Lived at Address: _____ Rent $_____ Security Deposit $_____

Landlord/Manager: _____

Landlord/Manager's Phone: _____

Reason for Leaving: _____

* By providing this fax number I agree to receive facsimile advertisements from the landlord or management company.

Previous Address: _____

Dates Lived at Address: _____ Rent $ _____ Security Deposit $ _____

Landlord/Manager: _____

Landlord/Manager's Phone: _____

Reason for Leaving: _____

Previous Address: _____

Dates Lived at Address: _____ Rent $ _____ Security Deposit $ _____

Landlord/Manager: _____

Landlord/Manager's Phone: _____

Reason for Leaving: _____

Employment History

SELF-EMPLOYED APPLICANTS: ATTACH TAX RETURNS FOR THE PAST TWO YEARS.

Name and Address of Current Employer: _____

_____ Phone: (___) _____

Name of Supervisor: _____ Supervisor's Phone: (___) _____

Dates Employed at This Job: _____ Position or Title: _____

Name and Address of Previous Employer: _____

_____ Phone: (___) _____

Name of Supervisor: _____ Supervisor's Phone: (___) _____

Dates Employed at This Job: _____ Position or Title: _____

ATTACH PAY STUBS FOR THE PAST TWO YEARS, FROM THIS EMPLOYER OR PRIOR EMPLOYERS.

Income

1. Your gross monthly employment income (before deductions): $_____

2. Average monthly amounts of other income (specify sources): $_____

   _____ $_____

   _____ $_____

                                    TOTAL: $_____

Bank/Financial Accounts

	Account Number	Bank/Institution	Branch
Savings Account:			
Money Market or Similar Account:			

Credit Card Accounts

Major Credit Card: ☐ VISA ☐ MC ☐ Discover Card ☐ Am Ex ☐ Other: _____

Issuer: _____ Account No. _____

Balance $_____ Average Monthly Payment $ _____

Major Credit Card: ☐ VISA ☐ MC ☐ Discover Card ☐ Am Ex ☐ Other: _____

Issuer: _____ Account No. _____

Balance $_____ Average Monthly Payment $ _____

Loans

Type of Loan (mortgage, car, student loan, etc.)	Name of Creditor	Account Number	Amount Owed	Monthly Payment

Other Major Obligations

Type	Payee		Amount Owed	Monthly Payment

Miscellaneous

Describe the number and type of pets you want to have in the rental property: _____

_____ .

Describe water-filled furniture you want to have in the rental property: _____

_____ .

Do you smoke?   ☐ yes   ☐ no

Have you ever: Filed for bankruptcy?   ☐ yes   ☐ no   How many times _____

Been sued?   ☐ yes   ☐ no   How many times _____

Sued someone else?   ☐ yes   ☐ no   How many times _____

Been evicted?   ☐ yes   ☐ no   How many times _____

Been convicted of a crime?   ☐ yes   ☐ no   How many times _____

Explain any "yes" listed above: _____

_____

_____

_____

References and Emergency Contact

Personal Reference: _____ Relationship: _____

Address: _____

_____ Phone: (_____) _____

Personal Reference: _____ Relationship: _____

Address: _____

_____ Phone: (_____) _____

Contact in Emergency: _____ Relationship: _____

Address: _____

_____ Phone: (_____) _____

Source

Where did you learn of this vacancy? _____

_____

I certify that all the information given above is true and correct and understand that my lease or rental agreement may be terminated if I have made any material false or incomplete statements in this application. I authorize verification of the information provided in this application from my credit sources, credit bureaus, current and previous landlords and employers, and personal references. This permission will survive the expiration of my tenancy.

_____   _____

Applicant   Date

Notes (Landlord/Manager): _____

_____

_____

_____

_____

_____

_____

Tenant References

Name of Applicant: _____

Address of Rental Unit: _____

Previous Landlord or Manager

Contact (name, property owner or manager, address of rental unit): _____

_____

_____

Date: _____

Questions

When did tenant rent from you (move-in and move-out dates)?_____

What was the monthly rent? _____ Did tenant pay rent on time? ☐ yes ☐ no

If rent was not paid on time, did you have to give tenant a legal notice demanding the rent? ☐ yes ☐ no

If rent was not paid on time, provide details _____

_____

Did you give tenant notice of any lease violation for other than nonpayment of rent? ☐ yes ☐ no

If you gave a lease violation notice, what was the outcome? _____

Was tenant considerate of neighbors—that is, no loud parties and fair, careful use of common areas?

_____

Did tenant have any pets? ☐ yes ☐ no

If so, were there any problems? _____

Did tenant make any unreasonable demands or complaints? ☐ yes ☐ no

If so, explain: _____

_____

Why did tenant leave? _____

Did tenant give the proper amount of notice before leaving? ☐ yes ☐ no

Did tenant leave the place in good condition? ☐ yes ☐ no

Did you need to use the security deposit to cover damage? ☐ yes ☐ no

Any particular problems you'd like to mention? _____

Would you rent to this person again? ☐ yes ☐ no

Other comments: _____

_____

Previous Landlord or Manager

When did tenant rent from you (move-in and move-out dates)?_____

What was the monthly rent? _____ Did tenant pay rent on time? ☐ yes ☐ no

If rent was not paid on time, did you have to give tenant a legal notice demanding the rent? ☐ yes ☐ no

If rent was not paid on time, provide details: _____

_____

Did you give tenant notice of any lease violation for other than nonpayment of rent? ☐ yes ☐ no

If you gave a lease violation notice, what was the outcome? _____

Was tenant considerate of neighbors—that is, no loud parties and fair, careful use of common areas?

_____

Did tenant have any pets? ☐ yes ☐ no

If so, were there any problems? _____

Did tenant make any unreasonable demands or complaints? ☐ yes ☐ no

If so, explain: _____

_____

Why did tenant leave? _____

Did tenant give the proper amount of notice before leaving? ☐ yes ☐ no

Did tenant leave the place in good condition? ☐ yes ☐ no

Did you need to use the security deposit to cover damage? ☐ yes ☐ no

Any particular problems you'd like to mention? _____

Would you rent to this person again? ☐ yes ☐ no

Other comments: _____

_____

Employment Verification

Contact (name, company, position): _____

Date: _____

Salary: _____

Dates of Employment: _____

Comments: _____

_____

_____

Personal Reference

Contact (name and relationship to applicant): _____

Date: _____

How long have you known the applicant? _____

Would you recommend this person as a prospective tenant? ☐ yes ☐ no

Comments: _____

_____

_____

Credit and Financial Information

_____

_____

_____

_____

_____

_____

_____

_____

_____

_____

Notes, Including Reasons for Rejecting Applicant

_____

_____

_____

_____

_____

_____

_____

_____

_____

_____

_____

_____

Landlord-Tenant Checklist

GENERAL CONDITION OF RENTAL UNIT AND PREMISES

Street Address _____ Unit No. ____ City _____

	Condition on Arrival	Condition on Departure	Estimated Cost of Cleaning/Repair/Replacement
Living Room			
Floors & Floor Coverings			
Drapes & Window Coverings			
Walls & Ceilings			
Light Fixtures			
Windows, Screens, & Doors			
Front Door & Locks			
Fireplace			
Other			
Other			
Kitchen			
Floors & Floor Coverings			
Walls & Ceilings			
Light Fixtures			
Cabinets			
Counters			
Stove/Oven			
Refrigerator			
Dishwasher			
Garbage Disposal			
Sink & Plumbing			
Windows, Screens, & Doors			
Other			
Other			
Dining Room			
Floors & Floor Covering			
Walls & Ceilings			
Light Fixtures			
Windows, Screens, & Doors			
Other			

	Condition on Arrival		Condition on Departure		Estimated Cost of Cleaning/Repair/ Replacement
Bathroom(s)	Bath #1	Bath #2	Bath #1	Bath #2	
Floors & Floor Coverings					
Walls & Ceilings					
Windows, Screens, & Doors					
Light Fixtures					
Bathtub/Shower					
Sink & Counters					
Toilet					
Other					
Other					

	Condition on Arrival			Condition on Departure			Estimated Cost of Cleaning/Repair/ Replacement
Bedroom(s)	Bdrm #1	Bdrm #2	Bdrm #3	Bdrm #1	Bdrm #2	Bdrm #3	
Floors & Floor Coverings							
Windows, Screens, & Doors							
Walls & Ceilings							
Light Fixtures							
Other							
Other							
Other							
Other							
Other Areas							
Heating System							
Air-Conditioning							
Lawn/Garden							
Stairs and Hallway							
Patio, Terrace, Deck, etc.							
Basement							
Parking Area							
Other							
Other							
Other							
Other							
Other							

☐ Tenants acknowledge that all smoke detectors and fire extinguishers were tested in their presence and found to be in working order, and that the testing procedure was explained to them. Tenants agree to test all detectors at least once a month and to report any problems to Landlord/Manager in writing. Tenants agree to replace all smoke detector batteries as necessary.

FURNISHED PROPERTY

	Condition on Arrival			Condition on Departure			Estimated Cost of Cleaning/Repair/ Replacement
Living Room							
Coffee Table							
End Tables							
Lamps							
Chairs							
Sofa							
Other							
Other							
Kitchen							
Broiler Pan							
Ice Trays							
Other							
Other							
Dining Room							
Chairs							
Stools							
Table							
Other							
Other							
Bathroom(s)	Bath #1	Bath #2		Bath #1	Bath #2		
Mirrors							
Shower Curtain							
Hamper							
Other							
Bedroom(s)	Bdrm #1	Bdrm #2	Bdrm #3	Bdrm #1	Bdrm #2	Bdrm #3	
Beds (single)							
Beds (double)							
Chairs							
Chests							
Dressing Tables							
Lamps							
Mirrors							
Night Tables							

	Condition on Arrival	Condition on Departure	Estimated Cost of Cleaning/Repair/ Replacement
Other			
Other			
Other Areas			
Bookcases			
Desks			
Pictures			
Other			
Other			

Use this space to provide any additional explanation:

_____

_____

_____

_____

_____

_____

_____

Landlord-Tenant Checklist completed on moving in on _____ and approved by:

_____ and _____
Landlord/Manager   Tenant

_____
Tenant

_____
Tenant

Landlord-Tenant Checklist completed on moving out on _____
and approved by:

_____ and _____
Landlord/Manager   Tenant

_____
Tenant

_____
Tenant

Move-In Letter

Date: _____

Tenant: _____

Street Address: _____

City and State: _____

Dear: _____ ,
                      Tenant

Welcome to _____

_____ [*address of rental unit*]. We hope you will enjoy living here.

This letter is to explain what you can expect from the management and what we'll be looking for from you.

1. Rent: _____
   _____
   _____ .

2. New Roommates: _____
   _____
   _____
   _____ .

3. Notice to End Tenancy: _____
   _____
   _____
   _____ .

4. Deposits: _____
   _____
   _____ .

5. Manager: _____
   _____
   _____
   _____ .

6. Landlord-Tenant Checklist: _____
   _____
   _____
   _____
   _____
   _____ .

7. Maintenance/Repair Problems: _____

_____

_____

_____

_____

_____

8. Semiannual Safety and Maintenance Update: _____

_____

_____

_____

_____

9. Annual Safety Inspection: _____

_____

_____

_____

10. Insurance: _____

_____

_____

_____

_____

11. Moving Out: _____

_____

_____

_____

12. Telephone Number Changes: _____

_____

_____

Please let us know if you have any questions.

Sincerely,

_____   _____
Landlord/Manager   Date

I have read and received a copy of this statement.

_____   _____
Tenant   Date

Notice of Needed Repairs

To: _____ [*name of landlord or manager*]

At: _____ [*address*]

From: _____ [*tenant*]

At: _____ [*address*]

I am writing to inform you of the following problem(s) in my rental unit:

_____

_____

_____

_____

_____

_____

_____

_____

_____

_____

_____

_____

_____

_____

_____

_____

_____ .

I would very much appreciate it if you would promptly look into the problem(s). Please contact me so that I'll know when to expect you or a repairperson. You can reach me as follows:

Work (daytime): _____ Home (evenings): _____

Email: _____

Thank you very much for your attention to this problem.

Signature: _____ Date: _____
                [*tenant*]

Semiannual Safety and Maintenance Update

Please complete the following checklist and note any safety or maintenance problems in your unit or on the premises.

Please describe the specific problems and the rooms or areas involved. Here are some examples of the types of things we want to know about: garage roof leaks, excessive mildew in rear bedroom closet, fuses blow out frequently, door lock sticks, water comes out too hot in shower, exhaust fan above stove doesn't work, smoke alarm malfunctions, peeling paint, and mice in basement. Please point out any potential safety and security problems in the neighborhood and anything you consider a serious nuisance.

Please indicate the approximate date when you first noticed the problem and list any other recommendations or suggestions for improvement.

Please return this form with this month's rent check. Thank you.—THE MANAGEMENT

Name: _____

Address: _____

_____

Please indicate (and explain below) problems with:

- ☐ Floors and floor coverings _____
- ☐ Walls and ceilings _____
- ☐ Windows, screens, and doors _____
- ☐ Window coverings (drapes, miniblinds, etc.) _____
- ☐ Electrical system and light fixtures _____
- ☐ Plumbing (sinks, bathtub, shower, or toilet) _____
- ☐ Heating or air-conditioning system _____
- ☐ Major appliances (stove, oven, dishwasher, refrigerator) _____
- ☐ Basement or attic _____
- ☐ Locks or security system _____
- ☐ Smoke detector _____
- ☐ Fireplace _____
- ☐ Cupboards, cabinets, and closets _____
- ☐ Furnishings (table, bed, mirrors, chairs) _____
- ☐ Laundry facilities _____
- ☐ Elevator _____
- ☐ Stairs and handrails _____
- ☐ Hallway, lobby, and common areas _____
- ☐ Garage _____
- ☐ Patio, terrace, or deck _____
- ☐ Lawn, fences, and grounds _____

☐ Pool and recreational facilities _____ Page 2 of 2

☐ Roof, exterior walls, and other structural elements_____

☐ Driveway and sidewalks _____

☐ Neighborhood _____

☐ Nuisances _____

☐ Other _____

_____

Specifics of problems: _____

_____

_____

_____

_____

Other comments: _____

_____

_____

_____

_____

_____

_____   _____

Tenant   Date

....

FOR MANAGEMENT USE

Action/Response: _____

_____

_____

_____

_____

_____

_____

_____

_____   _____

Landlord/Manager   Date

Landlord-Tenant Agreement to Terminate Lease

Landlord: _____ and

Tenant: _____

agree that the lease they entered into for the time period of _____ , _____ ,

to _____ , _____ , for premises at _____

_____ ,

will terminate on _____ .

Additional conditions for cancellation of lease: _____

_____

_____

Landlord's signature: _____ Date: _____

Print name: _____

Tenant 1's signature: _____ Date: _____

Print name: _____

Tenant 2's signature: _____ Date: _____

Print name: _____

Tenant 3's signature: _____ Date: _____

Print name: _____

Consent to Assignment of Lease

Landlord: _____

Tenant: _____

Assignee: _____

Landlord, Tenant, and Assignee agree as follows:

1. **Location of Premises**

    Tenant has leased the premises located at _____ from Landlord.

2. **Lease Beginning and Ending Dates**

    The lease was signed on _____ , _____ .

    It will expire on _____ , _____ .

3. **Assignment**

    Tenant is assigning the balance of Tenant's lease to Assignee, beginning on _____ ,

    _____ . It will end on _____ , _____ .

4. **Tenant's Future Liability**

    Tenant's financial responsibilities under the terms of the lease are ended by this assignment.
    Specifically, Tenant's responsibilities for future rent and future damage are ended.

5. **Tenant's Right to Occupy**

    As of the effective date of the assignment, Tenant permanently gives up the right to occupy the premises.

6. **Binding Nature of Agreement**

    Assignee is bound by every term and condition in the lease that is the subject of this assignment.

Landlord's signature: _____ Date: _____

Print name: _____

Tenant's signature: _____ Date: _____

Print name: _____

Assignee's signature: _____ Date: _____

Print name: _____

Tenant's Notice of Intent to Move Out

Date: _____

Landlord: _____

Street Address: _____

City and State: _____

Dear: _____ [*name of landlord*]:

This is to notify you that the undersigned tenants, _____

_____ , will be moving from

_____ ,

on _____ , or _____ days from today. This

provides at least _____ days' written notice as required in our rental

agreement.

Sincerely,

Tenant: _____

Tenant: _____

Tenant: _____

Demand for Return of Security Deposit

Date: _____

_____

_____

_____

_____

[*insert landlord's name and address*]

Dear _____ [*name of landlord*]:

On _____ [*date*], we vacated the rental unit at _____

_____

_____ [*address*]

and gave you our new address and phone number. As of today, we haven't received our $ _____

[*amount of security deposit owed*] security deposit, nor any accounting from you for that money. We were

entitled to receive our deposit by _____ [*date when deposit*

was due]. You are now _____ [*number of days or weeks*] late.

We left our rental unit clean and undamaged, paid all of our rent, and gave you proper notice of our intention to move. In these circumstances, it's difficult to understand your oversight in not promptly returning our money.

Perhaps your check is in the mail. If not, please send it promptly. Should we fail to hear from you by

_____ [*date*], we'll take this matter to small claims court. And please

understand that if we are compelled to do this, we will also sue you for any costs and additional punitive damages allowed by state law.

Please mail our deposit immediately to the above address. If you have any questions, please contact us at the number below.

Very truly yours,

Signature of tenant: _____ Date: _____

Signature of tenant: _____ Date: _____

Address: _____

_____

Home phone: _____ Cell or other phone: _____

Loan Comparison Worksheet

Purpose of loan: _____

Desired amount of loan: $ _____

	Loan 1	Loan 2	Loan 3
General Information			
Lender:	_____	_____	_____
Contact:	_____	_____	_____
Address:	_____	_____	_____
	_____	_____	_____
	_____	_____	_____
Loan Terms			
APR:	_____ %	_____ %	_____ %
Interest rate:	_____ %	_____ %	_____ %
Adjustable?	_____	_____	_____
Cap:	_____ %	_____ %	_____ %
No. of months:	_____	_____	_____
Monthly payment:	$ _____	$ _____	$ _____
Total payments (# of mos. × monthly payment):	$ _____	$ _____	$ _____
Other Costs			
Loan application fee:	$ _____	$ _____	$ _____
Credit check fee:	$ _____	$ _____	$ _____
Credit insurance:	$ _____	$ _____	$ _____
Other:	$ _____	$ _____	$ _____
Other Features			
Collateral required?	_____	_____	_____
If yes, specify:	_____	_____	_____
Balloon payment?	_____	_____	_____
Prepayment penalty?	_____	_____	_____
If yes, amount:	_____	_____	_____
Cosigner required?	_____	_____	_____
Payment due date:	_____	_____	_____
Grace period?	_____	_____	_____
Late fee?	_____	_____	_____
Possible loan discounts:	_____	_____	_____
Account with lender:	_____	_____	_____
Automatic deduction:	_____	_____	_____
On-time payments:	_____	_____	_____

Authorization to Check Credit and Employment References

I, the undersigned borrower, _____ [*name of borrower*],

authorize _____ [*name*]

_____ [*address*]

_____ [*phone*] to verify my employment, financial, and credit information

provided on this form.

Borrower

Full name—include generations (Jr., Sr., III): _____

Other names used: _____

Street address: _____

Mailing address: _____

City, state, and zip code: _____

Date moved into current address: _____

Home phone: _____

Previous address: _____

City, state, and zip code: _____

Dates there: _____

Date of birth: _____ Social Security number: _____

Driver's license number: _____

Employment History

Name and address of current employer: _____

_____

Position/title: _____

Name of supervisor: _____

Supervisor's phone: _____

Annual gross income: _____

Previous employment (if at current job less than 18 months): _____

_____

Credit and Financial Information

Bank/Financial Accounts

Provide account number, bank/institution, branch address.

Bank savings account: _____

_____

Bank checking account: _____

_____

Bank certificate of deposit: _____

_____

Mutual fund account: _____

_____

Brokerage account: _____

_____

Other: _____

_____

Other: _____

_____

Other: _____

_____

Credit Accounts & Loans

Provide type of account (auto loan, Visa, etc.), account number, name and address of creditor, amount owed, and monthly payment.

Credit card: _____

Credit card: _____

Loan (specify type): _____

Loan (specify type): _____

Loan (specify type): _____

Other (specify type): _____

I certify that the information given above is true and correct. I authorize the above employers, financial institutions, and creditors to verify my employment, financial, and credit information provided above, and to provide correct information if the above is incorrect. A copy of this signed form is valid for this purpose.

Signature of Borrower: _____ Date: _____

Monthly Payment Record

Name of lender: _____

Name of borrower: _____

Original amount borrowed: _____ Date loan made: _____

Month	(A) Beginning balance (or prior month ending balance)	(B) Annual interest rate divided by 12	(C) Interest due (A) × (B)	(D) Amount of payment made	(E) Principal reduction (D) – (C)	(F) New balance (A) – (E)
1						
2						
3						
4						
5						
6						
7						
8						
9						
10						
11						
12						
13						
14						
15						
16						
17						
18						
19						
20						
21						
22						
23						
24						
25						
26						
27						
28						
29						
30						

Promissory Note

Loan repayable in installments with interest

1. Borrower(s)

_____ [name of borrower 1]

_____ [name of borrower 2]

2. Lender

_____ [name of lender]

3. Loan

In return for a loan Borrower has received from Lender, Borrower promises to pay to Lender the amount of $_____ (principal), plus interest on unpaid principal at the rate of _____% per year from the date this note is signed until it is paid in full. If there is more than one borrower, they agree to be jointly and severally liable.

4. Monthly Payments

Borrower will pay back the loan in monthly installments, which include principal and interest, of not less than $_____ per month until the principal and interest are paid in full. Payments will be due on the first day of each month, beginning on _____ [date on which first installment payment is due]. Borrower will send all payments to _____ _____ [address where payments are to be sent].

5. Prepayments

Borrower may make extra payments of principal, in addition to the monthly installment payments, at any time. Borrower will identify any such payments, in writing, as prepayments of principal. Lender will use any prepayments to reduce the amount of principal owed by Borrower. Prepayments will not change the amount or due date of any future installment payments.

6. Late Payments

If any installment payment due under this note is not received by Lender within _____ days of its due date, Borrower will pay a late fee of five percent of the amount of the monthly payment. The late fee will be due immediately.

If any installment payment is not received by Lender within _____ days of its due date, Lender may demand, in writing, that Borrower repay the entire amount of unpaid principal immediately. After receiving Lender's demand, Borrower will immediately pay the entire unpaid principal.

7. Attorneys' Fees

If Lender sues Borrower to collect on this note, and wins, Borrower agrees to pay Lender's attorneys' fees in an amount the court finds to be fair and reasonable.

8. Entire Agreement

This note represents the entire agreement between Borrower and Lender. Any modifications must be in writing and signed by both Borrower and Lender.

9. Terminology

The term Borrower refers to one or more borrowers. The term Lender refers to more than one lender and to any person who legally holds this note, including a buyer in due course.

Borrowers' Signature(s)

Name: _____ Date: _____

Signature: _____

Location: [city or county where signed]_____

Name: _____ Date: _____

Signature: _____

Location: [city or county where signed]_____

[ATTACH NOTARY CERTIFICATE WHERE APPLICABLE]

Promissory Note

Loan repayable in installments with interest and balloon payment

1. Borrower(s)

_____ [name of borrower 1]

_____ [name of borrower 2]

2. Lender

_____ [name of lender]

3. Loan

In return for a loan Borrower has received from Lender, Borrower promises to pay to Lender the amount of $_____ (principal), plus interest on unpaid principal at the rate of _____% per year from the date this note is signed until it is paid in full. If there is more than one borrower, they agree to be jointly and severally liable.

4. Installment Payments and Balloon Payment

Borrower will make monthly installment payments, which include principal and interest, of not less than $_____ , beginning on _____ [date by which first installment payment must be made] and continuing on the first day of each month until _____ [date of the last regular monthly payment before "balloon" payment becomes due]. Borrower agrees to pay the remaining principal and interest on or before _____ [date on which the "balloon" payment is due]. Borrower will send all payments to _____ _____ [address where payments are to be sent].

5. Prepayments

Borrower may make extra payments of principal, in addition to the monthly installment payments, at any time. Borrower will identify any such payments, in writing, as prepayments of principal. Lender will use any prepayments to reduce the amount of principal owed by Borrower. Prepayments will not change the amount or due date of any future installment payments.

6. Late Payments

If any installment payment due under this note is not received by Lender within _____ days of its due date, Borrower will pay a late fee of five percent of the amount of the monthly payment. The late fee will be due immediately.

7. Attorneys' Fees

If Lender sues Borrower to collect on this note, and wins, Borrower agrees to pay Lender's attorneys' fees in an amount the court finds to be fair and reasonable.

8. Entire Agreement

This note represents the entire agreement between Borrower and Lender. Any modifications must be in writing and signed by both Borrower and Lender.

9. Terminology

The term Borrower refers to one or more borrowers. The term Lender refers to more than one lender and to any person who legally holds this note, including a buyer in due course.

Borrowers' Signature(s)

Name: _____ Date: _____

Signature: _____

Location: [*city or county where signed*]_____

Name: _____ Date: _____

Signature: _____

Location: [*city or county where signed*]_____

[ATTACH NOTARY CERTIFICATE WHERE APPLICABLE]

nolo
NOLO
© www.nolo.com

Form 37: Promissory Note
Installment Payments With Interest and Balloon Payment

Page 2 of 2

Promissory Note

Loan repayable in installments without interest

1. Borrower(s)

_____ [*name of borrower 1*]

_____ [*name of borrower 2*]

2. Lender

_____ [*name of lender*]

3. Loan

In return for a loan Borrower has received from Lender, Borrower promises to pay to Lender the amount of $_____ (principal). If there is more than one borrower, they agree to be jointly and severally liable.

4. Monthly Payments

Borrower will make equal installments of $_____ per month until the principal is paid in full. Payments will be due on the first day of each month, beginning on _____ [*date on which first payment is due*]. Borrower will send all payments to _____ _____ [*address where payments are to be sent*].

5. Late Payments

If any installment payment due under this note is not received by Lender within _____ days of its due date, Borrower will pay a late fee of five percent of the amount of the monthly payment. The late fee will be due immediately.

If any installment payment is not received by Lender within _____ days of its due date, Lender may demand that Borrower repay the entire amount of unpaid principal immediately. If Lender notifies Borrower, in writing, that the entire amount is now due and payable, Borrower will immediately pay the entire unpaid principal.

6. Attorneys' Fees

If Lender sues Borrower to collect on this note, and wins, Borrower agrees to pay Lender's attorneys' fees in an amount the court finds to be fair and reasonable.

7. Entire Agreement

This note represents the entire agreement between Borrower and Lender. Any modifications must be in writing and signed by both Borrower and Lender.

8. Terminology

The term Borrower refers to one or more borrowers. The term Lender refers to more than one lender and to any person who legally holds this note, including a buyer in due course.

Borrowers' Signature(s)

Name: _____ Date: _____

Signature: _____

Location: [*city or county where signed*]_____

Name: _____ Date: _____

Signature: _____

Location: [*city or county where signed*]_____

[ATTACH NOTARY CERTIFICATE WHERE APPLICABLE]

Promissory Note

Loan repayable in lump sum with interest

1. Borrower(s)

_____ [*name of borrower 1*]

_____ [*name of borrower 2*]

2. Lender

_____ [*name of lender*]

3. Loan

In return for a loan Borrower has received from Lender, Borrower promises to pay to Lender the amount of $_____ (principal), plus interest on unpaid principal at the rate of _____% per year from the date this note is signed until it is paid in full. If there is more than one borrower, they agree to be jointly and severally liable.

4. Due Date and Repayment Terms

Borrower will repay the entire amount by _____ . Borrower will send payment to _____ [*address where payment is to be sent*].

5. Prepayments

Borrower may make payments of principal at any time before the loan is due. Borrower will identify any such payments, in writing, as prepayments of principal. Lender will use any prepayments to reduce the amount of principal owed by Borrower.

6. Attorneys' Fees

If Lender sues Borrower to collect on this note, and wins, Borrower agrees to pay Lender's attorneys' fees in an amount the court finds to be fair and reasonable.

7. Entire Agreement

This note represents the entire agreement between Borrower and Lender. Any modifications must be in writing and signed by both Borrower and Lender.

8. Terminology

The term Borrower refers to one or more borrowers. The term Lender refers to more than one lender and to any person who legally holds this note, including a buyer in due course.

Borrowers' Signature(s)

Name: _____ Date: _____

Signature: _____

Location: [*city or county where signed*]_____

Name: _____ Date: _____

Signature: _____

Location: [*city or county where signed*]_____

[ATTACH NOTARY CERTIFICATE WHERE APPLICABLE]

Promissory Note

Loan repayable in lump sum without interest

1. Borrower(s)

_____ [*name of borrower 1*]

_____ [*name of borrower 2*]

2. Lender

_____ [*name of lender*]

3. Loan

In return for a loan Borrower has received from Lender, Borrower promises to pay to Lender the amount of $_____ by _____ [*date on which payment is due*] at _____ [*address where payment is to be sent*]. If there is more than one borrower, they agree to be jointly and severally liable.

4. Attorneys' Fees

If Lender sues Borrower to collect on this note, and wins, Borrower agrees to pay Lender's attorneys' fees in an amount the court finds to be fair and reasonable.

5. Entire Agreement

This note represents the entire agreement between Borrower and Lender. Any modifications must be in writing and signed by both Borrower and Lender.

6. Terminology

The term Borrower refers to one or more borrowers. The term Lender refers to more than one lender and to any person who legally holds this note, including a buyer in due course.

Borrowers' Signature(s)

Name: _____ Date: _____

Signature: _____

Location: [*city or county where signed*]_____

Name: _____ Date: _____

Signature: _____

Location: [*city or county where signed*]_____

[*ATTACH NOTARY CERTIFICATE WHERE APPLICABLE*]

Cosigner Provision

Name of Cosigner 1: _____

Name of Cosigner 2: _____

Name of Borrower 1: _____

Name of Borrower 2: _____

Name of Lender: _____

1. Borrower has agreed to pay Lender the amount indicated in the attached Promissory Note under the terms specified in that Note.

2. Cosigner agrees to guarantee this debt and understands this obligation means the following:

   - If Borrower doesn't pay the debt on time, that fact may become a part of Cosigner's credit record.
   - If Borrower doesn't pay the debt at all, Cosigner will be legally obligated to do so.
   - Cosigner may have to pay late fees or collection costs, which will increase the amount due.
   - Lender can collect this debt from Cosigner without first trying to collect from Borrower.
   - Lender can use the same collection methods against Cosigner that can be used against Borrower, including filing a lawsuit against Cosigner, and if the lawsuit is successful, garnishing Cosigner's wages, seizing other personal property of Cosigner, and putting a lien against Cosigner's house.

The term Cosigner refers to one or more cosigners. If there is more than one cosigner, they agree to be jointly and severally liable.

Cosigner 1's signature: _____ Date: _____

Print name: _____

Location [*city or county where signed*]: _____

Address: _____

Cosigner 2's signature: _____ Date: _____

Print name: _____

Location [*city or county where signed*]: _____

Address: _____

Security Agreement Provision for Promissory Note

Here are some examples of the kind of language to include in the security agreement provision.

[If a vehicle is security, use this language:]

Borrower agrees that until the principal and interest owed under this note are paid in full, the note is secured by the following security agreement:

Security agreement signed by: _____ *[name of owner]* on: _____ *[date signed]*, which gives title to:

_____ *[date, make, model, and VIN of vehicle]*.

[If other valuable personal property is security, use this language:]

Borrower agrees that until the principal and interest owed under this note are paid in full, the note is secured by the following security agreement:

Security agreement signed by: _____ *[name of owner]* on: _____ *[date signed]*, which gives a security interest in:

_____

_____ *[description of the personal property used as collateral]*.

Security Agreement for Borrowing Money

Name of Borrower: _____

Name of Lender: _____

1. **Grant of Security Interest.** Borrower grants to Lender a continuing security interest in the following personal property: _____
   _____ (the Secured Property). Borrower grants this security interest to secure performance of the promissory note dated _____ that Borrower executed in favor of Lender (the Note), which obligates Borrower to pay Lender $ _____ with interest at the rate of _____% per year, on the terms stated in the Note.

2. **Financing Statement.** Until the amount due under the Note is paid in full, the Note will be further secured by a Uniform Commercial Code (U.C.C.) Financing Statement. Borrower agrees to sign any other documents that Lender reasonably requests to protect Lender's security interest in the Secured Property.

3. **Use and Care of Secured Property.** Until the amount due under the Note is paid in full, Borrower agrees to:

   A. Maintain the Secured Property in good repair.

   B. Refrain from selling, transferring, or releasing the Secured Property without Lender's prior written consent.

   C. Pay all taxes on the Secured Property as they become due.

   D. Allow Lender to inspect the Secured Property at any reasonable time.

4. **Borrower's Default.** If Borrower is more than _____ days late in making any payment due under the Note, or if Buyer fails to correct any violations of Paragraph 3 within _____ days of receiving written notice from Lender, Borrower will be in default.

5. **Lender's Rights.** If Borrower is in default, Lender may exercise the remedies contained in the U.C.C. for the state of _____ and any other remedies legally available to Lender. Before exercising such remedies, Lender will provide at least ten days' advance notice, as provided in Paragraph 6. Lender may, for example:

   A. Remove the Secured Property from the place where it is then located.

   B. Require Borrower to make the Secured Property available to Lender at a place designated by Lender that is reasonably convenient to Borrower and Lender.

   C. Sell, lease, or otherwise dispose of the Secured Property.

6. **Notice.** Any notice may be delivered to a party at the address that follows a party's signature below, or to a new address that a party designates in writing. A notice may be delivered in person, by certified mail, or by overnight courier.

7. **Entire Agreement.** This is the entire agreement between the parties. It replaces and supersedes any and all oral agreements between the parties, as well as any prior writings.

8. **Successors and Assigns.** This agreement binds and benefits the parties' heirs, successors, and assigns.

9. **Governing Law.** This agreement will be governed by and construed in accordance with the laws of the state of _____ .

10. **Modification.** This agreement may be modified only in writing.

11. **Waiver.** If one party waives any term or provision of this agreement at any time, that waiver will be effective only for the specific instance and specific purpose for which the waiver was given. If either party fails to exercise or delays exercising any rights or remedies under this agreement, that party retains the right to enforce that term or provision at a later time.

12. **Severability.** If any court determines that any provision of this agreement is invalid or unenforceable, any such invalidity or unenforceability will affect only that provision and will not make any other provision of this agreement invalid or unenforceable, and such provision shall be modified, amended, or limited only to the extent necessary to render it valid and enforceable.

Lender's signature: _____ Date: _____

Print name: _____

Location [*city or county where signed*]: _____

Address: _____

_____

Borrower's signature: _____ Date: _____

Print name: _____

Location [*city or county where signed*]: _____

Address: _____

_____

Form 44

U.C.C. Financing Statement

This Financing Statement is presented for filing under the Uniform Commercial Code as adopted in

_____ [*name of your state*].

Name of Borrower: _____

Address of Borrower: _____

_____

Name of Lender/secured party: _____

Address of Lender/secured party: _____

_____

The term Borrower refers to one or more borrowers. If there is more than one borrower, they agree to be jointly and severally liable. The term Lender refers to any person who legally holds the promissory note, including a buyer in due course.

The property listed as collateral in the security agreement is as follows [*identify or describe*]:

_____

_____

This Financing Statement secures the following debt:

Promissory note dated: _____

Amount of debt: _____

Payback due date: _____

All other terms and conditions are stated in the promissory note, a copy of which is attached.

Borrower's signature: _____

Print name: _____

Location [*city or county where signed*]: _____

Date: _____

(For Use of the Filing Officer)

Date of filing: _____ Time of filing: _____

File number and address of filing office: _____

_____

Release of U.C.C. Financing Statement

This Release of Financing Statement is presented for filing under the Uniform Commercial Code as

adopted in _____ [*name of your state*].

Name of Borrower: _____

Address of Borrower: _____

_____

Name of Lender/secured party: _____

Address of Lender/secured party: _____

_____

The term Borrower refers to one or more borrowers. The term Lender refers to any person who legally holds the promissory note, including a buyer in due course.

The property listed as collateral in the security agreement is as follows [*identify or describe*]:

_____

_____

File number of Financing Statement: _____

Date filed: _____

Address of filing office: _____

Borrower's signature: _____

Print name: _____

Date: _____

(For Use of the Filing Officer)

Date of filing: _____ Time of filing: _____

File number and address of filing office: _____

_____

Agreement to Modify Promissory Note

Name of Borrower 1: _____

Name of Borrower 2: _____

Name of Lender: _____

1. This Agreement modifies the original promissory note dated _____ , _____ , under which Borrower promised to pay to Lender the amount of $_____ at the rate of _____% per year from the date the note was signed until _____ , _____ .

2. Lender and Borrower agree to the following modifications [*choose all that apply*]:

   ☐ Borrower has until _____ , _____ to pay the note in full.

   ☐ Borrower will make interest-only payments beginning on _____ , _____ until _____ , _____ , at which time the remaining principal balance will be reamortized over the remaining months of the note.

   ☐ Beginning on _____ , _____ , the interest rate will change to _____ %. The new monthly payments will be in the amount of $_____ .

   ☐ Other: _____

   _____ .

The term Borrower refers to one or more borrowers. If there is more than one borrower, they agree to be jointly and severally liable. The term Lender refers to any person who legally holds the promissory note, including a buyer in due course.

Borrower 1's signature _____ Date _____

Print name _____

Location [*city or county where signed*] _____

Address _____

_____

Borrower 2's signature _____ Date _____

Print name _____

Location [*city or county where signed*] _____

Address _____

_____

Lender's signature _____ Date _____

Print name _____

Location [*city or county where signed*] _____

Address _____

_____

Overdue Payment Demand

Date: _____

To: _____

_____

_____

_____

[insert name and address of person who borrowed money]

Re: Promissory note dated _____

Dear: _____

This is to notify you that I have not received the following payment(s) due under the promissory note referenced above ("the Note").

Amount: $ _____ Due date: _____

Amount: $ _____ Due date: _____

Total: $ _____

Please remit the outstanding balance within 15 days. If you fail to do so, I will have no choice but to assume that you do not intend to repay the amount that is due under the Note. I will proceed to enforce my rights under the Note, including possibly filing a lawsuit, to collect the entire balance.

Sincerely,

Signature of Lender _____

Print name of Lender _____

Address _____

_____

Home phone _____ Work phone _____

Demand to Make Good on Bad Check

Date: _____

To: _____

_____

_____

_____

[*insert name and address of check writer*]

Re: Check # _____ dated _____ , _____

Issuing financial institution: _____

Dear: _____ :

Your check was returned to my bank and refused payment for the following reason [*choose one*]:

☐ insufficient funds in the account on which the check was drawn to cover the amount of the check.

☐ the account on which the check was drawn has been closed.

☐ you stopped payment on the check.

Please pay the returned check amount of $ _____ within 30 days. If you fail to do so, I will have no choice but to assume that you do not intend to make this check good. I will proceed to enforce my rights, which may include filing a lawsuit. I will request that the court award me the maximum monetary damages allowed under state law, as well as:

☐ the amount of the check

☐ the bad-check processing fee charged by my bank

☐ the expenses incurred in attempting to collect on the check as allowed under state law

Sincerely,

Signature of check recipient _____

Print name of check recipient _____

Address _____

_____

Home phone _____ Work phone _____

Ideal House Profile

Upper price limit: _____

Maximum down payment: _____

Special financing needs: _____

	Must Have	Hope to Have
Neighborhood or location:		
_____	☐	☐
_____	☐	☐
School needs:		
_____	☐	☐
Desired neighborhood features:		
_____	☐	☐
_____	☐	☐
_____	☐	☐
_____	☐	☐
Length of commute:		
_____	☐	☐
Access to public transportation:		
_____	☐	☐
Size of house:		
_____	☐	☐
Number and type of rooms:		
_____	☐	☐
_____	☐	☐
Condition, age, and type of house:		
_____	☐	☐
_____	☐	☐
Type of yard and grounds:		
_____	☐	☐
_____	☐	☐
Other desired features:		
_____	☐	☐
_____	☐	☐
_____	☐	☐
Absolute no ways:		
_____	☐	☐
_____	☐	☐
_____	☐	☐
_____	☐	☐

House Priorities Worksheet

Date visited: _____

Address: _____

_____

Price: $ _____

Contact: _____ Phone: _____

Must have:

- [ ] _____
- [ ] _____
- [ ] _____
- [ ] _____
- [ ] _____
- [ ] _____
- [ ] _____
- [ ] _____

Hope to have:

- [ ] _____
- [ ] _____
- [ ] _____
- [ ] _____
- [ ] _____
- [ ] _____
- [ ] _____
- [ ] _____

Absolute no ways:

- [ ] _____
- [ ] _____
- [ ] _____

Comments about the house:

_____

_____

_____

_____

_____

_____

House Comparison Worksheet

House 1 _____

House 2 _____

House 3 _____

House 4 _____

	1	2	3	4

Must have:

Item	1	2	3	4
_____	☐	☐	☐	☐
_____	☐	☐	☐	☐
_____	☐	☐	☐	☐
_____	☐	☐	☐	☐
_____	☐	☐	☐	☐
_____	☐	☐	☐	☐
_____	☐	☐	☐	☐
_____	☐	☐	☐	☐
_____	☐	☐	☐	☐
_____	☐	☐	☐	☐
_____	☐	☐	☐	☐
_____	☐	☐	☐	☐
_____	☐	☐	☐	☐

Hope to have:

Item	1	2	3	4
_____	☐	☐	☐	☐
_____	☐	☐	☐	☐
_____	☐	☐	☐	☐
_____	☐	☐	☐	☐
_____	☐	☐	☐	☐
_____	☐	☐	☐	☐
_____	☐	☐	☐	☐
_____	☐	☐	☐	☐
_____	☐	☐	☐	☐

Absolutely no ways:

Item	1	2	3	4
_____	☐	☐	☐	☐
_____	☐	☐	☐	☐
_____	☐	☐	☐	☐
_____	☐	☐	☐	☐
_____	☐	☐	☐	☐

Family Financial Statement

	Borrower	**Coborrower**
Name:		
Address:		
Home phone number:		
Employer:		
Employer's address:		
Work phone number:		

Worksheet 1: Income and Expenses

	Borrower ($)	Coborrower ($)	Total
I. INCOME			
A. Monthly gross income			
1. Employment			
2. Public benefits			
3. Dividends			
4. Royalties			
5. Interest and other investment income			
6. Other (specify):			
B. Total monthly gross income			
II. MONTHLY EXPENSES			
A. Nonhousing			
1. Child care			
2. Clothing			
3. Food			
4. Insurance			
a. Auto			
b. Life			
c. Medical & dental			
5. Other medical			
6. Personal			
7. Education			
8. Taxes (nonhousing)			
9. Transportation			
10. Other (specify):			
B. Current Housing			
1. Mortgage			
2. Taxes			
3. Insurance			
4. Utilities			
5. Rent			
6. Other (specify):			
C. Total monthly expenses			

Worksheet 2: Assets and Liabilities

I. ASSETS (Cash or Market Value)	Borrower ($)	Coborrower ($)	Total
A. Cash & cash equivalents			
1. Cash	_____	_____	_____
2. Deposits (list):	_____	_____	_____
_____	_____	_____	_____
_____	_____	_____	_____
B. Marketable securities			
1. Stocks/bonds (bid price)	_____	_____	_____
2. Other securities	_____	_____	_____
3. Mutual funds	_____	_____	_____
4. Life insurance	_____	_____	_____
5. Other (specify):	_____	_____	_____
_____	_____	_____	_____
_____	_____	_____	_____
C. Total cash & marketable securities	_____	_____	_____
D. Nonliquid assets			
1. Real estate	_____	_____	_____
2. Retirement funds	_____	_____	_____
3. Business	_____	_____	_____
4. Motor vehicles	_____	_____	_____
5. Other (specify):	_____	_____	_____
_____	_____	_____	_____
_____	_____	_____	_____
E. Total nonliquid assets	_____	_____	_____
F. Total all assets	_____	_____	_____
II. LIABILITIES			
A. Debts			
1. Real estate loans	_____	_____	_____
2. Student loans	_____	_____	_____
3. Motor vehicle loans	_____	_____	_____
4. Child or spousal support	_____	_____	_____
5. Personal loans	_____	_____	_____
6. Credit cards (specify):	_____	_____	_____
_____	_____	_____	_____
_____	_____	_____	_____
_____	_____	_____	_____
7. Other (specify):	_____	_____	_____
_____	_____	_____	_____
_____	_____	_____	_____
B. Total liabilities	_____	_____	_____
III. NET WORTH (Total assets minus total liabilities)	_____	_____	_____

Monthly Carrying Costs Worksheet

1. Estimated purchase price $_____

2. Down payment $_____

3. Loan amount $_____

4. Interest rate   _____%

5. Monthly mortgage payment $_____

6. Homeowners' insurance [*monthly*] $_____

7. Property taxes [*monthly*] $_____

8. Total monthly housing costs [*add lines 5–7*] $_____

9. Other monthly debts

    _____ $_____

    _____ $_____

    _____ $_____

    _____ $_____

    Total monthly debts $_____

10. Private mortgage insurance [*if any*] $_____

11. Homeowners' association fee
    [*if in a planned unit development*] $_____

12. Total monthly housing costs and other debts
    [*add lines 8–11*] $_____

13. Lender qualifying ratio [*between 28% and 36%*]   _____%

14. Monthly gross income to qualify
    [*divide line 12 by line 13*] $_____

15. Yearly gross income to qualify
    [*multiply line 14 by the number 12*] $_____

Mortgage Rates and Terms Worksheet

Lender: _____ _____ _____

_____ _____ _____

Loan agent: _____ _____ _____

_____ _____ _____

Phone number: _____ _____ _____

Date: _____ _____ _____

1. General Information

Fixed or adjustable	☐ F ☐ A	☐ F ☐ A	☐ F ☐ A
Fixed interest rate	_____ %	_____ %	_____ %
Government financing	☐ Y ☐ N	☐ Y ☐ N	☐ Y ☐ N
Minimum down payment	_____ %	_____ %	_____ %
PMI required	☐ Y ☐ N	☐ Y ☐ N	☐ Y ☐ N
Impound account	☐ Y ☐ N	☐ Y ☐ N	☐ Y ☐ N
Term of mortgage	_____ Years	_____ Years	_____ Years
Assumable	☐ Y ☐ N	☐ Y ☐ N	☐ Y ☐ N
Rate lock-in available	☐ Y ☐ N	☐ Y ☐ N	☐ Y ☐ N
Cost to lock in	$ _____	$ _____	$ _____
21 days	$ _____	$ _____	$ _____
30 days	$ _____	$ _____	$ _____
45 days	$ _____	$ _____	$ _____

2. Debt-to-Income Ratios Information

Allowable monthly carrying costs as % of income	_____	_____	_____
Allowable monthly carrying costs plus long-term debts as % of monthly income	_____	_____	_____
Maximum loan you qualify for based on debt-to-income ratios	$ _____	$ _____	$ _____

3. Loan Costs

Number of points	_____	_____	_____
Cost of points	$ _____	$ _____	$ _____
PMI	$ _____	$ _____	$ _____
Additional loan fee	$ _____	$ _____	$ _____
Credit report	$ _____	$ _____	$ _____
Application fee	$ _____	$ _____	$ _____
Appraisal fee	$ _____	$ _____	$ _____
Miscellaneous fees	$ _____	$ _____	$ _____
Estimated total loan costs	$ _____	$ _____	$ _____

4. Time Limits

Credit/employment check	_____ Days	_____ Days	_____ Days
Lender appraisal	_____ Days	_____ Days	_____ Days
Loan approval	_____ Days	_____ Days	_____ Days
Loan funding	_____ Days	_____ Days	_____ Days
Loan due date each month	_____	_____	_____
Grace period	_____ Days	_____ Days	_____ Days
Late fee	_____ %	_____ %	_____ %

5. Other Features

[such as a discount for having an account with a certain bank, or a lender discount of interest rate on initial payments]

_____ _____ _____

_____ _____ _____

_____ _____ _____

6. Fixed Rate Two-Step Loans

Initial annual interest rate	_____ %	_____ %	_____ %
Over how many years	_____ Years	_____ Years	_____ Years

7. Fixed Rate Balloon Payment Loans

Interest rate	_____ %	_____ %	_____ %
Monthly payment	$ _____	$ _____	$ _____
Term of loan	_____ Years	_____ Years	_____ Years
Amount of balloon payment	_____	_____	_____

8. Adjustable Rate Mortgages (ARMs)

Index:

11th District COFI Index	☐ _____ %	☐ _____ %	☐ _____ %
6-Month T-Bill Index	☐ _____ %	☐ _____ %	☐ _____ %
1-Year T-Bill Index	☐ _____ %	☐ _____ %	☐ _____ %
Other:			
_____	☐ _____ %	☐ _____ %	☐ _____ %
Margin	☐ _____ %	☐ _____ %	☐ _____ %
Initial interest rate	☐ _____ %	☐ _____ %	☐ _____ %
How long	____ Mos. ____ Yrs.	____ Mos. ____ Yrs.	____ Mos. ____ Yrs.
Interest cap rate	☐ _____ %	☐ _____ %	☐ _____ %
Adjustment period	_____ Months	_____ Months	_____ Months
Life-of-loan (overall) cap	☐ _____ %	☐ _____ %	☐ _____ %
Initial payment	_____ Months	_____ Months	_____ Months
Payment cap	☐ _____ %	☐ _____ %	☐ _____ %
Payment cap period	_____ Months	_____ Months	_____ Months

Highest payment or interest rate in:

6 months	____ % $_____	____ % $_____	____ % $_____
12 months	____ % $_____	____ % $_____	____ % $_____
18 months	____ % $_____	____ % $_____	____ % $_____
24 months	____ % $_____	____ % $_____	____ % $_____
30 months	____ % $_____	____ % $_____	____ % $_____
36 months	____ % $_____	____ % $_____	____ % $_____

9. Hybrid Loans

Initial interest rate	_____ %	_____ %	_____ %
Term as a fixed rate loan	_____ Years	_____ Years	_____ Years
Interest rate at first adjustment period	_____ %	_____ %	_____ %

Moving Checklist

[Not all items on this list will apply to you. If you're moving within the same town, you probably won't have to transfer your kids to a new school, get references for a new job, or have your car serviced for travel. So just focus on the applicable items.]

I. Two Weeks Before Moving

☐ Check with your children's new school about what records and transcripts it will need; arrange for their transfer.

☐ Close or transfer bank and safe deposit box accounts.

☐ Cancel deliveries—newspaper, organic fruits and vegetables, laundry.

☐ Contact utilitiy companies—gas, electric, cable, phone, Internet, water, garbage; transfer services (if possible) or arrange new services; request deposit refunds.

☐ Get recommendations or find in advance (especially if a medical condition needs regular attention) new doctors, dentist, and veterinarian. Arrange for copying or digital transfer of important medical records.

☐ Get reference letters, if you'll need to find a job.

☐ Cancel membership (or transfer membership, if relevant) in religious, civic, and athletic organizations.

☐ Have car serviced for travel.

☐ Arrange to move pets.

☐ Finalize arrangements with moving company. (You should have gotten bids and made preliminary arrangements weeks earlier.)

☐ Tell close friends and relatives your schedule.

II. Things to Remember While Packing

☐ Before you pack, do a good inventory and sort through things. This way you can move less and won't end up throwing things away at your new home or needing storage space.

☐ Label boxes on top and side—your name, new city, room of house, and contents.

☐ Assemble moving kit—hammer, screwdriver, pliers, tape, nails, tape measure, scissors, flashlight, cleansers, cleaning cloths, rubber gloves, garbage bags, lightbulbs, and extension cords. If you're driving to your new home, pack a broom and pail in your car. Larger items that are handy when moving in, such as a step stool or vacuum cleaner, should go in the moving van, unless your new house is nearby and you're moving lots of things by car.

☐ Keep the basics handy—comfortable clothes, prescription medications, toiletries, towels, alarm clock, disposable plates, cups, and utensils, can opener, one pot, one pan, sponge, paper towels, dish soap, toilet paper, plastic containers, and toys for kids.

☐ Consider carrying jewelry, extremely fragile items, currency, and important documents.

☐ Make other arrangements if the moving company won't move antiques, art collections, crystal, other valuables, or plants.

III. Whom to Send Changes of Address To

- ☐ Friends and relatives
- ☐ Subscription services or publications
- ☐ Government agencies you regularly deal with—Veterans Administration, IRS, Social Security Administration, etc.
- ☐ Charge and credit accounts
- ☐ Installment debt—such as student loan or car loan
- ☐ Frequent flyer programs
- ☐ Brokers and mutual funds
- ☐ Insurance agent/companies (If you've moved to a better neighborhood, your car insurance rates might go down!)
- ☐ Medical providers—if you'll be able to use them after moving
- ☐ Catalogs you want to keep receiving
- ☐ Charities you wish to continue donating to
- ☐ School alumni office
- ☐ Post office (But don't count on it for consistent forwarding. If you're trying to get off of catalog and other direct mailing lists, have only first-class mail forwarded. Give your new address to those catalog companies on whose lists you want to remain, and don't forget to tell them not to trade or sell your name.)

IV. Things to Do After Moving In

- ☐ Open bank accounts.
- ☐ Open safe deposit box account.
- ☐ Begin deliveries—oil, newspaper, organic fruits and vegetables, laundry.
- ☐ Change the locks.
- ☐ Register to vote.
- ☐ Change (or get new) driver's license.
- ☐ Change auto registration.
- ☐ Install new batteries in existing smoke detectors (and install any additionally needed smoke detectors); buy fire extinguisher.
- ☐ Hold party for the people who helped you find your house and your moving helpers, and take yourself out for a congratulatory dinner!

Motor Vehicle Bill of Sale

1. Seller

Seller name: _____

Seller address: _____

_____

2. Buyer

Buyer name: _____

Buyer address: _____

_____

3. Terminology

The term Buyer refers to one or more buyers, and the term Seller refers to one or more sellers.

4. Vehicle Being Sold

Make: _____ Model: _____

Body type: _____ [i.e. sedan, SUV] Year: _____

Vehicle identification number (VIN): _____

Vehicle includes the following additional items: _____

_____ [List

any items that are included in the sale price of the vehicle, such as a bicycle rack, car cover, etc.]

5. Odometer

The odometer reading for Vehicle is: _____ .

6. Purchase Price

The full purchase price for Vehicle is: _____ .

 In exchange for Vehicle, Buyer has paid Seller: [choose one]

  ☐ the full purchase price.

  ☐ $_____ as a down payment. Buyer will pay the balance of the purchase price by

   _____ [date on which balance is due].

  ☐ $_____ as a down payment and has executed a promissory note for the balance

  of the purchase price.

7. Legal Owner

Seller warrants that Seller is the legal owner of Vehicle and that Vehicle is free of all liens or encumbrances.

8. Inspections

 Vehicle ☐ has been ☐ has not been inspected by an independent mechanic at Buyer's request.

9. Condition of Vehicle

Vehicle is sold "as is," and Seller does not make any express or implied warranties about its condition, except that to the best of Seller's knowledge, Vehicle: [*select a box for each declaration*]

☐ is   ☐ is not a salvage vehicle.

☐ has   ☐ has not been declared a total loss by an insurance company.

☐ has   ☐ has not been repaired under the terms of a Lemon Law.

10. Additional Terms of Sale

Additional terms of sale for Vehicle are: _____

_____

_____ [*enter any additional terms, or enter "none"*].

11. Signatures

Seller signature _____ Date _____

Seller signature _____ Date _____

Buyer signature _____ Date _____

Buyer signature _____ Date _____

[ATTACH NOTARY CERTIFICATE WHEN REQUIRED/PREFERRED]

Boat Bill of Sale

Seller 1: _____

Address: _____

Seller 2: _____

Address: _____

Buyer 1: _____

Address: _____

Buyer 2: _____

Address: _____

[If there is more than one buyer or seller, the use of the singular incorporates the plural.]

1. Seller sells the boat (Boat) described here to Buyer:

   Year: _____ Make: _____

   Model: _____ Length: _____

   Serial or hull ID number: _____ General type: _____

   Registration, CF, or document number: _____

2. Boat has the following types of engine(s) (Engines) [*provide details on engines including year, make, type, model, hours, and serial numbers*]: _____

   _____

   _____

   _____ .

3. Boat contains the following equipment (Equipment) included in this sale [*list and describe all that apply, including sails and rigging, safety equipment, electronics and navigation equipment, and deck equipment*]: _____

   _____

   _____

   _____ .

4. Seller believes Boat, Engines, and Equipment to be in good condition except for the following defects:

   _____

   _____ .

5. Boat and Engines ☐ have been ☐ have not been independently inspected or surveyed at Buyer's request. If an independent inspection or marine survey has been made, the inspection report or marine survey ☐ is attached to and made part of this bill of sale ☐ is not attached.

6. The full purchase price for Boat, Engines, and Equipment is $_____ . In exchange for Boat, Engines, and Equipment, Buyer has paid Seller [*choose one*]:

   ☐ single payment of the full purchase price.

   ☐ $ _____ as a down payment, balance of the purchase price due by

   _____ [*date*].

☐ $ _____ as a down payment and has executed a promissory note for the balance of the purchase price.

7. Seller warrants that Seller is the legal owner of Boat, Engines, and Equipment and that Boat, Engines, and Equipment are free of all liens and encumbrances except _____

_____ .

Seller agrees to remove any lien or encumbrance specified in this clause with the proceeds of this sale and other funds as necessary within _____ days of the date of this bill of sale.

8. Additional terms of sale for Boat, Engines, and Equipment are as follows: _____

_____

_____ .

Seller 1's signature _____ Date _____

Seller 2's signature _____ Date _____

Buyer 1's signature _____ Date _____

Buyer 2's signature _____ Date _____

[ATTACH NOTARY CERTIFICATE WHEN REQUIRED/PREFERRED]

General Bill of Sale

1. Seller and Buyer

Seller name: _____

Seller address: _____

_____

Buyer name: _____

Buyer address: _____

_____

2. Description of Goods

Seller sells the goods (Goods) described here to Buyer: _____

_____ [describe goods in reasonable detail].

3. Purchase Price

The full purchase price for Goods is $_____ . In exchange for Goods, Buyer has paid Seller: [choose one]

☐ the full purchase price.

☐ _____ as a down payment. Buyer will pay the balance of the purchase price by

_____ [date on which balance is due].

☐ _____ as a down payment and has executed a promissory note for the balance of the purchase price.

☐ other payment arrangement: _____

_____

_____ [describe payment arrangement, i.e. exchange of goods or services].

4. Ownership

Seller warrants that Seller is the legal owner of Goods and that Goods are free of all liens and encumbrances.

5. Condition of Goods

Seller believes Goods to be in good condition except for the following: _____

_____ [describe any significant defects in the goods].

6. Delivery of Goods

Goods will be delivered to Buyer in the following manner: [choose one]

☐ Buyer will take immediate possession of Goods.

☐ Buyer will pick up Goods from _____

_____ [address] by _____ [pickup date].

_____

☐ In exchange for an additional delivery charge of \$ _____ , receipt of which is

hereby acknowledged, Seller will deliver goods to _____

_____ [*address of delivery location*]

by _____ [*delivery date*].

7. Additional Terms

Additional terms of this sale are as follows: _____

_____

_____ [*enter any additional terms, or enter "none"*].

8. Signatures

Seller signature _____ Date _____

Buyer signature _____ Date _____

[ATTACH NOTARY CERTIFICATE WHEN REQUIRED/PREFERRED]

Bill of Sale for Dog

Seller 1: _____

Address: _____

Seller 2: _____

Address: _____

Buyer 1: _____

Address: _____

Buyer 2: _____

Address: _____

[If there is more than one buyer or seller, the use of the singular incorporates the plural.]

1. Seller sells to Buyer the dog (Dog) described as follows:

   Name: _____

   Breed: _____ Sex: _____

   Birth date *[estimate if specific date not known]*: _____

2. The full purchase price for Dog is $ _____ .

3. Buyer has paid Seller *[choose one]*:

   ☐ single payment of the full purchase price

   ☐ a down payment of $ _____ with the balance of $ _____

      due _____ *[date]*, or

   ☐ other: _____

      _____ *[explain]*.

4. Seller warrants that:

   a. Seller is the legal owner of Dog.

   b. Dog has had the following vaccinations *[list all the vaccinations Dog has received, including the date the vaccination was given and the name of the vet who gave it]*: _____

      _____

      _____ .

   c. Dog was *[choose one]*:

      ☐ bred by the Seller

      ☐ bought from a breeder _____

         _____

         [name of breeder] on _____ *[date]*.

      ☐ acquired from a previous private party owner _____

         _____

         _____ *[name]*.

d. Dog has had the following special training:_____.

e. Dog ☐ is ☐ is not purebred.

f. Dog is:

    ☐ male, neutered

    ☐ male, not neutered

    ☐ female, spayed

    ☐ female, not spayed

       ☐ pregnant

       ☐ not pregnant

g. Dog is [*check one*]:

    ☐ registered with the American Kennel Club or another entity [*provide details as appropriate*]

    _____.

    ☐ not registered with the American Kennel Club or another entity and is not eligible to be registered.

    ☐ not registered with the American Kennel Club or another entity but is eligible to be registered [*explain*] _____

    _____.

    Seller will provide Buyer with the necessary papers to process registration.

5. Seller believes that Dog is healthy and in good condition, except for the following known problems:

_____

_____.

6. If a licensed veterinarian certifies, in writing, that Dog has a serious disease or congenital defect that was present when Buyer took possession of Dog, Buyer may, within 14 days of taking possession of Dog [*choose one*]:

    ☐ return Dog to Seller. In this case, Seller will refund the purchase price plus any sales tax and reimburse Buyer for the cost of reasonable veterinary services directly related to the examination that showed Dog was ill, and emergency treatment to relieve suffering plus any sales tax.

    ☐ keep Dog. In this case, Seller will reimburse Buyer for the cost of reasonable veterinary services directly related to the examination that showed Dog was ill, and emergency treatment to relieve suffering, up to the amount of the purchase price plus any sales tax.

7. Dog will be delivered to Buyer in the following manner [*choose one*]:

    ☐ Buyer will take immediate possession of Dog.

    ☐ Buyer assumes responsibility for picking up Dog from _____

    _____

    by _____ [*date*].

    ☐ In exchange for an additional delivery charge of $_____ , Seller will deliver Dog by

    _____ [*date*] to the following location: _____

    _____.

8. Additional terms: _____

_____

_____

_____

_____

_____

_____ .

Seller 1's signature _____ Date _____

Seller 2's signature _____ Date _____

Buyer 1's signature _____ Date _____

Buyer 2's signature _____ Date _____

[ATTACH NOTARY CERTIFICATE WHEN REQUIRED/PREFERRED]

Personal Property Rental Agreement

Owner's name: _____ Home phone: _____

Address: _____ Cell phone: _____

Renter's name: _____ Home phone: _____

Address: _____ Cell phone: _____

If there is more than one owner or renter, the use of the singular incorporates the plural.

1. Property Being Rented; Use

Owner agrees to rent to Renter, and Renter agrees to rent from Owner, the following property ("the Property"): _____ .

Renter will use the Property for the following purpose only: _____

_____ .

Owner may cancel this agreement and require that Renter return the Property immediately if it is used for any other purpose.

2. Duration of Rental Period

This rental will begin at _____ o'clock a.m./p.m. on _____ , _____

and will end at _____ o'clock a.m./p.m. on _____ , _____ .

3. Rental Amount

The rental amount will be $_____ per _____ [*specify hour, day, week, or month*].

4. Payment

Renter has paid $_____ to Owner to cover the rental period specified in Clause 2.

☐ **Security deposit** [*optional*]. In addition to the rent, Renter has deposited $_____ with Owner. This deposit will be applied toward any additional rent, late return fees, and any amounts owed for damage to or loss of the Property, which Owner and Renter agree has the current value stated in Clause 8. Owner will return to Renter any unused portion of the deposit within 24 hours of the return of the Property. Owner will deposit in the U.S. mail a refund check made out to Renter at the address shown above or deliver the payment in person.

5. Delivery

[*choose one*]

☐ Renter will pick up the Property from Owner at [*specify address*] _____

_____ .

☐ Owner will deliver the Property to Renter ☐ at no charge ☐ for a fee of $_____

on _____ , _____ at [*specify address*] _____

_____

_____ .

☐ Other delivery arrangements: _____

_____

_____ .

6. Late Return

If Renter returns the Property to Owner after the time and date when the rental period ends, Renter will pay Owner a rental charge of $_____ per day for each day or partial day beyond the end of the rental period until the Property is returned. Owner may subtract this charge from the security deposit (if any).

7. Condition of Property

Renter acknowledges receiving the Property in good condition, except for the following defects or damage: _____

_____ .

8. Damage or Loss

Renter will return the Property to Owner in good condition except as noted in Clause 7. If the Property is damaged while in Renter's possession due to Renter's negligent, reckless, or intentional act, Renter will be responsible for the cost of repair, up to the current value of the Property. If the Property is lost while in Renter's possession, Renter will pay Owner its current value. Owner and Renter agree that the current value of the Property is [*list value of items individually as well as total*]

$ _____ .

9. Disputes. (*This clause applies only to disputes regarding damage to the property or failure to return it, but not to disputes regarding personal injuries or damage to other property.*)

[*choose one*]:

☐ **Litigation.** If a dispute arises, either Owner or Renter may take the matter to court.

☐ **Mediation and possible litigation.** If a dispute arises, Owner and Renter will try in good faith to settle it through mediation conducted by [*choose one*]:

    ☐ _____ [*name of mediator*].

    ☐ a mediator to be mutually selected.

    Owner and Renter will share the costs of the mediator equally. If the dispute is not resolved within 30 days after it is referred to the mediator, either Owner or Renter may take the matter to court.

☐ **Mediation and possible arbitration.** If a dispute arises, Owner and Renter will try in good faith to settle it through mediation conducted by [*choose one*]:

    ☐ _____ [*name of mediator*].

    ☐ a mediator to be mutually selected.

    Owner and Renter will share the costs of the mediator equally. If the dispute is not resolved within 30 days after it is referred to the mediator, either Owner or Renter may take the matter to

[*choose one*]:

    ☐ _____ [*name of arbitrator*].

    ☐ an arbitrator to be mutually selected.

    The arbitrator's decision will be binding and judgment on the arbitration award may be entered in any court that has jurisdiction over the matter. Costs of arbitration, including lawyers' fees, will be allocated by the arbitrator.

Owner's signature _____ Date _____

Renter's signature _____ Date _____

Notice of Termination of Personal Property Rental Agreement

To _____ [*name of person to whom notice is being sent*]:

1. Notice of Termination

This is a notice that as of _____ , _____ , I am terminating

the following rental agreement:

Name of Owner: _____

Name of Renter: _____

Property covered by agreement: _____

_____

Date agreement signed: _____ , _____

2. Reason for Termination

The reasons for the termination are as follows [*optional, unless a reason to terminate is required by the*

rental agreement]: _____

_____

_____

_____

_____

_____

_____ .

3. Return of Property

[*choose one*]:

☐ [*for renters*] I will return the Property to Owner on or before _____ , _____ .

☐ [*for owners*] Please return the Property to Owner on or before _____ , _____ .

4. Return of Security Deposit

☐ Renter has deposited $_____ with Owner. Owner agrees to inspect the Property for

damage and refund Renter any unused portion of the security deposit. Within 24 hours of the

return of the Property, Owner will deposit in the U.S. mail a refund check made out to Renter at

the following address: _____

_____ .

Date _____

Signature _____ , ☐ Owner ☐ Renter

Print name _____

Storage Contract

Property Owner: _____

Address: _____

Property Custodian: _____

Address: _____

[If there is more than one owner or custodian, the use of the singular incorporates the plural.]

1. Property

Owner desires to store with Custodian, and Custodian agrees to accept and store for Owner, the following property ("the Property"): _____

_____

_____

_____

_____

_____

Photographs of ☐ some ☐ all of the items are attached.

2. Storage Location

The Property will be stored at the following location: _____

_____

Custodian agrees that the Property will not be removed from this location without prior written notice to and written consent of Owner.

3. Storage Term and Payment

[choose one]:

☐ Custodian agrees to store the Property on a _____ *[daily, weekly, or monthly]* basis in exchange for payment of $_____ per _____ , payable on the first day of each such period.

☐ Custodian agrees to store the Property for payment of $_____ . Payment will be made on or before _____ , _____ .

4. Beginning and Ending Dates

[choose one]:

☐ Storage will begin on _____ , _____ , and will continue until Owner claims the Property or Custodian serves Owner with a _____-day written notice terminating this storage agreement.

☐ Storage will begin on _____ , _____ , and will continue until _____ , _____ , or until Owner claims the Property, whichever occurs first.

5. Use of Property

Custodian will not use the Property, or permit it to be used by anyone else, without Owner's prior written consent. Notwithstanding Clause 13, Custodian is liable for any damage to the Property during use without Owner's prior written consent.

6. Reclaiming Property

Owner may reclaim the Property at any time, but not later than the date specified in Clause 4, or the date specified in the Custodian's notice of termination under that clause. Custodian will make the Property available to Owner, but may first require Owner to pay Custodian any unpaid charges allowed by Clauses 3 and 7.

Custodian may refuse delivery if Custodian has received any notice of attachment, levy, or similar notice and has given notice to Owner under Clause 15, or is instructed to withhold delivery by a court or law enforcement officer.

7. Failure to Reclaim Property

If Owner fails to reclaim the Property on or before the last day of storage indicated in the Custodian's notice of termination or in Clause 4, Custodian will [*choose one*]:

☐ continue to store the Property at the rate of $_____ per _____
until Owner reclaims the Property. Custodian may require owner to pay accrued storage fees before turning over the Property.

☐ send to Owner's last known address by first-class mail a notice to reclaim the Property, and wait 30 days; if Owner does not make arrangements to reclaim the Property during the 30 days, Custodian may deem the Property abandoned, sell it to pay for outstanding storage fees, and hold the balance (minus reasonable costs of sale) for Owner.

8. Early Reclaiming

If Owner reclaims the Property during a period for which payment has been made, no pro rata refund will be made.

9. Delivery to Someone Other Than Owner

Custodian will not deliver the Property to any person other than Owner without prior written permission from Owner. If Owner dies while this agreement is in effect, Owner instructs Custodian to deliver the Property to _____
upon proper proof of that person's identity and documentation of Owner's death, unless Custodian is instructed otherwise by a court or law enforcement official.

10. More Than One Owner

If more than one Owner is listed at the beginning of this form [*choose one*]:

☐ Custodian may deliver the Property only to all of the Owners.

☐ Custodian may deliver the Property to _____
[*state Owner's name*] rather than all of the Owners.

11. Value of the Property

Owner and Custodian agree that the approximate ☐ replacement value ☐ fair market value of each item of Property on the date this agreement is signed is [*list items and their value*]:

Item	Value

12. Condition of the Property

The Property being stored appears to be in good condition except for the following defects or damage [*provide details on each item of property being stored*]: _____

_____

_____

_____

_____

13. Care During Storage Period

Custodian agrees to exercise reasonable care to protect the Property from loss, theft, or damage. Custodian agrees to be liable for loss, theft, or damage to the Property caused by Custodian's negligent, reckless, or intentional act. Owner agrees to be liable for damage to the Property or the storage location caused by inherent or defective condition of the Property.

☐ Owner will insure the Property.

☐ Custodian will insure the Property to the extent allowable under Custodian's homeowners' or other insurance policy.

14. Title to the Property

The title to the Property will remain at all times in Owner.

15. Notice of Attachment

Custodian agrees to notify Owner promptly in writing if custodian receives any notice of attachment, levy, or similar notice.

16. Disputes

[*choose one*]:

☐ **Litigation.** If a dispute arises, either Owner or Custodian may take the matter to court.

☐ **Mediation and possible litigation.** If a dispute arises, Owner and Custodian will try in good faith to settle it through mediation conducted by [*choose one*]:

☐ _____ [*name of mediator*].

☐ a mediator to be mutually selected.

Owner and Custodian will share the costs of the mediator equally. If the dispute is not resolved within 30 days after it is referred to the mediator, either Owner or Custodian may take the matter to court.

☐ **Mediation and possible arbitration.** If a dispute arises, Owner and Custodian will try in good faith to settle it through mediation conducted by [*choose one*]:

☐ _____ [*name of mediator*].

☐ a mediator to be mutually selected.

Owner and Custodian will share the costs of the mediator equally. If the dispute is not resolved within 30 days after it is referred to the mediator, it will be arbitrated by [*choose one*]:

☐ _____ [*name of arbitrator*].

☐ an arbitrator to be mutually selected.

The arbitrator's decision will be binding and judgment on the arbitration award may be entered in any court that has jurisdiction over the matter. Costs of arbitration, including lawyers' fees, will be allocated by the arbitrator.

17. Modification of This Agreement

All agreements between the parties related to storage of the Property are incorporated in this contract. Any modification to this contract must be in writing signed by Owner and Custodian.

18. Additional Terms

Additional terms for the storage of the Property are as follows: _____

_____

_____

_____

_____ .

Owner's signature _____ Date _____

Custodian's signature _____ Date _____

Home Maintenance Agreement

Homeowner's name: _____

Address: _____

Home phone: _____ Work: _____

Cell: _____ Email: _____

Contractor's name: _____

Address: _____

_____ Business phone: _____

Cell: _____ Email: _____

Contractor's license number (if applicable): _____

Homeowner desires to contract with Contractor to perform certain work on property located at:

_____

_____ .

1. Work to Be Done

The work to be performed under this agreement consists of the following: _____

_____

_____

_____

_____

_____ .

2. Payment

In exchange for the work specified in Clause 1, Homeowner agrees to pay Contractor as follows [*choose one*]:

☐ $ _____ , payable upon completion of the specified work by ☐ cash ☐ check ☐ credit card ☐ other.

☐ $ _____ , payable one half at the beginning of the specified work and one half at the completion of the specified work by ☐ cash ☐ check ☐ credit card ☐ other.

☐ $ _____ per hour for each hour of work performed, up to a maximum of $ _____ , payable at the following times and in the following manner: _____

_____ .

☐ Other: _____

_____ .

3. Time

The work specified in this contract shall [*check the boxes and provide dates*]:

☐ begin on _____ , _____ .

☐ be completed on _____ , _____ .

4. Additional Terms

Homeowner and Contractor additionally agree that:_____

_____

_____

_____

_____ .

All agreements between Homeowner and Contractor related to the specified work are incorporated in this contract. Any modification to the contract must be in writing.

Homeowner's signature _____ Date_____

Contractor's signature _____ Date _____

Home Repairs Agreement

Homeowner's name: _____

Address: _____

Home phone: _____ Work: _____

Cell: _____ Email: _____

Contractor's name: _____

Address: _____

_____ Business phone: _____

Cell: _____ Email: _____

Homeowner and Contractor agree that contractor will perform certain work on property located at:

_____

_____ .

1. Work to Be Done

The work to be performed under this agreement consists of the following: _____

_____

_____

_____

_____

_____

_____

_____

_____

_____ .

2. Payment

In exchange for the work specified in Clause 1, Homeowner agrees to pay Contractor as follows [*choose one*]:

☐ $ _____ , payable upon completion of the specified work by ☐ cash ☐ check ☐ credit card ☐ other.

☐ $ _____ , payable by ☐ cash ☐ check ☐ credit card ☐ other as follows:

_____% payable when the following occurs: _____

_____% payable when the following occurs: _____

_____% payable when the following occurs: _____ .

☐ $_____ per hour for each hour of work performed, up to a maximum of $ _____ ,

payable at the following times and in the following manner: _____

_____

_____ .

☐ Other: _____

_____ .

3. Time

The work specified in Clause 1 will [*check the boxes and provide dates*]:

☐ begin on _____ , _____ .

☐ be completed on _____ , _____ .

Time is of the essence.

4. Licensing and Registration Requirements

Contractor will comply with all state and local licensing and registration requirements for the type of activity involved in the specified work [*check one box and provide description*]:

☐ Contractor's state license or registration is for the following type of work and carries the following number: _____ .

☐ Contractor's local license or registration is for the following type of work and carries the following number: _____ .

☐ Contractor is not required to have a license or registration for the specified work, for the following reasons: _____
_____ .

5. Permits and Approvals

[*check all appropriate boxes*]:

☐ Contractor ☐ Homeowner will be responsible for determining which permits are necessary and for obtaining those permits.

☐ Contractor ☐ Homeowner will pay for all state and local permits necessary for performing the specified work.

☐ Contractor ☐ Homeowner will be responsible for obtaining approval from the local homeowners' association, if required.

6. Injury to Contractor

Contractor will carry insurance. If Contractor is injured in the course of performing the specified work, Homeowner will be exempt from liability for those injuries to the fullest extent allowed by law.

7. Additional Terms

Homeowner and Contractor additionally agree that: _____
_____
_____
_____
_____
_____ .

All agreements between Homeowner and Contractor related to the specified work are incorporated in this contract. Any modification to the contract must be in writing.

Homeowner's signature _____ Date _____

Contractor's signature _____ Date _____

Contractor Mid-Job Worksheet

Date	Issue/Question	Response	Additional cost?	Resolved?	Initials

Daily Expenses

Week of _____

Sunday		Monday		Tuesday		Wednesday	
Expenses	Cost	Expenses	Cost	Expenses	Cost	Expenses	Cost
Daily Total:	_____	**Daily Total:**	_____	**Daily Total:**	_____	**Daily Total:**	_____

Thursday		Friday		Saturday		Other	
Expenses	Cost	Expenses	Cost	Expenses	Cost	Expenses	Cost
Daily Total:	_____	**Daily Total:**	_____	**Daily Total:**	_____	**Daily Total:**	_____

Total for the Week $ _____

Monthly Income

Source of income	Description	Amount of each payment	Time period covered by each payment	Monthly income
A. Wages or Salary				
Job 1: _____	Gross pay, including overtime:	$_____		
	Subtract:			
	Federal taxes	_____		
	State taxes	_____		
	Social Security (FICA)	_____		
	Medicare	_____		
	Union dues	_____		
	Insurance payments	_____		
	Child support withholding	_____		
	Other deductions (specify):			
	Subtotal Job 1	$_____	_____	$_____
Job 2: _____	Gross pay, including overtime:	$_____		
	Subtract:			
	Federal taxes	_____		
	State taxes	_____		
	Social Security (FICA)	_____		
	Medicare	_____		
	Union dues	_____		
	Insurance payments	_____		
	Child support withholding	_____		
	Other deductions (specify):			
	Subtotal Job 2	$_____	_____	$_____
Job 3: _____	Gross pay, including overtime:	$_____		
	Subtract:			
	Federal taxes	_____		
	State taxes	_____		
	Social Security (FICA)	_____		
	Medicare	_____		
	Union dues	_____		
	Insurance payments	_____		
	Child support withholding	_____		
	Other deductions (specify):			
	Subtotal Job 3	$_____	_____	$_____
	Total Wages and Salary			$_____

Source of income	Description	Amount of each payment	Time period covered by each payment	Monthly income
B. Self-Employment Income				
Job 1: _____	Gross pay, including overtime:	$_____		
	Subtract:			
	Federal taxes	_____		
	State taxes	_____		
	Self-employment taxes	_____		
	Other deductions (specify):			
	_____	_____		
	Subtotal Job 1	$_____	_____	$_____
Job 2: _____	Gross pay, including overtime:	$_____		
	Subtract:			
	Federal taxes	_____		
	State taxes	_____		
	Self-employment taxes	_____		
	Other deductions (specify):			
	_____	_____		
	Subtotal Job 2	$_____	_____	$_____
	Total Self-Employment Income			$_____
C. Investment Income	Dividends	$_____	_____	$_____
	Interest	$_____	_____	$_____
	Leases	$_____	_____	$_____
	Licenses	$_____	_____	$_____
	Rent	$_____	_____	$_____
	Royalties	$_____	_____	$_____
	Other deductions (specify):			_____
	_____	$_____		$_____
	Total Investment Income			$_____
D. Other Income	Bonuses	$_____	_____	$_____
	Note or trust income	$_____	_____	$_____
	Alimony or child support	$_____	_____	$_____
	Pension/retirement income	$_____	_____	$_____
	Social Security	$_____	_____	$_____
	Other public assistance	$_____	_____	$_____
	Other (specify):			
	_____	$_____	_____	$_____
	_____	$_____	_____	$_____
	Total Other Income			$_____
	Grand Total Monthly Income			$_____

Monthly Budget

	Proj.	Jan.	Feb.	Mar.	April	May	June	July	Aug.	Sept.	Oct.	Nov.	Dec.
Home													
rent/mortgage													
property taxes													
renters' ins.													
homeowners' ins.													
homeowners' association dues													
telephone													
gas & electric													
water & sewer													
cable TV													
Internet access													
garbage													
household supplies													
housewares													
furniture & appliances													
cleaning													
yard or pool care													
maintenance & repairs													
Credit and Loans													
credit card payments													
personal loan payments													
other loan payments													
Food													
groceries													
breakfast out													
lunch out													
dinner out													
coffee/tea													
snacks													
Clothing													
clothing, shoes, & accessories													
laundry, dry cleaning, & mending													
Self-Care													
toiletries & cosmetics													
haircuts													
massage													
health club membership													
donations													

	Proj.	Jan.	Feb.	Mar.	April	May	June	July	Aug.	Sept.	Oct.	Nov.	Dec.

Health Care

insurance

medications

vitamins

doctors

dentist

eye care

therapy

Transportation

car payment

insurance

road service club

registration

gasoline

maintenance & repairs

car wash

parking & tolls

public transit & cabs

parking tickets

Entertainment

music

movies & rentals

concerts, theater,
 & ballet

museums

sporting events

hobbies & lessons

club dues or
 membership

books, magazines,
 & newspapers

software & games

Dependent Care

child care

clothing

allowance

school expenses

toys

entertainment

Form 68

	Proj.	Jan.	Feb.	Mar.	April	May	June	July	Aug.	Sept.	Oct.	Nov.	Dec.

Pet Care

grooming

vet

food

toys & supplies

Education

tuition or loan payments

books & supplies

Travel

Gifts & Cards

holidays

birthdays & anniversaries

weddings & showers

Personal Business

supplies

photocopying

postage

bank & credit card fees

lawyer

accountant

taxes

savings

Savings and Investments

deposit to savings

deposit to retirement account

deposit to annuity

purchase of stock

purchase of mutual funds

other

Total Expenses

Total Income

Difference

Statement of Assets and Liabilities

(as of _____)

Assets	Date of Purchase	Account Number (if relevant)	Current Market Value ($)
Cash and Cash Equivalents			
Cash	_____	_____	_____
Checking accounts	_____	_____	_____
Savings accounts	_____	_____	_____
Money market accounts	_____	_____	_____
Other	_____	_____	_____
Subtotal			_____
Real Estate			
House/condo/co-op	_____	_____	_____
Vacation home	_____	_____	_____
Income properties	_____	_____	_____
Unimproved lot	_____	_____	_____
Other lot	_____	_____	_____
Subtotal			_____
Personal Property			
Motor vehicles	_____	_____	_____
Furniture	_____	_____	_____
Home furnishings	_____	_____	_____
Electronic equipment	_____	_____	_____
Computer equipment	_____	_____	_____
Jewelry	_____	_____	_____
Clothing	_____	_____	_____
Collections (coin, stamp, etc.)	_____	_____	_____
Animals	_____	_____	_____
Other	_____	_____	_____
Subtotal			_____
Investments and Miscellaneous Assets			
Life insurance (term cash value)	_____	_____	_____
Life insurance (whole policies)	_____	_____	_____
Stocks	_____	_____	_____
Bonds	_____	_____	_____
Mutual funds	_____	_____	_____
Annuities	_____	_____	_____
IRAs	_____	_____	_____
Keoghs	_____	_____	_____
401(k) plans	_____	_____	_____
Other retirement plans	_____	_____	_____
Partnerships	_____	_____	_____
Accounts receivable	_____	_____	_____
Other	_____	_____	_____
Subtotal			_____

Liabilities	Date Incurred	Account Number	Total Balance Due ($)
Secured			
Mortgage			
Mortgage			
Deeds of trust			
Home equity loans			
Liens			
Motor vehicle loans			
Bank loans			
Personal loans			
Other			
Subtotal			
Unsecured			
Student loans			
Bank loans			
Personal loans			
Credit card balances			
Judgments			
Taxes			
Support arrears			
Other			
Subtotal			

Net Worth Summary

Total Assets

Cash Subtotal $ _____

Real Estate Subtotal _____

Personal Property Subtotal _____

Investments Subtotal _____

Total Assets $_____

Total Liabilities

Secured Subtotal _____

Unsecured Subtotal _____

Total Liabilities $_____

Net Worth _____

(Assets minus liabilities) $_____

Assignment of Rights

Assignor 1's name: _____

Address: _____

Assignor 2's name: _____

Address: _____

Assignee 1's name: _____

Address: _____

Assignee 2's name: _____

Address: _____

If there is more than one assignor or assignee, the use of the singular incorporates the plural.

1. Assignor transfers to Assignee all of the following rights of Assignor [*describe the rights you are assigning*]: _____

   _____

   _____

   _____ .

2. Evidence of Assignor's rights can be found in the following document [*describe the document, such as a promissory note, providing details of document name, parties, and date*]: _____

   _____

   _____ .

   Evidence of Assignor's right ☐ is ☐ is not attached to this Assignment of Rights form.

3. This assignment takes effect on: _____ .

4. This assignment lasts until: _____ [*specify date or event that ends assignment*].

Assignor 1's signature _____ Date _____

Print name _____

Location [*city or county where signed*] _____

Address _____

Assignor 2's signature _____ Date _____

Print name _____

Location [*city or county where signed*] _____

Address _____

Assignee 1's signature _____ Date _____

Print name _____

Location [*city or county where signed*] _____

Address _____

Assignee 2's signature _____ Date _____

Print name _____

Location [*city or county where signed*] _____

Address _____

Notice to Terminate Joint Account

Date: _____

_____

_____

_____

_____

[*name and address of creditor*]

Names on account: _____

Account number: _____

To Whom It May Concern:

With this letter, I am requesting that you close the account referenced above, effective immediately.

I am requesting a "hard close" of the account so that neither party to the account may incur new charges. If you do not hard close the account, please be informed that as of the date of this letter, I will not be responsible for any new charges made to this account.

If my account has an outstanding balance, you may keep the account open for billing purposes only. Nevertheless, I request that you keep the account inactive so that neither party to the account can incur new charges.

Please acknowledge receipt of this notice by signing the duplicate of this letter and returning it to me in the enclosed stamped, self-addressed envelope.

Thank you for your assistance with this matter.

Signature _____ Date _____

Printed or typed name _____

Address _____

_____

Home phone _____ Work phone _____

Receipt acknowledged by:

Signature _____ Date _____

Printed or typed name _____

Title _____

Outstanding balance _____ As of _____

Notice to Stop Payment of Check

Date: _____

_____

_____

_____

_____

[*name and address of financial institution*]

Re: Stop payment of check

To Whom It May Concern:

This letter is to confirm my telephone request of _____ [*date*] that you stop payment on the following check:

Name(s) on account: _____

Account number: _____ Check number: _____

Payable to: _____

Date written: _____ Amount of check: _____

Please acknowledge receipt of this notice by signing the duplicate of this letter and returning it to me in the enclosed stamped, self-addressed envelope.

Thank you for your assistance.

Signature _____ Date _____

Printed or typed name _____

Address _____

_____

Home phone _____ Work phone _____

Receipt acknowledged by:

Signature _____ Date _____

Printed or typed name _____

Title _____

Request for Credit Report

Date: _____

_____

_____

_____

_____

[*name and address of credit bureau*]

To Whom It May Concern:

Please send me a copy of my credit report.

Full name: _____

Date of birth _____ Social Security number: _____

Spouse's name: _____

Telephone number: _____

Current address: _____

_____

Previous address: _____

_____

[*check one*]:

☐ Because of information in my credit file, _____
took the following action on _____ , 20____ (I enclose a copy of the notice
I received):

  ☐ Denied me credit.

  ☐ Granted me credit, but not near the amount or on the terms that I requested.

  ☐ Terminated my credit account.

  ☐ Made unfavorable changes to my account (but did not change the terms of all, or substantially
  all of the consumer accounts of the same type).

  ☐ Took the following adverse action or determination in connection with my application for

  _____

  _____ [*the application and adverse action*].

  ☐ Took the following adverse action or determination in connection with _____

  _____

  _____ [*the transaction and the adverse action*].

☐ I hereby swear that I am unemployed and intend to apply for a job within the next 60 days.
Enclosed is a copy of a document verifying my unemployment.

☐ I hereby swear that I receive public assistance/welfare. Enclosed is a copy of my most recent public
assistance check as verification.

☐ I hereby swear that I believe there is erroneous information in my file due to fraud.

☐ I am unaware of anything that would entitle me to a free copy of my report. Enclosed is a copy of a document identifying me by my name and address and a check for $ _____ .

Thank you for your attention to this matter.

Sincerely,

Signature _____

Request Reinvestigation of Credit Report Entry

Date: _____

_____

_____

_____

_____

[name and address of credit bureau]

This is a request for you to reinvestigate the following items that appear on my credit report:

☐ The following personal information about me is incorrect:

Erroneous Information	Correct Information

☐ The following accounts are not mine:

Creditor's Name	Account Number	Explanation

☐ The account status is incorrect for the following accounts:

Creditor's Name	Account Number	Correct Status

☐ The following information is too old to be included in my report:

Creditor's Name	Account Number	Date of Last Activity

☐ The following inquiries are older than two years:

Creditor's Name	Date of Inquiry

☐ The following inquiries were not authorized:

Creditor's Name   Date of Inquiry   Explanation

_____   _____   _____

_____   _____   _____

_____   _____   _____

☐ The following accounts were closed at my request and should say so:

Creditor's Name   Account Number

_____   _____

_____   _____

_____   _____

_____   _____

☐ Other incorrect information:

Explanation

_____

_____

_____

_____

_____

_____

_____

_____

I understand that you will check each specified item, above, with the credit grantor reporting the information, remove any information the credit grantor cannot verify, or modify information that is incorrect or incomplete. I further understand that [*choose the one that applies to you*]:

☐ because I am requesting this reinvestigation after receiving my free annual credit report from you, you must complete your reinvestigation within 45 days of receipt of this letter. (15 U.S.C. § 1681j(a)(3).)

☐ you must complete your reinvestigation within 30 days of receipt of this letter. (15 U.S.C. § 1681i(a).)

Sincerely,

Signature _____ Date _____

Printed or typed name _____

Address _____

_____

Home phone _____ Work phone _____

Social Security number _____

Dispute Credit Card Charge

Date: _____

_____

_____

_____

_____

[name and address of the company or financial institution that issued credit card]

Re: Account number:

    Names(s) on account: _____

To Whom It May Concern:

I am writing to dispute the following charge that appears on my billing statement dated _____ .

    Merchant's name: _____

    Amount in dispute: _____ .

I am withholding payment of $ _____ , which represents the unpaid balance on the disputed item.

I am disputing this amount for the following reason(s): _____

_____

_____

_____

_____

_____ .

As required by law, I have tried in good faith to resolve this dispute with the merchant. *[Describe your efforts]*

_____

_____

_____

_____

_____ .

[For purchases made with a credit card, such as Visa or MasterCard, not issued by the seller]:

☐ This purchase was for more than $50 and was made in the state in which I live or within 100 miles of my home. Please remove the charge for this item, and all associated late and interest charges from my account.

Sincerely,

Signature _____

Printed or typed name _____

Address _____

_____

Home phone _____

Demand Collection Agency Cease Contact

Date: _____

_____

_____

_____

_____

[name and address of collection agency, including name of individual collector, if known]

Name(s) on account: _____

Account number: _____

Creditor: _____

To _____ :

Since approximately _____ *[date]*, I have received several phone calls and letters from you concerning my account with the above-named creditor.

Under 15 U.S.C. § 1692c, this is my formal notice to you to cease all further communications with me except for the reasons specifically set forth in the federal law.

Signature _____

Printed or typed name _____

Address _____

_____

Home phone_____

Telemarketing Phone Call Log

Date	Time	Company	Telemarketer's name and phone number	Product	Said "Put me on a 'do not call' list"	Followed up with letter

Notice to Put Name on Company's "Do Not Call" List

Date: _____

_____

_____

_____

_____

[name and address of company on whose behalf call was made]

To Whom It May Concern:

This letter is a follow-up to the telemarketing phone call I received from _____

_____ *[name of person who*

placed the call to you] on behalf of your company on _____ *[date]*.

As I stated at that time, I do not wish to receive telemarketing phone calls. Please put me on your "do not
call" list immediately.

Sincerely,

Signature _____

Printed or typed name _____

Address _____

_____

Home phone _____

Demand for Damages for Excessive Calls

Date: _____

_____

_____

_____

_____

[*name and address of company on whose behalf the calls were made*]

To Whom It May Concern:

Since _____ [*date*], I have received multiple phone calls from telemarketers calling on behalf of your company. I am giving your company the opportunity to settle my claim against you before I sue you in small claims court.

On or about _____ [*date*], I received a telephone call at my home from a telemarketer by the name of _____ , who stated that ☐ he ☐ she was calling on behalf of your company. I told this person that I was not interested in your company's product, and asked that my name be placed on the "do not call" list for calls made on behalf of your company.

On or about _____ [*date*], I received a second telephone call at my home from a telemarketer by the name of _____ , who stated that ☐ he ☐ she was calling on behalf of your company. I told this person that I was not interested in your company's product, and asked that my name be placed on a "do not call" list for calls made on behalf of your company.

[*Repeat the above paragraph as needed, changing the word "second" to "third," "fourth," etc.*]

Section 64.1200(d)(3) of Title 47 of the Code of Federal Regulations states, in pertinent part:

> If a person or entity making a call for telemarketing purposes (or on whose behalf such a call is made) receives a request from a residential telephone subscriber not to receive calls from that person or entity, the person or entity must record the request and place the subscriber's name, if provided, and telephone number on the do-not-call list at the time the request is made. Persons or entities making calls for telemarketing purposes (or on whose behalf such calls are made) must honor a residential subscriber's do-not-call request within a reasonable time from the date such request is made. **If such requests are recorded or maintained by a party other than the person or entity on whose behalf the telemarketing call is made, the person or entity on whose behalf the telemarketing call is made will be liable for any failures to honor the do-not-call request.**

A violation of this regulation is actionable under 47 U.S.C. § 227(c)(5). That section provides that:

> A person who has received more than one telephone call within any 12-month period by or on behalf of the same entity in violation of the regulations prescribed under this subsection may ... bring in an appropriate court of that state

(A) an action based on a violation of the regulations prescribed under this subsection to enjoin such violation,

(B) an action to recover for actual monetary loss from such a violation, or to receive up to $500 in damages for each such violation, whichever is greater, or

(C) both such actions.

In addition, treble damages may be awarded for knowing and willful violations.

Your company clearly violated the law on _____ separate occasions. I am entitled to $500 for each violation, for a total of $_____ .

[*Optional clause*]

Your company also violated state law. I am entitled to damages and/or civil penalties for those violations as well.

[*End of optional clause*]

I am willing to forgo my right to seek an injunction and treble damages against your company if you send me a cashier's check for the amount stated above within the next 30 days. If I do not hear from you within that time, I will seek all appropriate remedies in a court of law.

Sincerely,

Signature _____

Printed or typed name _____

Address _____

_____

Home phone _____

Notice to Remove Name From List

Date: _____

_____

_____

_____

_____

[*name and address of list maintainer*]

To Whom It May Concern:

Please permanently remove all members of this household from all lists you maintain, sell, trade, share, or use in any other capacity for direct marketing, telemarketing, credit card prescreening, or any other promotional purpose.

Name 1 _____

Address _____

Home phone (with area code) _____

Date of birth _____

Social Security number [*provide only when contacting a credit bureau*] _____

Name 2 _____

Address _____

Date of birth _____ Social Security number _____

Name 3 _____

Address _____

Date of birth _____ Social Security number _____

Sincerely,

Signature _____

Print name _____

Notice to Add or Retain Name but Not Sell or Trade It

Date: _____

_____

_____

_____

_____

[name and address of list maintainer]

To Whom It May Concern:

Please ☐ add ☐ retain   my name on your mailing list. ***Please do not sell, trade, or share my name or address with any other company or business.***

☐ I will accept telemarketing phone calls from your company.

☐ I do not wish to receive telemarketing phone calls from your company. Put me on your "do not call" list.

Sincerely,

Signature _____

Printed or typed name _____

Address _____

_____

Home phone _____

Child Care Agreement

1. **Parent or Legal Guardian**

   Parent(s)' name(s): _____

   Address(es): _____

   _____

   Home phone number(s): _____

   Work phone number(s): _____

   Cell phone: _____ Email: _____

2. **Child Care Provider**

   Child Care Provider's name: _____

   Address: _____

   _____ Home phone number: _____

   Cell phone: _____ Email: _____

3. **Children**

   Parent(s) desire(s) to contract with Child Care Provider to provide child care for: _____

   _____

   _____ [*names and birthdates of the children*].

4. **Location and Schedule of Care**

   Care will be provided at: _____

   _____ [*your address or other location where care is to be given*].

   Days and hours of child care will be as follows (unless Parents and Child Care Provider agree to a

   temporary schedule change): _____

   _____ .

5. **Beginning Date**

   Employment will begin on _____ [*date*].

6. **Training or Probation Period**

   There will be a training/probation period during the first _____ [*length of

   training period*] of employment. At the end of the period, Parents will let Child Care Provider know

   whether they will continue the employment relationship. Neither Parents nor Child Care Provider is

   obligated to continue the employment relationship through the entire probationary period.

7. **Responsibilities**

   The care to be provided under this agreement consists of the following responsibilities [*describe and

   provide details*]: _____

   _____

   _____

   _____

   _____ .

8. **Wage or Salary**

Child Care Provider will be paid as follows:

☐ $ _____ per ☐ hour ☐ week

☐ $ _____ per hour when Child Care Provider is required to do overtime

☐ other: _____

Parents will withhold federal [*and state, if any*] taxes from Child Care Provider's paychecks.

9. **Payment Schedule**

Child Care Provider will be paid on the following intervals and dates:

☐ once a week on every _____

☐ twice a month on _____

☐ once a month on _____

☐ other: _____

10. **Benefits**

Parent(s) will provide Child Care Provider with the following benefits [*describe and provide details*]:

_____

_____

_____

_____.

11. **Termination Policy**

Either Parent(s) or Child Care Provider may terminate this agreement at any time, for any reason, without notice.

12. **Confidentiality**

Child Care Provider will not share any health, financial, relationship, or other personal matters concerning this family with outsiders.

13. **Additional Provisions**

Parent(s) and Child Care Provider agree to the following additional terms: _____

_____

_____

_____.

14. **Modifications in Writing**

To be binding, any modifications to this contract must be in writing and signed by both parties to the agreement.

Signatures

Parent 1's signature: _____ Date _____

Parent 2's signature: _____ Date _____

Child Care Provider's signature: _____ Date _____

Child Care Instructions

1. **Home and Family Information**

   Parent(s)' name(s) [*list any parents who live at this address; other parents may be listed under
   Emergency Contacts*]: _____

   Names of children: _____

   Address: _____

   _____ Home phone number: _____

   Cell phone: _____ Email: _____

2. **Parent(s)' Work Information**

   [*list name and address of employer, work phone number, and regular work hours for each parent*]

   _____

   _____

3. **Child's Personal and Care Information**

   [*provide the following information for each child*]

   Name of child: _____

   Date of birth: _____

   Allergies and other medical conditions: _____

   Medications: _____

   Meals, naps, and bedtime schedule: _____

   Other comments: _____

   _____

4. **Child's Health Care Providers**

   [*list names, addresses, and phone numbers*]

   Doctor: _____

   Dentist: _____

   Other medical providers: _____

5. **Emergency Contacts**

   [*list names, addresses, and phone numbers of people whom babysitter can contact if unable to reach
   you in an emergency; specify their relationship to your family, such as children's aunt or neighbor*]

   _____

   _____.

   IN CASE OF EMERGENCY, CALL 911.

6. **Other Important Information:** _____

Elder Care Agreement

1. Employer

Employer(s)' name(s): _____

Address(es): _____

_____

Phone number(s): _____

Email: _____

2. Caregiver

Caregiver's name: _____

Address: _____

_____

Phone number: _____ Email: _____

3. Location and Schedule of Care

Caregiver agrees to care for _____ *[name*

of person for whom you're arranging care] at _____

_____ *[address or other location where care is to be given]*

according to the following schedule: _____

_____ .

4. Beginning Date

Employment will begin on _____ *[date]*.

5. Responsibilities

The caregiver's responsibilities will include *[provide as much detail as you think is necessary]*:

_____

_____

_____ .

6. Compensation

Caregiver will be compensated as follows:

☐ $ _____ per ☐ hour ☐ week ☐ month

☐ other: _____

Employer will withhold federal *[and state, if any]* taxes from Caregiver paychecks.

7. Payment Schedule

Caregiver will be paid on the following schedule:

☐ once a week on _____

☐ twice a month on _____

☐ once a month on _____

☐ other: _____

8. Benefits

Employer(s) will provide Caregiver with the following benefits [*describe and provide details or enter "none"*]:

_____

_____

_____

_____ .

9. Termination Policy

Employer(s) or Caregiver may terminate this agreement at any time, for any reason, without notice.

10. Additional Provisions

Employer(s) and Caregiver agree to the following additional terms [*specify any other elements of your agreement or enter "none"*]: _____

_____

_____

_____

_____

_____ .

11. Modifications in Writing

To be binding, any modifications to this agreement must be in writing and signed by both parties to the agreement.

Signatures

Employer(s)' signature(s): _____ Date _____

Caregiver's signature: _____ Date _____

Housekeeping Services Agreement

1. Employer

Employer(s)' name(s): _____

Address(es): _____

_____

Home phone number(s): _____

Work phone number(s): _____

Cell phone: _____ Email: _____

2. Housekeeper

Housekeeper's name: _____

Address: _____

_____ Home phone number: _____

Cell phone: _____

Email: _____

3. Location and Schedule of Work

Employer desires to contract with Housekeeper to work at: _____

_____ [*your address*].

Days and hours of cleaning will be as follows: _____

_____ .

4. Beginning Date

Employment will begin on _____ [*date*].

5. Housecleaning Responsibilities

The services to be provided under this agreement consist of cleaning the following [*describe and provide details*]: _____

_____

_____

_____

_____

_____

_____

_____

_____

_____

_____

_____

_____

_____ .

6. Other Responsibilities

Housekeeper also agrees to do the following types of work [*describe and provide details regarding cooking, laundry, and other noncleaning responsibilities*]: _____

_____

_____

_____

_____

_____

_____ .

7. Wage or Salary

Housekeeper will be paid as follows:

☐ $ _____ per ☐ hour ☐ week ☐ month

☐ other: _____

8. Payment Schedule

Housekeeper will be paid on the following intervals and dates:

☐ once a week on every _____

☐ twice a month on _____

☐ once a month on _____

☐ other: _____

9. Benefits

Employer(s) will provide Housekeeper with the following benefits [*describe and provide details*]:

_____

_____

_____ .

10. Termination Policy

Either Employer(s) or Housekeeper may terminate this agreement at any time, for any reason, without notice.

11. Additional Provisions

Employer(s) and Housekeeper agree to the following additional terms: _____

_____

_____

_____ .

12. Modifications in Writing

To be binding, any modifications to this contract must be in writing and signed by both parties.

Signatures

Employer(s)' signature(s): _____ Date_____

Housekeeper's signature: _____ Date _____

Agreement to Keep Property Separate

Partner 1's name: _____

Partner 2's name: _____

We agree as follows:

1. This contract sets forth our rights and obligations toward each other. We intend to abide by them in a spirit of cooperation and good faith.

2. All property owned by either of us as of the date of this agreement will remain the separate property of its owner and cannot be transferred to the other person except in writing. We have each attached to this contract a list of our major items of separate property.

3. The income each of us earns—as well as any items or investments either of us purchases with our income—belongs absolutely to the person who earns the money unless there is a written joint ownership agreement as provided in Clause 6.

4. We shall each maintain our own separate bank, credit card, investment, and retirement accounts, and neither of us shall in any way be responsible for the debts of the other. If we register legally as domestic partners and, by so doing, the law requires us to be responsible for each other's basic living expenses, we agree to assume no more than the minimum level of reciprocal responsibility for living expenses, as required by the law.

5. Expenses for routine household items and services, which include groceries, utilities, rent, and cleaning supplies, shall be shared equally.

6. From time to time, we may decide to keep a joint checking or savings account for a specific purpose (for example, to pay household expenses), or to own some property jointly (for example, to purchase a television). If so, the details of our joint ownership agreement shall be put in writing in a written contract or a deed, title slip, or other joint ownership document.

7. Should either of us receive real or personal property by gift or inheritance, the property belongs absolutely to the person receiving the gift or inheritance and cannot be transferred to the other except in writing.

8. In the event we separate, each of us shall be entitled to immediate possession of our separate property.

9. Any dispute arising out of this contract will be mediated by a third person mutually acceptable to both of us. The mediator's role will be to help us arrive at our solution, not to impose one on us. If good-faith efforts to arrive at our own solution to all issues in dispute with the help of a mediator prove to be fruitless, either of us may pursue other legal remedies.

10. This agreement represents our complete understanding regarding our living together and replaces any and all prior agreements, written or oral. It can be amended, but only in writing, and any amendment must be signed by both of us.

11. If a court finds any portion of this contract to be illegal or otherwise unenforceable, the remainder of the contract is still in full force and effect.

Partner 1's signature _____ Date _____

Partner 2's signature _____ Date _____

[OPTIONAL: ATTACH NOTARY CERTIFICATE]

Attachment A

Separate personal property of _____ :

_____

_____

_____

_____

_____

_____

_____

_____

_____

_____

_____

_____

Attachment B

Separate personal property of _____ :

_____

_____

_____

_____

_____

_____

_____

_____

_____

_____

_____

_____

_____

_____

Agreement for a Joint Purchase

Partner 1's name: _____

Partner 2's name: _____

We agree as follows:

1. We will jointly acquire and own _____

    _____

    [*describe the property*] at a cost of $_____ .

2. We will own the Property in the following shares:

    Partner 1 will own _____% of the Property and Partner 2 will own _____% of the Property.

3. If we separate and stop living together, one of the following will occur:

    (a) If one of us wants the Property and the other doesn't, the person who wants the Property will pay the other the fair market value (see Clause 4) of the Property.

    (b) If both of us want the Property, the decision will be made in the following way [*choose one*]:

    ☐ Right of First Refusal. _____

    [*specify either Partner 1 or 2*] shall have the right of first refusal and may purchase _____

    _____ 's [*specify either Partner 1 or 2*]

    share of the Property for its fair market value (see Clause 4). _____

    _____ [*specify either Partner 1 or 2*] will then become sole owner of the Property.

    ☐ Coin Toss Method. We will flip a coin to determine who is entitled to the Property. The winner, upon paying the loser fair market value for the loser's share of ownership, will become the sole owner of the Property.

    ☐ Other: _____

    _____ .

4. Should either of us decide to end the relationship, we will do our best to agree on the fair current market value of the Property. If we can't agree on a price, we will jointly choose a neutral appraiser and abide by the appraiser's decision.

5. If we separate and neither of us wants the Property—or if we can't agree on a fair price—we will advertise it to the public, sell it to the highest bidder, and divide the money according to our respective ownership shares as set forth in Clause 2.

6. Should either of us die while we are living together, the Property will belong absolutely to the survivor. If either of us makes a will or other estate plan, this agreement shall be reflected in that document.

7. This agreement can be changed, but only in writing, and any changes must be signed by both of us.

8. Any dispute arising out of this contract will be mediated by a third person mutually acceptable to both of us. The mediator's role will be to help us arrive at our solution, not to impose one on us. If good faith efforts to arrive at our own solution to all issues in dispute with the help of a mediator prove to be fruitless, either of us may pursue other legal remedies.

9. If a court finds any portion of this contract to be illegal or otherwise enforceable, the remainder of the contract is still in full force and effect.

Partner 1's signature _____ Date _____

Partner 2's signature _____ Date _____

Agreement to Share Property

Partner 1's name: _____

Partner 2's name: _____

We agree as follows:

1. This contract sets forth our rights and obligations toward each other. We intend to abide by them in a spirit of cooperation and good faith.

2. All earned income received by either of us after the date of this contract and all property purchased with this income belongs in equal shares to both of us with the following exceptions: _____

   _____

   _____

   _____

   _____

   _____ .

3. All real or personal property earned or accumulated by either of us before the date of this agreement (except jointly owned property listed in Attachment C of this agreement), including all future income such property produces, is the separate property of the person who earned or accumulated it and cannot be transferred to the other except in writing. Attached to this agreement in the form of Attachments A, B, and C, respectively, are lists of the major items of property each of us owns separately and both of us own jointly as of the date this agreement is made.

4. Should either of us receive real or personal property by gift or inheritance, that property, including all future income it produces, belongs absolutely to the person receiving the gift or inheritance and cannot be transferred to the other except in writing.

5. In the event we separate, all jointly owned property shall be divided equally.

6. Any dispute arising out of this contract will be mediated by a third person mutually acceptable to both of us. The mediator's role will be to help us arrive at our solution, not to impose one on us. If good faith efforts to arrive at our own solution to all issues in dispute with the help of a mediator prove to be fruitless, either of us may pursue other legal remedies.

7. This agreement represents our complete understanding regarding our living together and replaces any and all prior agreements, written or oral. It can be amended, but only in writing, and any amendments must be signed by both of us.

8. If a court finds any portion of this contract to be illegal or otherwise unenforceable, the remainder of the contract is still in full force and effect.

Partner 1's signature _____ Date _____

Partner 2's signature _____ Date _____

[OPTIONAL: ATTACH NOTARY CERTIFICATE]

Attachment A

Separate personal property of _____ :

_____

_____

_____

_____

_____

_____

_____

_____

_____

_____

_____

_____

_____

Attachment B

Separate personal property of _____ :

_____

_____

_____

_____

_____

_____

_____

_____

_____

_____

_____

_____

_____

Attachment C

Joint owned property acquired prior to _____ [*date of the Agreement*]:

_____

_____

_____

_____

_____

_____

_____

_____

_____

_____

_____

_____

_____

_____

Declaration of Legal Name Change

I, the undersigned, declare that I am 18 years of age or older and further declare:

1. I,_____ [*name currently used*],

   was born _____ [*name on birth certificate*]

   in the County of_____ [*county where born*]

   in the State of _____ [*state where born*]

   on _____ [*birthdate, including year*].

2. I hereby declare that I have changed my legal name, and from now on will be exclusively known as

   _____ [*new name*].

3. My legal name change was completed by order of the _____

   County Superior Court in case no. _____ on

   _____ , _____ . A copy of the court order is attached to this declaration.

4. Notice is hereby given to all agencies of the State of _____

   [*state where you reside*], all agencies of the federal government, all creditors, and all private persons,

   groups, businesses, corporations, and associations of said legal name change.

5. Please revise all relevant records accordingly.

I declare under penalty of perjury under the laws of the State of _____

[*state where you reside*] that the foregoing is true and correct.

Signature, new name _____ Date_____

Signature, old name _____ Date _____

Demand Letter

Date: _____

To: _____

_____

_____

[name and address of person or business to whom you are writing]

I am requesting compensation and/or a remedy in connection with the following problem: *[Describe in your own words exactly what happened. Specify dates, names of people you dealt with, what was said and done, any harm or damages that resulted, and anything else that may be relevant]*

_____

_____

_____

_____

_____

_____

_____

_____

_____ .

In light of the above, *[choose one]*:

☐ please send me a check or money order in the amount of $_____ by _____ *[enter date]*.

☐ please _____

_____ *[state exactly what you want done, i.e. "repair my dishwasher properly and fix the damage caused by your faulty work" or "replace the defective television you sold me with a new and properly functioning television of equal or greater retail value"]*.

☐ please send me a check or money order in the amount of $ _____ by _____ *[enter date for payment]*. By _____ *[date for action]*, please also _____

_____ *[description of action you're demanding]*.

If the problem is not resolved to my satisfaction as outlined above, I will take this dispute to court unless you notify me that you are willing to try to resolve it through mediation. In that case, I am willing to meet with a neutral third party, agreed to by both of us, in a good-faith attempt to resolve the dispute without court action.

[Note: Use the above paragraph if you are willing to use mediation to resolve your dispute. If you do not want to propose mediation, simply say "If the problem is not resolved to my satisfaction as outlined above, I will promptly take this dispute to court."]

Thank you for your immediate attention to this matter.

Sincerely,

Signature _____

Cell phone_____ Home phone _____

Email _____

Online Auction Buyer Demand Letter

To: _____ [name of seller]

_____

_____ [address]

I am writing to you regarding a dispute over _____
[description of item purchased] for which I was high bidder on the auction at _____
_____ [name of auction site] as Item No.
_____ [number of item at auction site].

   A dispute exists because [describe the reason you are dissatisfied with your purchase in as much detail as possible] _____
_____ .

   I would like to resolve the matter as follows [choose one]:

☐ I will return the item to you via _____ [describe the shipping method] and request compensation from you in the amount of $ _____ , which includes the following costs [list all costs for which you are seeking compensation, for example, shipping item to you, shipping item back to seller, amount paid for item, etc.] _____
_____
_____ .

☐ I will keep the item, but I request a partial refund of $_____ for the following reasons [specify reasons for price reduction, for example, partial damage or not as advertised, and include proof such as photos of item] _____
_____ .

☐ I seek a full refund of all monies paid as I never received the item.

   Please make payment by [specify the method by which payment shall be made to you. For example, if payment to seller was made by credit card, seek a charge back. If payment was made by money order, seek a money order, etc.] _____ .

   If you disagree with my request and would like to resolve the matter through a third-party dispute resolution procedure, I am prepared to use online dispute resolution procedures at:

☐ iCourthouse (www.i-courthouse.com)

☐ myADR (www.namadr.com)

☐ other [list online dispute resolution website] _____

   If I do not hear back from you by [date] _____ I will conclude that you do not wish to resolve the matter and I will [check as many as apply]:

☐ [if payment was made by credit card] seek a charge back on my credit card.

☐ file an online incident report at the National Consumer League's Fraud Center (www.fraud.org).

☐ post negative feedback at your online auction site.

Signature: _____

Address: _____

Email: _____

_____

Request for Refund or Repair of Goods Under Warranty

Date: _____

To: _____

_____

_____

_____

[*name and address of seller or manufacturer*]

ATTN: Customer Service Department

Re: _____

_____ [*description of item purchased, including serial number, if any*]

To Whom It May Concern:

I am writing to request compensation for the item described above, which I purchased for $_____

on _____ [*date*] from _____

_____ [*specify place of purchase*].

My reason for demanding compensation is as follows [*describe the reason you are dissatisfied with your purchase, in as much detail as possible. List anything included with this request, such as a copy of the warranty, purchase receipt, or the item itself*]: _____

_____

_____

_____

_____ .

Specifically, I request the following compensation [*explain what you want, such as a refund of the full purchase price, a replacement item, or a repair*]: _____

_____

_____ .

Please process this request by _____ [*specify a deadline for processing your request, such as date within 30 days*]. If I don't receive compensation by then, I will take further action, which may include filing a court action.

Thank you for your immediate attention to this matter.

Sincerely,

Signature _____

Address _____

_____ Cell phone _____

Home phone _____ Email _____

_____

Accident Claim Worksheet

What Happened

Date of accident: _____

Description of accident: _____

_____

Names of parties involved: _____

_____

Names of witnesses: _____

_____

Location of accident: _____

_____

Time of accident: _____

Weather conditions (if outside): _____

People Responsible for the Accident

Name: _____

Address: _____

_____

Cell Phone: _____ Home Phone: _____

Work Phone: _____

Insurance company: _____

Policy number: _____ Driver's license: _____

What person did: _____

_____

_____

_____

_____

Name: _____

Address: _____

_____

Cell Phone: _____ Home Phone: _____

Work Phone: _____

Insurance company: _____

Policy number: _____ Driver's license: _____

What person did: _____

_____

_____

_____

_____

Name: _____

Address: _____

_____

Cell Phone: _____ Home Phone: _____

Work Phone: _____

Insurance company: _____

Policy number: _____ Driver's license: _____

What person did: _____

_____

_____

_____

_____

_____

Witnesses

Name: _____

Address: _____

_____

Cell Phone: _____ Home Phone: _____

Work Phone: _____ Date of first contact: _____

Written statement: ☐ yes ☐ no

What person saw: _____

_____

_____

_____

_____

_____

_____

Name: _____

Address: _____

_____

Cell Phone: _____ Home Phone: _____

Work Phone: _____ Date of first contact: _____

Written statement: ☐ yes ☐ no

What person saw: _____

_____

_____

_____

_____

_____

Name: _____

Address: _____

_____

Cell Phone: _____ Home Phone: _____

Work Phone: _____ Date of first contact: _____

Written statement: ☐ yes ☐ no

What person saw: _____

_____

_____

_____

_____

_____

_____

Medical Treatment Providers

Name: _____

Address: _____

_____ Telephone: _____

Date of first visit: _____ Date of most recent or last visit: _____

Person to be contacted for medical records: _____

Date requested: _____ Date received: _____

Person to be contacted for medical billing: _____

Date requested: _____ Date received: _____

Reason for treatment and prognosis: _____

_____

_____

_____

_____ .

Name: _____

Address: _____

_____ Telephone: _____

Date of first visit: _____ Date of most recent or last visit: _____

Person to be contacted for medical records: _____

Date requested: _____ Date received: _____

Person to be contacted for medical billing: _____

Date requested: _____ Date received: _____

Reason for treatment and prognosis: _____

_____

_____

_____

_____

Name: _____

Address: _____

_____ Telephone: _____

Date of first visit: _____ Date of most recent or last visit: _____

Person to be contacted for medical records: _____

Date requested: _____ Date received: _____

Person to be contacted for medical billing: _____

Date requested: _____ Date received: _____

Reason for treatment and prognosis: _____

_____

_____

_____

_____ .

Other Party's Insurance Company (First Party)

Company name: _____

Address: _____

_____ Telephone: _____

Claim number: _____ Insured: _____

Adjuster: _____ Date demand letter was sent: _____

Settlement amount: _____ Date accepted: _____

Other Party's Insurance Company (Second Party)

Company name: _____

Address: _____

_____ Telephone: _____

Claim number: _____ Insured: _____

Adjuster: _____ Date demand letter was sent: _____

Settlement amount: _____ Date accepted: _____

Communications With Insurer

Date: _____ Name of Employee: _____

If oral, what was said: _____

_____

_____

_____ .

Date: _____ Name of Employee: _____

If oral, what was said: _____

_____

_____

_____ .

Date: _____ Name of Employee: _____

If oral, what was said: _____

_____

_____

_____ .

Date: _____ Name of Employee: _____

If oral, what was said: _____

_____

_____

_____ .

Losses

Describe damage to your property: _____

_____

Do you have photos showing damage? ☐ yes ☐ no

If Repairable

Estimates for repairs (name of repair shop and amounts of estimates): _____

_____

Actual

Repair bills (name of repair shop and amounts of bills): _____

_____

If totaled

Value at the time destroyed: _____ Documentation of value: _____

General Release

Releasor: _____

Address: _____

_____

Releasee: _____

Address: _____

_____

1. Releasor voluntarily and knowingly signs this release with the express intention of canceling Releasee's legal liabilities and obligations as described below.

2. Releasor hereby releases Releasee from all claims, known or unknown, that have arisen or may arise from the following occurrence: _____

_____

_____.

    Releasor understands that, as to claims that are known to the parties when the release is signed, any statutory provisions that would otherwise apply to limit this general release are hereby waived. Releasor also understands that this release extends to claims arising out of this incident that are *not* known by Releasor at the time this release is signed.

3. In exchange for granting this release, Releasor has received the following payment or other considerations: _____

_____

_____

_____.

4. By signing this release, Releasor additionally intends to bind his or her spouse, heirs, legal representatives, assigns, and anyone else claiming under him or her. Releasor has not assigned any claim covered by this release to any other party. Releasor intends that this release apply to the heirs, personal representatives, assigns, insurers, and successors of Releasee as well as to the Releasee.

Releasor's signature _____ Date _____

Print name _____ County of residence _____

Releasor's spouse's signature _____ Date _____

Print name _____ County of residence _____

Releasee's signature _____ Date _____

Print name _____ County of residence _____

Releasee's spouse's signature _____ Date _____

Print name _____ County of residence _____

[OPTIONAL: ATTACH NOTARY CERTIFICATE]

General Mutual Release

Party 1: _____

Address: _____

_____

Party 2: _____

Address: _____

_____

1. We voluntarily and knowingly sign this mutual release with the express intention of eliminating the liabilities and obligations described below.

2. Disputes and differences that we both desire to settle exist between us with respect to the following:

   _____

   _____

   _____ .

3. The value (consideration) for this mutual release consists of our mutual relinquishment of our respective legal rights involved in the disputes described above.

4. In addition, the following payment or other consideration will be provided or paid [*check and explain any that apply*]:

   ☐ Party 1 will receive from Party 2: _____

   _____ .

   ☐ Party 2 will receive from Party 1: _____

   _____ .

5. By signing this release, we both intend to bind our spouses, heirs, legal representatives, assigns, and anyone else claiming under us, in addition to ourselves. Each party understands that, as to claims that are known to that party when the release is signed, any statutory provisions that would otherwise apply to limit this general release are hereby waived. Each party also understands that this release extends to claims arising out of this incident that are *not* known at the time this release is signed.

Party 1's signature _____ Date _____

Print name _____ County of residence _____

Party 1's spouse's signature _____ Date _____

Print name _____ County of residence _____

Party 2's signature _____ Date _____

Print name _____ County of residence _____

Party 2's spouse's signature _____ Date _____

Print name _____ County of residence _____

[*OPTIONAL: ATTACH NOTARY CERTIFICATE*]

Release for Damage to Real Estate

Releasor: _____

Address: _____

_____

Releasee: _____

Address: _____

_____

1. Releasor is the owner of certain property (Property) located at _____
   _____ , which specifically consists of the following:
   _____
   _____ .

2. Releasor voluntarily and knowingly signs this release with the intention of eliminating Releasee's liabilities and obligations as described below.

3. Releasor hereby releases Releasee from all claims, known or unknown, that have arisen or may arise from the occurrence described in Clause 4. Releasor understands that, as to claims that are known to the parties when the release is signed, any statutory provisions that would otherwise apply to limit this general release are hereby waived. Releasor also understands that this release extends to claims arising out of this incident that are *not* known by Releasor at the time this release is signed.

4. Releasor has alleged that Property suffered damage in the approximate amount of $ _____
   as a result of the following activity of Releasee: _____
   _____
   _____

5. By signing this release, Releasor additionally intends to bind his or her spouse, heirs, legal representatives, assigns, and anyone else claiming under him or her. Releasor has not assigned any claim arising from the transaction described in Clause 4 to another party. Releasor intends that this release apply to the heirs, personal representatives, assigns, insurers, and successors of Releasee as well as to the Releasee.

6. Releasor has received good and adequate value (consideration) for this release in the form of:
   _____
   _____ .

Releasor's signature _____ Date _____

Print name _____ County of residence _____

Releasor's spouse's signature _____ Date _____

Print name _____ County of residence _____

Releasee's signature _____ Date _____

Print name _____ County of residence _____

Releasee's spouse's signature _____ Date _____

Print name _____ County of residence _____

[*OPTIONAL: ATTACH NOTARY CERTIFICATE*]

Release for Property Damage in Auto Accident

Releasor: _____

Address: _____

_____

Releasee: _____

Address: _____

_____

1. Releasor voluntarily and knowingly signs this release with the express intention of eliminating Releasee's liabilities and obligations as described below.

2. Releasor hereby releases Releasee from all liability for claims, known and unknown, arising from property damage sustained by Releasor in an automobile accident that occurred on _____ _____ [date] at _____ _____ [location] involving a vehicle owned by Releasee or driven by Releasee or Releasee's agent. Releasor understands that, as to claims that are known to the parties when the release is signed, any statutory provisions that would otherwise apply to limit this general release are hereby waived. Releasor also understands that this release extends to claims arising out of this incident that are *not* known by Releasor at the time this release is signed.

3. By signing this release, Releasor does not give up any claim that he or she may now or hereafter have against any person, firm, or corporation other than Releasee and those persons and entities specified in Clause 6.

4. Releasor understands that Releasee does not, by providing the value described below, admit any liability or responsibility for the accident described in Clause 2 or its consequences.

5. Releasor has received good and adequate value (consideration) for this release in the form of:

_____ .

6. By signing this release, Releasor additionally intends to bind his or her spouse, heirs, legal representatives, assigns, and anyone else claiming under him or her. Releasor has not assigned any claim arising from the accident described in Clause 2 to any other party. This release applies to Releasee's heirs, legal representatives, insurers, and successors, as well as to Releasee.

Releasor's signature _____ Date _____

Print name _____ County of residence _____

Releasor's spouse's signature _____ Date _____

Print name _____ County of residence _____

Releasee's signature _____ Date _____

Print name _____ County of residence _____

Releasee's spouse's signature _____ Date _____

Print name _____ County of residence _____

[OPTIONAL: ATTACH NOTARY CERTIFICATE]

Release for Personal Injury

Releasor: _____

Address: _____

_____

Releasee: _____

Address: _____

_____

1. Releasor voluntarily and knowingly executes this release with the intention of eliminating Releasee's liabilities and obligations as described below.

2. Releasor hereby releases Releasee from all liability for claims, known and unknown, arising from injuries, mental and/or physical, sustained by Releasor as follows: _____

_____

_____

_____ .

   Releasor understands that, as to claims that are known to the parties when this release is signed, any statutory provisions that would otherwise apply to limit this general release are hereby waived. Releasor also understands that this release extends to claims arising out of this incident that are *not* known by Releasor at the time this release is signed.

3. Releasor has been examined by a licensed physician or other health care professional competent to diagnose [*choose one or both*]:

   ☐ physical injuries and disabilities.

   ☐ mental and emotional injuries and disabilities.

   Releasor has been informed by this physician or health care professional that the injury described in Clause 2 has completely healed without causing permanent damage.

4. By executing this release Releasor does not give up any claim that he or she may now or hereafter have against any person, firm, or corporation other than Releasee and those persons specified in Clause 7.

5. Releasor understands that Releasee does not, by providing the value described in Clause 6 below, admit any liability or responsibility for the above described injury or its consequences.

6. Releasor has received good and adequate value (consideration) for this release in the form of:

_____

_____

_____ .

7. By signing this release, Releasor additionally intends to bind his or her spouse, heirs, legal representatives, assigns, and anyone else claiming under him or her. Releasor has not assigned any claim arising from the accident described in Clause 2 to any other party. This release applies to Releasee's heirs, legal representatives, insurers, and successors, as well as to Releasee.

Releasor's signature _____ Date _____

Print name _____ County of residence _____

Releasor's spouse's signature _____ Date _____

Print name _____ County of residence _____

Releasee's signature _____ Date _____

Print name _____ County of residence _____

Releasee's spouse's signature _____ Date _____

Print name _____ County of residence _____

[OPTIONAL: ATTACH NOTARY CERTIFICATE]

Mutual Release of Contract Claims

Party 1: _____

Address: _____

_____

Party 2: _____

Address: _____

_____

1. We voluntarily and knowingly sign this mutual release with the intention of eliminating the liabilities and obligations described below.

2. Disputes and differences have arisen between us with respect to an agreement entered into between us on _____ [*date*], under which we agreed to the following:

   _____

   _____

   _____ .

   This agreement is hereby made a part of this release and incorporated by reference. A copy of the agreement (if written) is attached to this release.

3. We each hereby expressly release the other from all claims and demands, known and unknown, arising out of the agreement specified in Clause 2. Each party understands that, as to claims that are known to that party when the release is signed, any statutory provisions that would otherwise apply to limit this general release are hereby waived. Each party also understands that this release extends to claims arising out of this incident that are *not* known at the time this release is signed.

4. This release additionally applies to our heirs, legal representatives, and successors and is binding on our spouses, heirs, legal representatives, assigns, and anyone else claiming under us. Neither of us has assigned to another party any claim arising under or out of the contract specified in Clause 2.

5. The value (consideration) for this mutual release binds our mutual agreement to forgo our respective legal rights with reference to the disputes and differences described above.

6. We also agree that the contract specified in Clause 2 shall be and is hereby rescinded, terminated, and canceled as of _____ [*date*].

Party 1's signature _____ Date _____

Print name _____ County of residence _____

Party 1's spouse's signature _____ Date _____

Print name _____ County of residence _____

Party 2's signature _____ Date _____

Print name _____ County of residence _____

Party 2's spouse's signature _____ Date _____

Print name _____ County of residence _____

[OPTIONAL: ATTACH NOTARY CERTIFICATE]

Complaint Letter

Date: _____

To: _____

_____

_____

_____

[*name and address of consumer protection office*]

To Whom It May Concern:

I wish to lodge a complaint about the following company:

Name: _____

Address: _____

_____

Phone number: _____ Website: _____

Name of person with whom I dealt: _____

The details of my complaint are as follows [*attach additional sheets if necessary*]: _____

_____

_____

_____

_____

_____

_____

_____

_____ .

Please investigate this matter and inform me of the results.

Sincerely,

Signature _____

Printed name _____

Address _____

_____

Email _____ Cell phone _____

Home phone _____

cc: _____

_____

_____

Notice of Insurance Claim

Date: _____

To: _____

_____

_____

_____

[name and address of insurance company]

Name of your insured: _____

Policy number: _____

To Whom It May Concern:

Please be advised that ☐ I received injuries ☐ I sustained property damage in an accident on

_____ [date], at approximately _____ [time], at the following location:

_____

_____ [place].

The accident involved:

☐ two or more motor vehicles

☐ motor vehicle and pedestrian

☐ motor vehicle and bicycle

☐ motor vehicle and property

[for all motor vehicles involved other than your own, give]:

Make, model, year, and color of vehicle: _____

License plate number and state of issuance: _____

Vehicle identification number: _____

Name of driver (if different from name of insured above): _____

Driver's license number and state of issuance: _____

☐ slip and fall

☐ animal bite, claw, knockdown, etc.

☐ dangerous or defective product

☐ other (specify): _____

Your insured named above was involved in the incident. Please confirm in writing to the address below your liability coverage of the insured identified above. Please also advise whether your insured contends that anyone other than your insured may be in whole or in part legally responsible for accidents on or near the premises or for this accident.

As requested, please respond in writing. If necessary, I may be reached by telephone at the number below.

Thank you for your prompt attention to this matter.

Sincerely,

Signature _____ Date _____

Printed name _____

Address _____

Email _____ Phone _____

Notice to Cancel Certain Contracts

To Whom It May Concern:

This letter constitutes written notice to you that I am canceling the following contract:

Seller: _____

Address: _____

_____

Buyer: _____

Address: _____

_____

Contract pertains to the following goods/services purchased:_____

_____ .

Date contract signed for these goods/services: _____ .

Please acknowledge receipt of this letter by signing below and returning the acknowledgment to me in the enclosed envelope. I understand that under the law, you must refund my money within _____ days. Furthermore, if applicable, I understand that you must either pick up the items purchased, or reimburse me within _____ days for my expense of mailing the goods back to you. If you do not pick up the goods within that time, I am entitled to keep them.

Buyer's signature _____ Date _____

Print name _____

Acknowledgment

Seller's signature _____ Date _____

Print name _____

Cancel Membership or Subscription Notice

Date: _____

To: _____

_____

_____

_____

[*name and address of publication or organization; include name of department if available*]

Re: _____ [*subscription or membership number*]

This letter is to notify you that I would like to cancel my _____

_____ [*specify what you are canceling, such as a subscription to publication or membership in organization*] effective _____ [*date of cancellation*].

The reason for this cancellation is _____

_____ [*specify reason for cancellation*].

Thank you for your prompt assistance.

Signature _____

Print name _____

Address _____

_____

Subscription or account number _____

Request to Begin Special Education Process

Date: _____

To: _____

_____

_____

_____

[*name and address of special education administrator*]

Re: _____ [*name of child*]

Child's school: _____

Child's teacher: _____ Child's grade: _____

I am writing because my child is experiencing difficulties in school, including [*describe difficulties*] _____

_____

_____

_____

_____

_____

_____

_____ .

I am formally requesting that the school immediately begin its special education process, including initial assessment for eligibility. I understand that you will send me an assessment plan explaining the tests that may be given to my child. Because I realize the assessment can take some time, I would appreciate receiving the assessment plan within ten days. I would also appreciate any other information you have regarding assessments, how eligibility is determined, and the general IEP process.

I am also requesting that you make available to me a complete copy of my child's school file, including all tests, reports, assessments, grades, notes by teachers or other staff members, and any other information contained in the file. I understand that I am entitled to these records under the Family Educational Rights and Privacy Act (FERPA) (20 U.S.C. Section 1232 [g]). I would greatly appreciate having these files within the next five days. I will call you to discuss how and when I will get the copies.

Thank you very much for your assistance. I look forward to working with you and your staff.

Sincerely,

Signature of parent _____

Printed name _____

Address _____

_____

Email _____ Cell phone _____

Home phone _____

Identity Theft Worksheet

Credit Bureaus

☐ Experian: www.experian.com

Date of Contact	Type of Contact	Comments

☐ Equifax: www.equifax.com

Date of Contact	Type of Contact	Comments

☐ TransUnion: www.transunion.com

Date of Contact	Type of Contact	Comments

Financial Institutions

Credit Card Companies

Name of Company	Phone Number or Website	Date of Contact	Contact Person or Method	Comments

Banks

Name of Bank	Phone Number or Website	Date of Contact	Contact Person or Method	Comments

Other Service Providers

Name of Institution	Phone Number or Website	Date of Contact	Contact Person or Method	Comments

Law Enforcement Agencies

Local Police Department

Name of Department	Phone Number or Website	Date of Contact	Name of Person or Officer Contacted	Comments

Federal Trade Commission: www.ftc.gov

Date of Contact	Contact Method	Comments

Other Law Enforcement Agencies

Name of Agency	Phone Number or Website	Date of Contact	Contact Person or Method	Comments

Other Contacts

Postal Inspector: https://postalinspectors.uspis.gov

Phone Number or Website	Date of Contact	Contact Person or Method	Comments

Social Security Administration: 800-772-1213

Date of Contact	Contact Person or Method	Comments

Debt Collectors

Name of Collection Agency	Phone Number	Date of Contact	Contact Person	Comments

U.S. State Department: 877-487-2778 or https://travel.state.gov/content/passports/en/passports/lost-stolen.html

Date of Contact	Contact Person or Method	Comments

Department of Motor Vehicles

DMV Location	Phone Number or Website	Date of Contact	Contact Person or Method	Comments

Additional Conversations/Correspondence

Name of Institution	Phone Number or Website	Date of Contact	Contact Person or Method	Comments

Expenses Incurred

Date Expense Incurred	Reason for Expense	Cost
		$
		$
		$
		$
	Total Costs:	$

Index

N

Names
  in forms and contracts, 5
  name change declaration, 123
Nannies, 112, 114. *See also* Household employees
National Do Not Call Registry, 105
Neighbor disputes, 133
Net worth, 68, 70
  family financial statement, 68–70
  statement of assets and liabilities, 94
New hire reporting, household employees, 113
Nonpurchase money security agreements, 59
Notarization, 6, 7–8. *See also specific forms*
Notice forms
  death notifications, 37, 38, 39–40
  notice of insurance claim, 137–138
  notice of needed repairs (rentals), 46–47
  notice of revocation of power of attorney, 20, 25
  notice of termination of personal property rental agreement, 83
  notice to add or retain name but not sell or trade it, 108, 109
  notice to cancel certain contracts, 138–139
  notice to cancel membership or subscription, 139–140
  notice to put name on company's "do not call" list, 107
  notice to remove name from (mailing) list, 38, 108–109
  notice to stop payment of check, 96–97
  notice to terminate joint account, 95–96
  tenant's notice of intent to move out, 49

O

Obituary information fact sheet, 38–39
Online auction buyer demand letter, 127–128
Online resources
  consumer complaints to government agencies, 105, 136, 137
  consumer privacy rights, 104
  contract cancellation rights, 139

credit card disputes, 100
credit report requests, 97
death certificates, 36
dispute resolution, 10
estate planning, 30
identity theft, 142, 143, 144
independent contractor status, 87
landlord-tenant law and documents, 42
lawyer referrals, 10
legal research, 10
legal updates, 3, 10
loan payment calculators, 56–57
minimum wage law, 113
obituaries and online memorials, 39
online auction purchases, 127
real estate and home buying, 66, 72
small claims court, 10, 50
unwanted mail and phone calls, 104, 105, 107, 108, 109
vehicle ownership and history, 77
vehicle values, 70
Oral contracts, 3, 133
  mutual release of contract claims, 134
  unmarried couples and, 120
Oral notice of intent to move out of rental, 49
Overdue payment demand, 62–63
Overtime pay, household employees, 112–113

P

Passports, stolen or fraudulently obtained, 144
Payment demand forms, 62–63
Payment record form (loans), 54
Perfecting a lien, 60, 61
Permits, for home repairs, 87, 88
Personal finances, 92–101
  assignment of rights, 94–95
  daily expenses form, 92–93
  demanding that a collection agency cease contact, 100–101
  family financial statement, 68–70
  monthly budget, 93–94
  monthly income form, 93